THE ROLE OF PARENTS IN THE ONTOGENY OF ACHIEVEMENT-RELATED MOTIVATION AND BEHAVIORAL CHOICES

EDITED BY

Sandra D. Simpkins Jennifer A. Fredricks and Jacquelynne S. Eccles

WITH COMMENTARY BY

Aletha C. Huston

Patricia J. Bauer
Series Editor

MONOGRAPHS OF THE SOCIETY FOR RESEARCH IN CHILD DEVELOPMENT

Serial No. 317, Vol. 80, No. 2, 2015

THE ROLE OF PARENTS IN THE ONTOGENY OF ACHIEVEMENT-RELATED MOTIVATION AND BEHAVIORAL CHOICES

CONTENTS

COMMENTARY

ABSTRACT

Parents believe what they do matters. But, how does it matter? How do parents' beliefs about their children early on translate into the choices those children make as adolescents? The Eccles's expectancy–value model asserts that parents' beliefs about their children during childhood predict adolescents' achievement-related choices through a sequence of processes that operate in a cumulative, cascading fashion over time. Specifically, parents' beliefs predict parents' behaviors that predict their children's motivational beliefs. Those beliefs predict children's subsequent choices. Using data from the Childhood and Beyond Study (92% European American; $N = 723$), we tested these predictions in the achievement domains of sports, instrumental music, mathematics, and reading across a 12-year period. In testing these predictions, we looked closely at the idea of reciprocal influences and at the role of child gender as a moderator. The cross-lagged models generally supported the bidirectional influences described in Eccles's expectancy–value model. Furthermore, the findings demonstrated that: (a) these relations were stronger in the leisure domains than in the academic domains, (b) these relations did not consistently vary based on youth gender, (c) parents were stronger predictors of their children's beliefs than vice versa, and (d) adolescents' beliefs were stronger predictors of their behaviors than the reverse. The findings presented in this monograph extend our understanding of the complexity of families, developmental processes that unfold over time, and the extent to which these processes are universal across domains and child gender.

Corresponding author: Sandra Simpkins, T. Denny Sanford School of Social and Family Dynamics, Arizona State University, Tempe, AZ, 85287; email: Sandra.simpkins@asu.edu
Author Note: Sandra D. Simpkins, T. Denny Sanford School of Social and Family Dynamics, Arizona State University; Jennifer Fredricks, Department of Human Development, Connecticut College; and Jacquelynne S. Eccles, School of Education, University of California at Irvine. This research was supported by Grant HD17553 from the National Institute for Child Health and Human Development to Jacquelynne Eccles, Allan Wigfield, Phyllis Blumenfeld, and Rena Harold, Grant 0089972 from the National Science Foundation to Jacquelynne Eccles and Pamela Davis-Kean, and grants from the MacArthur Network on Successful Pathways through Middle Childhood to Eccles. We would like to thank the principals, teachers, students, and parents of the cooperating school districts for their participation in this project. We would also like to thank the following people for their work on the project: Amy Arbreton, Phyllis Blumenfeld, Carol Freedman-Doan, Rena Harold, Janis Jacobs, Toby Jayaratne, Mina Vida, Allan Wigfield, and Kwang Suk Yoon. Simpkins's work on this monograph was also supported by a William T. Grant Young Scholars Award (#7936) and a CAREER grant from the National Science Foundation (DRL-1054798).

Why do children and adolescents choose such different achievement-related activities and have such different achievement-related goals and interests? Why, for example, do some children prefer math to reading or instrumental music to sports or sports to academics? Why do children with fairly similar ability levels have different opinions of their abilities? Why, for example, do girls develop lower estimates of their math ability than boys, even though they get equivalent or higher grades? Most importantly for this monograph, what role do parents play in the socialization of these individual and group differences?

Questions such as these are at the heart of our understanding of the socialization of motivated behavior. Beginning with Winterbottom (1958), developmentalists have been interested in the role that parents play in socializing achievement-related motivation and behavior (see Simpkins, Fredricks, & Eccles, 2015, for a recent review). This work focused on the socialization of what was assumed to be general achievement motivation and demonstrated the importance of four components of parenting: (1) high expectations for children's performance, (2) the provision of developmentally appropriate but challenging tasks, (3) a warm supportive emotional climate, (4) and strong role models of high achievement-oriented behaviors (Crandall, Dewey, Katkovsky, & Preston, 1964; Winterbottom, 1958). These themes continued to be reflected in the work linking parenting styles to school achievement outcomes in Baumrind's seminal studies (Baumrind, 1971; Steinberg, Lamborn, Dornbursch, & Darling, 1992) and in the work based on self-determination theory (Grolnick, Gurland, DeCourcey, & Jacob, 2002; Grolnick & Ryan, 1989). The importance of role models, parental expectations, and the provision of specific experiences has been salient in the work on both gender and social class-related socialization as well (Bradley & Corwyn, 2006; Davis-Kean, Malanchuk, Peck, & Eccles, 2003; Ruble, Martin, & Berenbaum, 2006).

With the social cognitive revolution in the 1960s, much greater attention was placed on beliefs as key to the motivated behaviors of parents and their children, as well as the need for domain specificity rather than a focus on general motivational constructs such as achievement. Developmentalists became interested in the role of parents' specific beliefs about their children's differential abilities and causal attributions for their children's performances. They proposed several variations of social cognitive models of parental influence, though this work focused primarily on academic achievement-related behaviors and outcomes (Alexander & Entwisle, 1988; Eccles [Parsons], Adler, & Kaczala, 1982; Goodnow & Collins, 1990; Grolnick & Slowiaczek, 1994; Holloway, 1988; Marjoribanks, 2002).

In an effort to address the kinds of questions outlined in our first paragraph in a systematic way, Eccles and her colleagues developed two comprehensive models of achievement-related choices to guide subsequent research efforts (Eccles [Parsons] et al., 1983). The first model, depicted in Figure 1a, focused on the psychological processes linked to achievement-related behaviors and choices (see Figure 1a). It draws heavily from classic theories of expectancy and value, interest, and efficacy models of performance and task choice (Atkinson, 1964; Bandura, 1997; Csikszentmihalyi, 1988; Weiner, 1979). In the second model, depicted in Figure 1b, Eccles and her colleagues elaborated on the diverse pathways through which parents might influence their children's achievement-related activity choices and motivational beliefs (see Eccles, 1993). They proposed that parents can shape children's motivational beliefs (e.g., self-concept of ability, task value) and achievement-related choices through a variety of child-specific beliefs and activity-specific behaviors.

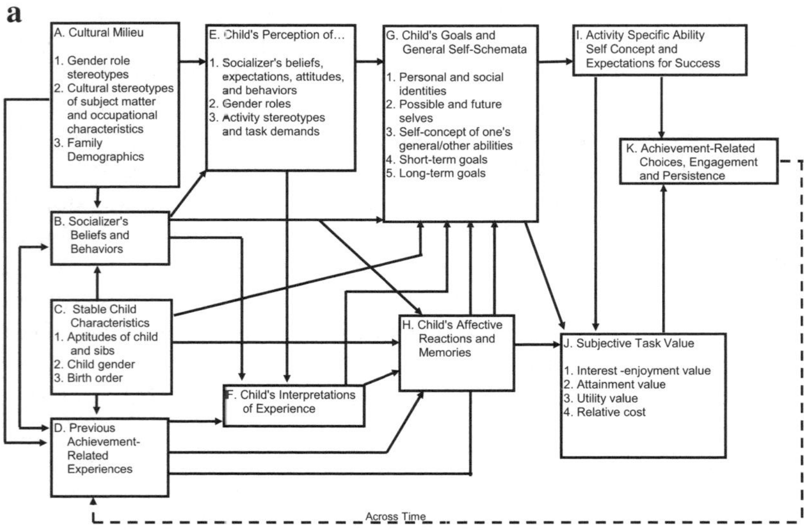

FIGURE 1A.—Expectancy-value model of achievement choices.

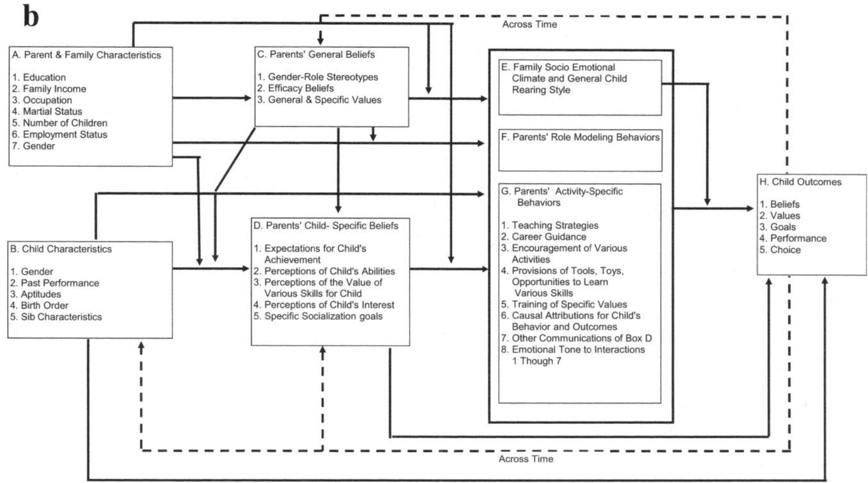

Figure 1b.—Model of parents influence on children's achievement related to self-perceptions, values, and behaviors.

In this monograph, we use both of these theoretical frameworks to examine the role of the family in the ontogeny of European American, middle-class adolescents' achievement-related choices. To this end, we tested a developmental model spanning 12 years describing the processes by which parents' beliefs about their children become associated with their adolescent's later achievement-related choices.

Although there has been extensive research on particular subcomponents of this model, this monograph extends previous work in several critical regards. First, few studies, even Simpkins and her colleagues (2012)—the most comparable study to this monograph, address questions about the direction of influence between both mothers' and fathers' beliefs and behaviors, and children's beliefs and achievement-related activity choices from childhood through adolescence. Second, parents' beliefs and behaviors have often been examined in separate studies. Third, much of the research on parents' beliefs is quite general. Fourth, much of the research in motivation has focused on children's academic motivation and school achievement. Fifth, few researchers have examined whether children's gender moderates the strength of relations within the theoretical model being tested. Sixth, and perhaps most importantly, we investigate the responsiveness of parents' beliefs and behaviors to their children's characteristics.

In this monograph, we focus on four achievement domains: sports, instrumental music, math, and reading because comparisons across these domains are related to several important theoretical debates and because participation in each domain has implications for individuals' well-being into adulthood. Adolescents' motivational beliefs and engagement in math and reading have clear implications for educational achievement, college majors, and occupational choices. With regard to sports and instrumental music, adolescents who participate in either of these skill-based domains often evidence more positive adjustment than adolescents who do not participate in these leisure domains (Burton, Horowitz, & Abeles, 2000; Fredricks & Eccles, 2006; Kahn et al., 2008; North, Hargreaves, & O'Neill, 2000; Pedersen & Seidman, 2005; Pfeiffer et al., 2006). Participation in these domains also can play a key role in identity formation leading to a positive and agentic view of one's self.

These four domains were also chosen because they cover theoretically important distinctions. First, these domains vary in terms of whether they are generally stereotyped as a masculine (i.e., math and sports) or feminine (i.e., reading) domain (Eccles, Wigfield, & Schiefele, 1998; Wigfield, Eccles, Schiefele, Roeser, & Davis-Kean, 2006). Second, these domains include mandated academic pursuits (i.e., math and reading) and voluntary but highly skilled leisure pursuits (i.e., sports and instrumental music). These distinctions are theoretically important in that the predictors may vary for particular groups (e.g., girls, thus helping us understand gender role socialization better) and/or for particular types of domains (e.g., leisure pursuits, thus helping us understand the role of context in achievement socialization). Inclusion of domains that cover the distinctions created by gender and academic/leisure pursuit provides insight into the generalizability of findings across key dimensions of achievement-related choices, as well as provides tests of specific hypotheses about gender and domain differences.

THEORETICAL PERSPECTIVES ON ACHIEVEMENT-RELATED BEHAVIORAL CHOICES

Our main focus in this monograph is on understanding the precursors of adolescents' achievement-related choices and engagement during high school. Studying choices and engagement during adolescence is important for several reasons. First, these choices are related to well-being during adolescence (see Eccles & Gootman, 2002). Second, adolescents' choices will shape the options available to them as they move into and through their adulthood (Bates, 1987; Eccles & Gootman, 2002). Adolescence is a critical developmental stage in terms of increased opportunities for decision-making (Eccles, Jacobs, et al., 1993; Smetana, 2010). Adolescents also have an increasing sense of who they are and whom they would like to become (Eccles, 2009; Erikson, 1982).

4

There are also several sociocultural changes that make the high school years a particularly important time for studying differential engagement across various achievement-related activities (Eccles, Jacobs, et al., 1993). Adolescents typically have more opportunities to make choices among high school courses than they had as elementary and middle school students. These choices can have significant implications for subsequent educational and occupational pathways (Farmer, Wardrop, Anderson, & Risinger, 1995). In addition, adolescents' after-school environments become more competitive than those during childhood (e.g., a slot on the football team), often requiring a greater skill and time investment. Adolescents also have greater demands on their after-school time than do younger children, such as paid employment (Larson & Verma, 1999). These shifts make adolescence a particularly interesting period to study achievement-related choices because it is both a time of greater opportunity to make choices and a time in which these choices become more consequential.

According to ecological theory and expectancy–value theory, adolescents' achievement-related choices are shaped by the immediate contexts in which they are embedded and their prior developmental history, as well as by the broader culture in which they live (Bronfenbrenner & Morris, 2006). Certainly, sociocultural studies have shown that the broader cultural setting shapes the likelihood that adolescents will pursue specific activity domains (Rogoff, 2003). Furthermore, the larger contexts in which adolescents and families are embedded, such as adolescents' school or neighborhoods, influence children and families (Furstenberg et al., 1999). However, what is really interesting is the variability within similar contexts. For example, not all adolescents from families with high resources participate in organized activities even though they are likely to have the resources to support participation (Mahoney & Eccles, 2007; Simpkins, Ripke, Huston, & Eccles, 2005). More importantly, some children and adolescents in families with very limited resources participate in organized activities (Lareau, 2003; Mahoney & Eccles, 2007; Simpkins, Ripke, et al., 2005). Several researchers have shown that parents' beliefs and behaviors are key determinants of how children invest their time within and after school (Eccles, 1993; Fredricks & Eccles, 2005; Lareau, 2003; Simpkins, Ripke, et al., 2005). However, few studies have been couched within a broad and integrative theoretical model.

Adolescents' choices also are based on a developmental process with roots in childhood. Several motivational theories note that adolescents' choices are based, in part, on their prior ability self-concepts and values as shown in Figure 1a (Deci & Ryan, 1985; Eccles, 1993; Marsh & Craven, 1997). One of the next critical questions is: What are the contextual factors that promote adolescents' ability self-concepts and values? Many social cognitively oriented socialization theorists argue that parents shape children's motivational beliefs and choices through their own beliefs and behaviors (Eccles,

1993; Eccles [Parsons] et al., 1983; Goodnow & Collins, 1990; Grolnick, Ryan, & Deci, 1991; McGillicuddy-DeLisi, 1982). The family socialization model illustrated in Figure 1b summarizes these theoretical perspectives (Eccles, 1993). This perspective on the socialization and enactment of behavioral choices is consistent with recent theoretical work focused on cascades of experience and outcomes (Masten & Coatsworth, 1998; Masten et al., 2005). According to a cascade perspective, experiences have immediate and long-term consequences because they set in motion processes that change individual's developmental trajectories through their impact on options, skills, assets, and risks across time.

Foundational Issues in the Expectancy–Value Model

In this next section, we discuss three important theoretical debates concerning the relations outlined in the Eccles's socialization model that we address in this monograph: (1) origin of parents' beliefs, (2) direction of influence, and (3) gender. A full review of the literature relevant to these issues is included later in the introduction where specific components of the model are discussed.

Origins of Parents' Beliefs

Inherent in the Eccles's et al. model illustrated in Figure 1b, as well as in other sociocultural theories of social development, is the idea that parents' beliefs and behaviors do not emerge in a vacuum (Furstenberg et al., 1999; McLoyd, 1990). They are influenced by characteristics of their children and by their own circumstances, values, histories of experience, and sociocultural positioning (see the boxes to the far left). For example, two characteristics that should influence parents' beliefs and behaviors is the child's gender and abilities. In fact, one could argue that these characteristics, circumstances, and histories begin the cascade. But they can also influence all subsequent steps in the socialization stream through ongoing feedback loops. For example, parents' estimates of their children's abilities in various domains should be responsive to information they receive about their children's performance in these domains—information obtained from others like teachers or coaches, as well as information obtained through parents' own interactions with their children. Similarly, the value parents attach to their children acquiring particular competencies or interests should be responsive to information they get about their children's competencies and the emerging interests their children develop over time.

Direction of Influence

The importance of feedback systems was initially discussed most extensively by Bell (1968) who argued that we should not assume that the statistical associations we find between parenting constructs and children's characteristics reflect a unidirectional influence from parents to children. Instead, we should consider the possibility that parents are responding to characteristics of their children. This view is now widely endorsed and most developmental theoreticians now argue for the importance of taking a reciprocal view of parent–child patterns of influence (Bronfenbrenner & Morris, 2006; Bugental & Johnston, 2000; Mischel, 1973; Pardini, 2008; Rogoff, 2003; Sameroff, 2000). Although the influence of children on parents has been at the forefront of research on some areas of development, such as child temperament (Bates, 1987; Belsky, 1984), children's effects on their parents have not received much attention in the field of achievement-related motivation and behavior, even in studies based on the Eccles model (Simpkins, Fredricks, & Eccles, 2012). One of our goals is to fill this gap with regard to the possible influence of children's gender, competencies, and beliefs on their parents' beliefs and behaviors.

A secondary feedback system detailed in the Eccles's expectancy–value model is the reciprocal relations between individuals' beliefs and their behaviors over time. As in most social cognitive theories of behavior, Eccles et al. (1983) assume that beliefs cause behaviors. However, there is a long tradition within the social psychology of the link between attitudes and behaviors in which scholars question this assumption. For example, in his classic work, Bem (1970) argued that people infer their beliefs from their behaviors. Scholars within the attitude behavior tradition, now argue that the association between beliefs and behaviors are stronger when the attitudes are quite specific and directly tied to the behaviors being studied (Eagly & Chaiken, 1993). In this monograph, we investigated several of these possibilities.

Gender

Gender differences are a pervasive theme throughout the literatures on achievement-related engagement and performance. This is particularly true in the domains of sports, math, and reading. These three domains, plus instrumental music, were selected, in part, due to the traditional gender stereotypes associated with each of these areas. Sports and math are often considered to be masculine domains, whereas reading/English and instrumental music are often deemed as feminine domains during childhood (Wigfield et al., 2006). In fact, particular initiatives have been developed to try to reduce these gender differences. For example, Title IX addresses equality in school sports opportunities for boys and girls. The National Science Foundation also has placed a spotlight on increasing women's and ethnic minority individual's pursuit of science, technology, engineering, and math. Furthermore, the underachievement of boys in reading and English is receiving renewed attention (Fredricks, 2014).

Gender differences in youths' behavioral engagement in each of these domains emerge early in elementary school. Boys are more physically active and more likely to participate in organized sports than girls (Duncan, Duncan, & Strycker, 2005; Fredricks & Eccles, 2006; Jacobs, Vernon, & Eccles, 2005; Kahn et al., 2008). In contrast, girls are more likely to participate in music (Jacobs et al., 2005) and reading during out-of-school time than boys (Baker & Wigfield, 1999; Coles & Hall, 2002; Nippold, Duthie, & Larsen, 2005). The findings for math depend on whether it is in school or out of school; boys are *less* likely to engage in math activities outside of school (Eccles & Harold, 1991; Simpkins, Davis-Kean, & Eccles, 2005), but *more* likely to enroll in the most advanced math courses during high school than girls (Eccles [Parsons] et al., 1984; Farmer et al., 1995; Updegraff, Eccles, Barber, & O'Brien, 1996). The gender differences in instrumental music may also change during adolescence when boys become increasingly interested in rock music and garage bands. The next critical step that we undertake in this monograph is to understand the role of gender in the precursors of these gendered choices.

Gender effects can take two forms: (a) mean-level differences between girls and boys on key constructs and (b) differences in the patterns of associations among constructs. The existing research has largely focused on mean-level gender differences in the types of constructs included in this investigation. Mean-level differences speak to whether boys or girls, on average, are more likely to engage in certain activities or hold different motivational beliefs. These findings are critical to identify areas of discrepancy and to pinpoint particular segments of the population that should be targeted with policy and practice initiatives.

It is equally important, however, to understand if the nature of the associations among constructs for the various groups are similar. For example, it is important to know if the subjective task value an individual places on math versus English is an equally powerful predictor of taking advanced math courses for boys and girls. Eccles and her colleagues found that it was not—subjective task values were more powerful predictors for girls' than for boys' intentions to take more math courses—in contrast, ability self-concepts were more powerful predictors for boys than for girls (Eccles [Parsons] et al., 1983). Other research suggests there may not be differences in the predictors between girls and boys (Simpkins, Davis-Kean, & Eccles, 2006). If policy makers and practitioners want to change outcomes, they need to know whether the same program or intervention should be designed for both genders. This type of information is gathered by testing whether gender is a moderator of the relations among constructs. Relatively few such studies have been done.

It is important to note that moderation can occur regardless of mean-level differences. In math, boys have higher math motivational beliefs and enroll in a higher number of elective advanced math and physical science high school and college courses than girls (Updegraff et al., 1996). Despite these differences, the associations between math beliefs and the number of math courses are similar for both boys and girls (Simpkins, Davis-Kean, et al., 2006). In other words, if an adolescent believes s/he is good at math, he *or* she is more likely to enroll in a math course than an adolescent who does not believe s/he is good at math. Thus, boys and girls with high beliefs about their math abilities are likely to enroll in math courses (i.e., lack of moderation based on gender). However, boys are more likely than girls to have high math-related ability beliefs (i.e., significant mean-level differences based on gender). Although we have consistent research findings on mean-level gender differences, particularly in sports and math, much less is known concerning whether the relations among indicators vary based on gender. In the next two sections, we review the support for the relations between (a) parenting and children's motivational beliefs, and (b) children's motivational beliefs and choices.

A MORE DETAILED PERSPECTIVE ON PARENTING BELIEFS AND BEHAVIORS

As children's first socializers, parents play an important role in the creation of gender-differentiated beliefs and values by giving children their first messages about gender roles and by providing them with opportunities and experiences that support the development of certain competencies (Coltrane & Adams, 1997; Eccles, 1993; Eccles [Parsons] et al., 1983). Many developmentalists believe these early experiences play an important role in shaping children's views of their capabilities (Bandura, 1997; Eccles, 1993; Goodnow & Collins, 1990; Harter, 1999). Parents may be particularly influential in shaping children's beliefs and abilities when they are in elementary school because children are highly focused on these activities as well as on forming their ability self-concepts around these activities during this period (Eccles & Midgley, 1989; Erikson, 1982; Stipek & MacIver, 1989).

Another factor that contributes to parents' importance in elementary school is the degree of control they have over the kinds of experiences their children are exposed to and how they spend their time (Eccles, 1993; Parke et al., 2003). When children are young, parents play an important role in getting their children initially involved in activities, such as by buying equipment and books to support their continued involvement, and spending time with them to develop their skills. As children get older, parents begin to relinquish some control and give children more responsibility for making their own decisions. Children begin to play a role in planning their activities during the after-school hours near the end of elementary school (Savage & Gauvain, 1998).

Parent Beliefs

Parents can play a role in shaping children's competence and value beliefs by conveying general messages to children about their view of the world and more specific messages about children's varying abilities in different activity domains. As shown in Figure 1b, parents convey these messages to children in a variety of ways including: (1) causal attributions about children's success in various domains, (2) specific expectations for success, (3) perceptions of the value of various activities, and (4) perceptions of the difficulty of various tasks (Eccles, 1993). In this study, we focus on parents' perceptions of their children's ability and perceptions of the value of each domain as they are the two dimensions that have received the most attention in prior research.

Parents' estimates of their children's academic competencies have been found to be important predictors of children's own ability self-concepts and actual performance (Alexander & Entwisle, 1988; Eccles, 1993). There is an extensive literature linking parents' ratings of their children's ability to children's estimates of their ability and interest in sports, math, and English (Andre, Whigham, Hendrickson, & Chambers, 1999; Bhanot & Jovanovic, 2005; Bleeker & Jacobs, 2004; Fredricks & Eccles, 2002, 2005; Frome & Eccles, 1998; McCullagh, Matzkanin, Shaw, & Maldonado, 1993; Simpkins et al., 2012; Shumow & Lomax, 2002; Tiedemann, 2000). In fact, parents' beliefs of children's math and sport abilities predicted slower declines in children's competence beliefs from grades 1–12 using the same data as is reported in this monograph (Fredricks & Eccles, 2002). Very little comparable work has been done in the domain of instrumental music, though scholars have suggested parents' perceptions of their children's musical ability and talent may be important factors in children's music motivation (Dai & Schader, 2002; Davidson, Howe, Moore, & Sloboda, 1996; Eccles, 1993; Simpkins et al., 2012). Furthermore, researchers have yet to link these experiences in a cascading fashion to achievement-related choices made during adolescence.

Parents' value of a domain may also predict their children's own competence and value beliefs, but less research has addressed this question. When parents perceived that participating in schoolwork and sports was important, elementary and junior high school students had increased academic and sport competence beliefs (Bandura, Barbaranelli, Caprara, & Pastorelli, 1996; Eccles & Harold, 1991; Fredricks & Eccles, 2005; Simpkins et al., 2012) as well as increased participation in sports (Fredricks & Eccles, 2005; Kahn et al., 2008). In contrast, other studies have failed to document a relation between parents' perception of importance and children's ability self-concepts and interest in math and reading (Andre et al., 1999; Simpkins et al., 2012) and between parents' value beliefs and children's sport participation (Eccles & Harold, 1991; Kimiecik & Horn, 1998). Preliminary evidence is also mixed on whether these relations differ depending on the gender of the parent and gender of the child (Fredricks & Eccles, 2005; McGrath & Repetti, 2000).

10

In contrast to the extensive literature on parents' general beliefs (e.g., the valuing of achievement and school competence, child rearing beliefs, values and goals, gender-typed beliefs, and cultural-based beliefs), only a handful of studies have examined the links between parents' child-specific beliefs (i.e., perceptions of their child's competence and value) and parenting practices. In a previous study using the same data as this monograph, researchers tested portions of the Eccles's parental socialization model in sports, instrumental music, math, and reading (Simpkins et al., 2012); mothers' behaviors mediated the link between mothers' and youth's beliefs in sports, music, and math, but not in reading. Additionally, Jodl and coworkers (2001) found that in sports, fathers' behaviors mediated the relation between parents' and youth's sport values. In contrast, they also found that parents' values in academics predicted adolescents' values directly rather than indirectly through their behaviors.

Parent Behaviors

Historically, family researchers have largely focused on face-to-face interactions and parenting styles. Parents also promote children's development by managing children's environments through such strategies as choosing where to live, designing peer networks, providing objects that structure children's activities, and seeking specific experiences outside of their home (Bradley et al., 1989; Eccles, 1993; Furstenberg et al., 1999; Parke et al., 2003). Theories of sociocultural psychology and motivation, posit that parents play a central role in adolescents' choices through these types of promotive behaviors (Rogoff, 1990). According to the Eccles's socialization model (Eccles, 1993), parents influence their children's beliefs through five basic mechanisms: (1) role modeling, (2) encouragement and reinforcement, (3) interpreting their children's experiences and the events they observe around them, (4) provision of activity-related experiences (e.g., sport equipment), and (5) parent–child coactivity (e.g., parents practicing sports with their child).

Modeling

Parents' leisure pursuits, or their modeling of behavioral choices, have the potential to influence their children's choices through processes associated with observational learning and with the desire to be like their parents (Bandura, 1997; Eccles, 1993). The process of role modeling has been suggested as one of the ways in which children absorb social norms, especially those associated with gender-typed choices (Maccoby & Jacklin, 1974). The handful of studies on the effects of role modeling on academic outcomes has not found strong associations (Andre et al., 1999; Eccles [Parsons] et al., 1982), though adult modeling may have a modest influence on children's reading (Neuman, 1986; Pluck, Ghafari, Glynn, McNaughton, 1984). The findings concerning the effects of role modeling in sports and music are also mixed. Some studies have shown significant relations between parents' and children's activity level, especially with young children (Kahn et al., 2008; Moore et al., 1991; Sallis, Prochaska, Taylor, Hill, & Geraci, 1999; Vilhjalmsson & Thorlindsson, 1998), whereas others found no relation between parent and child activity level (Dempsey, Kimiecik, & Horn, 1993; Fredricks & Eccles, 2005; Kimiecik & Horn, 1998; Welk, Woods, & Morss, 2003). Finally, although only a minority of parents are performing musicians or play an instrument themselves (McPherson & Davidson, 2006; Sloboda & Howe, 1991), parental modeling in terms of listening to music predicted children's music competence (Davidson et al., 1996). There are a variety of reasons for the mixed findings concerning modeling. Parental modeling may be a weak unique predictor relative to other behaviors (e.g., coactivity) because it is likely to occur with other behaviors. In contrast, modeling may have a weak influence on activities that are more cognitive in nature and require instruction, such as completing a math problem or reading a book.

Encouragement

Parental encouragement can directly promote children's ability self-concepts and values through positive reinforcement (Eccles, 1993). Encouragement may also indirectly support children's ability self-concepts and values by creating a positive affective association with particular activities. Studies consistently highlight the importance of parental encouragement. Talented adolescents and elite adult athletes, artists, and musicians reported that parental encouragement was one of the key dimensions of parenting that shaped their pathways (Bloom, 1985; Csikszentmihalyi, Rathunde, & Whalen, 1993; Sosniak, 1990). Parental encouragement and support in reading and math has been linked to children's time spent reading (Neuman, 1986) as well as math self-efficacy beliefs, perceptions of the importance of math, and career interests in math and science (Ferry, Fouad, & Smith, 2000; Turner, Stewart, & Lapan, 2004). Several studies have linked parental encouragement in sports to children's sport interest and athletic participation (Bauer, Nelson, Boutelle, & Neumark-Sztainer, 2008; Brustad, 1993; Fredricks & Eccles, 2005; Pugliese & Tinsley, 2007; Sallis et al., 1999). In addition, individuals who achieved high musical competence reported having had supportive parents who provided ongoing encouragement and general support for music practice (Davidson et al., 1996; Howe & Sloboda, 1991; McPherson & Davidson, 2002; Sosniak, 1985).

Provision of Materials

According to sociocultural theory, materials in the home expose children to particular experiences and value systems (Vygotsky, 1978). Parents actively manage the home environment as a way to structure children's experiences

12

through the provision of toys, equipment, books, and other learning activities (Furstenberg et al., 1999; Parke et al., 2003). Higher exposure leads to children's comfort, engagement, and learning in a domain, as well as engagement in a domain with their parents (e.g., reading a book with their parents). Materials provided in the home have been core to the research on supporting children's academic achievement as noted in the work by Bradley et al. (1989), research on family involvement in children's education (Epstein, 1995), and research on the socialization of gender-typed activity patterns and preferences (Ruble et al., 2006).

Indicators of logistic support, such as sport equipment and transportation, predicted adolescents' sport motivational beliefs and physical activity (Davison, Cutting, & Birch, 2003; Dowda, Dishman, Pfeiffer, & Pate, 2007; Fredricks & Eccles, 2005; Pugliese & Tinsley, 2007). Furthermore, children who had increased access to literature-related activities in the home had more positive attitudes about reading, engage in more leisure reading, and had increased reading achievement (Neuman, 1986; Rowe, 1991; Whitehurst & Lonigan, 2001). Provision of music opportunities, in terms of purchasing instruments, books, and CDs, also is critical for children's ongoing music participation (McPherson, 2009; McPherson & Davidson, 2006). However, few studies have looked at the provision of materials as part of a larger model of parental influence and none have looked at this type of influence across activity domains.

Coactivity

Parent–child participation in an activity together (i.e., coactivity) is another strategy parents might use to promote children's activity participation. Parent–child coactivity can occur through informal activities at home, involvement in organized activities such as being a coach or going to a museum together, and attending a community event together (Simpkins, Vest, Dawes, & Neuman, 2010). Parent–child coactivity provides a context for parents to offer verbal encouragement, convey the value of an activity, provide feedback, and both model and teach skills.

Parents' involvement in children's sport activities (e.g., attending children's sporting events) predicted children's sport interest, ability self-concept, and participation (Babkes & Weiss, 1999; Duncan et al., 2005; Fredricks & Eccles, 2005). In music, parents' involvement in music lessons, going to concerts together, or informal music activities with the child was important for children's music success and persistence in both prospective and retrospective studies (Davidson et al., 1996; Howe & Sloboda, 1991; Sloboda & Howe, 1991; Sosniak, 1985, 1990; Zdzinski, 1994, 1996). Family joint reading in the home has also been related to young children's motivation to read (Baker, Scher, & Mackler, 1997; Bus, 1994; Morrow, 1983), though a few studies have failed to document a relation between parents' involvement and children's reading motivation (Baker & Scher, 2002; Loera, Rueda, & Nakamoto, 2011). Finally, parent–child math coactivity predicted children's math knowledge and fluency (LeFevre et al., 2009).

How Do These Parental Behaviors Work Together?

Multiple parental behaviors can influence children. However, few studies have adopted a holistic integrated view of the family context. Instead, much of the previous research predicting activity participation from parental indicators has focused on only one or two behaviors, one parent, and/or one activity domain (Fredricks & Eccles, 2005; Simpkins et al., 2012). The qualitative literature on talent development demonstrates that families influence children simultaneously through multiple behaviors. For example, Bloom (1985) found that parents in the homes of elite athletes, musicians, and artists supported children's talents through multiple strategies, including helping to gain access to special teachers or coaches, helping to develop plans for practicing their skills, and providing money for lessons and equipment. Other scholars have also pointed to the importance of a holistic perspective on parenting that takes into account the variety of ways in which parents can interact with and influence their children (Lareau, 2003; Rogoff, 1990).

Most quantitative studies, however, include only a limited subset of parental behaviors and many use regression techniques that assess the unique contribution of each predictor adjusting for the other variables in the model rather than taking a more holistic view. Such analytic models are based on the assumption that influences relate additively to the outcome being studied and that the most important thing to understand is the unique effect of each individual component. Although this is a quite acceptable approach to studying multiple influences on a particular outcome as well as being the theoretical underpinning of multiple linear regression approaches to data analysis, it does reflect a strong theoretical stance regarding the nature of parental influences on their children—one that should be open to questioning in light of the qualitative studies that highlight a more nuanced and integrative perspective on family influences (Laureau, 2003; Rogoff, 1990).

The multiple regression approach also is being questioned for mathematical reasons. Including moderately to highly correlated predictors in regression models can obscure meaningful associations of individual predictors and the outcome variable due to deflated parameter estimates (Mosteller & Tukey, 1977). Given these theoretical and methodological considerations, we believe a holistic or pattern-centered approach, such as cluster analysis, multidimensional scaling, and cumulative models hold promise for assessing the more synergistic nature of families. In this methodological approach, individual factors are examined in conjunction with other factors rather than comparing the relative importance of each individual variable (Bergman, Magnusson, & El-Khouri, 2003).

There are three areas of research on family socialization that have taken a holistic approach to examining parental socialization. First, several scholars examining the parental correlates of children's physical activities have incorporated multiple indicators of parental behaviors, including indicators of praise, coactivity, encouragement, provision of necessary sport equipment/ transportation, and parent's physical activity into an overall scale of parental support. This overall indicator predicts children's self-efficacy (Dowda et al., 2007) and physical activity (Beets, Vogel, Forlaw, Pitetti, & Cardinal, 2006; Davison et al., 2003; Dowda et al., 2007). A recent meta-analysis showed that an overall indicator of parents' behaviors had a small, but significant relation to children's physical activity (Pugliese & Tinsley, 2007).

Second, the literature on family involvement in children's education exemplifies a multivariate approach to studying families. For example, several scholars have argued that parents influence their children's academic performance through a variety of mechanisms, such as coactivity, involvement in the school, and providing an educationally enriching environment inside and outside of the home (Eccles, 1993; Eccles [Parsons] et al., 1983; Epstein, 1995; Lareau, 2003; Saracho, 2002). Parents' behaviors across these areas were predictive of children's academic achievement and motivational beliefs (see Jeynes, 2007, for a meta-analysis).

The other notable exception is work on parental socialization and achievement motivation by Eccles and her colleagues using the same dataset as used in this monograph (Fredricks & Eccles, 2005; Fredricks, Simpkins, & Eccles, 2005; Simpkins, Fredricks, Davis-Kean, & Eccles, 2006). Building on risk and resilience models (Rutter, 1988; Sameroff, Bartko, Baldwin, Baldwin, & Seifer, 1998), the researchers created indicators representing the extent to which a family included no, a few, or many supports for children's domain-specific competence beliefs, value beliefs, and activity engagement. This single indicator of parental support was linearly related to increases over time in children's ability self-concepts, values, and activity participation in math, sports, music, and science. This finding contradicted analyses with the same set of parental variables using regression techniques. These analyses showed that many of the behavioral socialization factors, such as time spent doing sports with children, were not related to children's competence and value beliefs after controlling for parents' beliefs and the children's actual competence.

Direction of Influence

The socialization of children is not a unidirectional process by which parents simply shape children. Although Bell emphasized this point as early as 1968, the majority of research has focused on how indicators of parenting predict children's adjustment (Bell, 1968). In the few relevant studies testing the influence of children's beliefs and choices on parents, researchers have found that parents' promotive behaviors were predicted by children's previous sport ability self-concepts (Davison et al., 2003) and music involvement (Davidson et al., 1996). Similarly, Simpkins and her colleagues (2010) used latent growth curve modeling to examine the association between children's motivational beliefs and changes in parents' behavior in sports and instrumental music. They found that high child sport motivational beliefs predicted slower increases in fathers' sport-related behavior from grades 1–6. In contrast, fathers had steeper increases in behavior if their sons expressed an interest in instrumental music. Finally, using cross-lagged SEM, Eccles and her colleagues found that mothers' perceptions of their elementary school-aged children's ability more strongly predicted changes in children's ability self-perceptions across a 2-year period than vice versa (Eccles, Freedman-Doan, Frome, Jacobs, & Yoon, 2000).

Gender

Parents use a variety of factors including objective indicators to form their beliefs about their child's competencies and interests. Gender is one such salient characteristic that parents attend to in forming an impression of their child. Parents hold certain beliefs about girls' and boys' abilities in different domains, which may be partly influenced by the larger cultural beliefs about appropriate gender roles (e.g., men excel in mathematics and science).

The findings concerning differences in parents' beliefs based on children's gender in all domains are mixed. There is some evidence that parents rated children's math ability (Bhanot & Jovanovic, 2005; Eccles, Jacobs, & Harold, 1990; Herbert & Stipek, 2005; Jacobs & Eccles, 1992; Tiedemann, 2000) as well as sport competence and importance beliefs (Brustad, 1993; Eccles, 1993; Fredricks & Eccles, 2005; Jacobs & Eccles, 1992) higher for sons than daughters in childhood and adolescence. Additionally, there is evidence that parents of daughters rated their children as more competent in reading than do parents of sons (Bhanot & Jovanovic, 2005; Eccles, Jacobs, et al., 1993; Frome & Eccles, 1998; Lummis & Stevenson, 1990). However, it is important to note that other studies have failed to document gender differences in parents' perceptions of ability in and importance of math (Andre et al., 1999; Eccles et al., 1993; Frome & Eccles, 1998; Jacobs & Eccles, 1992), sports (Babkes & Weiss, 1999; Bois, Sarrazin, Brustad, Trouilloud, & Cury, 2002; Kimiecik & Horn, 1998), and reading (Andre et al., 1999; Herbert & Stipek, 2005).

The evidence that parents treat daughters and sons differently depends on the activity domain. Several researchers have shown that parents' differential engagement in behaviors for their sons and daughters follow traditional gender stereotypes (Eccles & Hoffman, 1984; Lytton & Romney, 1991; Tenebaum & Leaper, 2003). For example, parents were more likely to purchase math and science items for their sons than their daughters in both childhood and adolescence (Bleeker & Jacobs, 2004; Jacobs et al., 2005). Additionally, parents have been found to provide more sport opportunities for boys than for girls (Fredricks & Eccles, 2005; Greendorfer, Lewko, & Rosengren, 1996; Welk et al., 2003), though a small number of studies on physical activity (which is broader than organized sports) showed no differences in behaviors based on child gender (Bauer et al., 2008; Duncan et al., 2005; Pugliese, & Tinsley, 2007). In contrast, parents reported similar reading-related behaviors for their sons and daughters (Neuman, 1986). The limited research testing gender as a moderator of the associations between parents' behaviors and children's outcomes indicated that parents' activity-related behaviors had similar associations with boys' and girls' beliefs and participation in a variety of activities (Fredricks et al., 2005; Simpkins, Davis-Kean, et al., 2005; Simpkins et al., 2010, 2012).

Parent gender also is important. Mothers and fathers may play different roles in gender socialization. According to reciprocal role theory (Johnson, 1975), fathers socialization practices are more likely to promote sex-typing in children because fathers tend to make a greater distinction between their sons and daughters. The evidence in support of reciprocal role theory is mixed. Delineating the role mothers *and* fathers play in socialization is complicated by the limited number of studies that have collected data from fathers. Additionally, some studies include mothers and fathers in the same model and suggest that fathers make a relatively minimal contribution to child development. We know this is not the case. Our goal in this monograph is to contribute to the literature by testing the parental processes at hand for mothers and for fathers. As such, our hypotheses and analyses focus on similar processes for each parent, but do not focus on the comparison across parents or the relative contribution of each parent.

A MORE DETAILED PERSPECTIVE ON CHILDREN'S AND ADOLESCENTS' MOTIVATIONAL BELIEFS AND PARTICIPATION

According to the Eccles's expectancy–value model, contextual influences on adolescents' choices are mediated by adolescents' motivational beliefs (Eccles [Parsons] et al., 1983). According to this model (see Figure 1a), there are two key motivational beliefs underlying adolescents' participation in academic and nonacademic skill-based activities: individuals' confidence in their ability to be successful at an activity (now assessed in terms of the individuals' ability self-concepts) and the subjective task value they attach to engaging in an activity. Consistent with social constructivist perspectives, individual differences in self- and task-perceptions come not from reality itself, but from children's interpretation of reality.

Competence Beliefs

Ability self-concept is defined as children's beliefs about their competence in different areas as well as how well they expect to do on the task (Eccles [Parsons] et al., 1983). Ability self-concept has been the cornerstone of many other theories whose goal is to predict performance and choices, including Bandura's (1977) seminal work on self-efficacy, Covington's self-worth theory (1992), and Marsh's reciprocal effects model (Marsh, Gerlach, Trautwein, Lüdtke, & Brettschneider, 2007). In fact, according to self-determination theory, people's need for competence will drive them to seek out situations in which they can express and build their competencies (Ryan & Deci, 2000). Harter (1999) also asserted that children's ability self-concepts have implications beyond choices; such that, ability self-concepts in highly valued activity domains are the building blocks of one's overall self-esteem.

Although several studies have linked ability self-concepts to choice, effort, persistence, and performance in mathematics, English, computer activities, and sports (Marsh, Chanal, Sarrin, & Bois, 2006; Marsh et al., 2007; Wigfield et al., 2006), the findings are mixed across domains. For example, math ability self-concept did not predict the number of math and science courses taken in high school once actual performance history was controlled in some studies (Joyce & Farenga, 1999; Updegraff et al., 1996), but it was predictive in other studies (Simpkins, Davis-Kean, et al., 2006). Ability self-concept in reading was associated with the amount and breadth of leisure time reading in elementary school (Baker & Wigfield, 1999; Guthrie & Wigfield, 2000; Wigfield & Guthrie, 1997) as well as the number of language courses taken and time spent reading for pleasure in high school (Durik, Vida, & Eccles, 2006). Furthermore, children's self-concept of sport ability predicted children's athletic participation (Bois et al., 2002; Fredricks & Eccles, 2005; Kimiecik & Horn, 1998; Sabiston & Crocker, 2008). Finally, there is limited evidence that self-concept of music ability predicts interest and participation for both in-school and out-of-school music activities (Austin, 1990; Klinedinst, 1991; Simpkins et al., 2012). No studies have looked at multiple domains simultaneously so we do not know whether these inconsistencies across studies and domains reflect methodological or substantive issues.

Value Beliefs

Eccles and her colleagues have developed the most extensive theory of subjective task value (see Eccles [Parsons] et al., 1983; Wigfield & Eccles, 1992, for a full description). Subjective task value is broadly defined as the relative

18

value individuals attach to doing different tasks. Individuals should engage in tasks they positively value and avoid tasks that they do not highly value. Subjective task value is a function of at least four distinct components: intrinsic value (enjoyment of the activity), attainment value (importance of doing well on the task for confirming aspects of one's self-schema), utility value/importance (importance of task for current or future goals), and cost (negative aspects of engaging in task) (Eccles [Parsons] et al., 1983). Intrinsic value is related to the construct of intrinsic motivation (Deci & Ryan, 1985; Harter, 1981), and to the constructs of interests and flow (Csikszentmihalyi, 1988; Renninger, 2000; Schiefele, 1991). In contrast, attainment value and utility value are related to the link of the task to other short- and long-term goals. In this investigation, we focus on intrinsic value (henceforth labeled interest) and attainment/utility value (henceforth labeled importance) as they are the two dimensions that have received the most attention in prior research.

There is strong empirical support for interest and importance being central to children's choices. Adolescents' values (i.e., a combination of interest and importance) were strong predictors of their *intentions* to enroll in elective math and science courses (Atwater, Wiggins, & Gardner, 1995; Crombie et al., 2005; Ethington, 1991) and the actual number of math and science courses adolescents took in high school (Joyce & Farenga, 1999; Simpkins, Davis-Kean, et al., 2006; Simpkins et al., 2012; Updegraff et al., 1996). Math values were also important in whether adults pursue a career in science (Farmer et al., 1999). The findings for reading are mixed. Interest in reading was related to time spent reading for pleasure, but not to time spent reading in school (Cox & Guthrie, 2001; Durik et al., 2006). In addition, some studies have linked reading importance to reading time use and course taking (Durik et al., 2006; Simpkins et al., 2012), whereas others have failed to document a relation between reading importance and time spent reading for pleasure (Baker & Wigfield, 1999; Wigfield & Guthrie, 1997). Furthermore, children's values were positively associated with sport involvement (Eccles & Harold, 1991; Sabiston & Crocker, 2008; Simpkins et al., 2012) and negatively associated with dropping out of athletics (Guillet, Sarrazin, Fontayne, & Brustad, 2006). Finally, a few studies have linked music task value to time spent practicing music (McPherson & McCormick, 1999; O'Neill, 1999; Simpkins et al., 2012).

Direction of Influence

Up to this point, we have discussed the relations between adolescents' motivational beliefs and choices in terms of how adolescents' motivational beliefs predict their choices. Motivation models explicitly state that the relations between beliefs and choices are reciprocal across time (Eccles, 1993; Marsh, Byrne, & Yeung, 1999; Marsh & Craven, 2006). The research that has been conducted focuses on the reciprocal associations between motivational beliefs and performance, not choices. For example, in a series of studies in both academic and non-academic domains, Marsh (1990), Marsh and Perry (2005), Marsh and his colleagues (2006, 2007) found that ability self-concept was associated with increases in performance, and in turn, that higher performance was related to increased ability self-concept.

Participation in math out-of-school activities and the number of high school elective math and science courses has been found to predict adolescents' subsequent motivational beliefs in math and science (Farmer et al., 1995; Jacobs, Finken, Griffin, & Wright, 1998; Simpkins, Davis-Kean, et al., 2006). Participation in sports also positively predicted subsequent sport interest, importance, and self-concept of ability (Fredricks, 1999; Simpkins, Fredricks et al., 2006; Simpkins et al., 2010). Although these studies provide preliminary evidence that children's choices are associated with beliefs. One central goal of this study is to test the strength of the reciprocal relations between choices and motivational beliefs across time through a series of cross-lagged models.

Gender

Boys' and girls' domain-specific ability self-concepts differ in gender role stereotypic ways during childhood and adolescence. For example, several studies have shown that girls have lower math ability self-concepts even though boys and girls perform equally well in this domain (Evans, Schweingruber, & Stevenson, 2002; Fredricks & Eccles, 2002; Herbert & Stipek, 2005; Jacobs, Lanza, Osgood, Eccles, & Wigfield, 2002; Marsh & Yeung, 1998; Tiedemann, 2000; Watt, 2005). In addition, girls have consistently reported lower self-concepts of sport ability than boys in both childhood and adolescence (Eccles & Harold, 1991; Evans et al., 2002; Fredricks & Eccles, 2002, 2005; Klomsten, Skaalivk, & Espnes, 2004; Sabiston & Crocker, 2008). In contrast, girls have reported higher reading and language arts ability self-concepts than do boys (Andre et al., 1999; Baker & Wigfield, 1999; Evans et al., 2002; Lummis & Stevenson, 1990; Marsh, 1989). Finally, limited research suggests that elementary school-aged girls had more positive self-concepts of ability in instrumental music than do boys (Eccles, Wigfield, Harold, & Blumenfeld, 1993; Evans et al., 2002).

Gender differences in the value children and adolescents attach to different activities also tend to follow gender norms and stereotypes. Consistent differences in values are evident in sports and reading across a variety of ages. Boys placed greater value on sports than girls (Eccles, Wigfield, et al., 1993; Fredricks & Eccles, 2002; Jacobs et al., 2002; Klomsten, Marsh, & Skaalvik, 2005; Sabiston & Crocker, 2008; Wigfield et al., 1997), whereas, boys placed lower value on reading and language arts than girls (Andre et al., 1999; Baker & Wigfield, 1999; Evans et al., 2002; Jacobs et al., 2002; Marinak &

20

Gambell, 2010; VanSchooter, Oostdam, & de Glopper, 2001; Wigfield et al., 1997). The findings regarding gender differences in math value have been mixed. Some studies show no gender differences in math value (Eccles, Wigfield, et al., 1993; Fredricks & Eccles, 2002; Jacobs et al., 2002). In contrast, other studies show that boys report greater interest in math in high school (Hyde, Fennema, Ryan, Frost, & Hopp, 1990) and rate the importance of math higher than do girls (Andre et al., 1999). Very little research has addressed gender differences in instrumental music value. One exception is work by Eccles and her colleagues (1993) who found that girls had more positive value beliefs in music than did boys.

The majority of research addressing gender differences in motivational beliefs has examined whether boys and girls differ according to their means. A second and completely independent question is whether gender moderates or alters the associations between the constructs in the models. Tests of gender moderation examine if similar processes operate for girls and boys. If the various self- and task-related beliefs of the early adolescents predict subsequent activity choices differently for girls and boys, then interventions aimed to increase the participation of girls and boys in math and science, for example, will need to focus on different beliefs. More specifically, if the task value beliefs are stronger predictors of girls' than of boys' subsequent course-taking in math and vice versa for math ability self-concepts, then interventions to increase girls' enrollments will need to focus on task value beliefs whereas interventions to increase boys' enrollments should focus on raising their ability self-concepts. The few researchers who have tested gender as a moderator have found that the relation between youths' motivational beliefs with participation and performance are similar for boys and girls in academic and nonacademic domains (Marsh et al., 2007; Sabiston & Crocker, 2008; Simpkins, Davis-Kean, et al., 2006; Valentine, Dubois, & Cooper, 2004). Given the small but growing literature on adolescent gender as a moderator of these relations and the potential importance of the issue for designing effective interventions, we explored whether child gender moderated relations between motivational beliefs and participation.

OUR HYPOTHESES

Our overarching goal in this monograph is to test the predicted relations outlined in Figure 1b. Consistent with cascade-type models of human development, this model includes three main portions: the first focuses on the association of child characteristics with their parents' beliefs, the second focuses on parents' possible influence on their children's beliefs, and the third focuses on the relations of children's beliefs to their own achievement-related task engagement. Because we assume that the first two portions precede the third in developmental time, we use data from early elementary school to investigate the first parts of the model and data from late elementary school through high school to investigate the second half of the model. Throughout, we control for the exogenous characteristics shown in the far left boxes of Figure 1b in order to provide as strong a test as possible of the proposed causal linkages. In addition, we use cross-lagged analytic techniques to provide a further test of the proposed causal links in the model. We examine these hypotheses across two mandatory school-based achievement domains (math and reading) and two voluntary but highly skilled leisure activities (sports and instrumental music), all four of which are gender-typed in the United States.

We have five general hypotheses. First, parents' views of their children's abilities will be reciprocally related to the teachers' estimates of their children's natural talent in each domain and to the gender of their child. Second, parents' beliefs will positively predict changes in their children's motivational beliefs and participation. Third, parents' beliefs will positively predict changes in their own behaviors over time (i.e., role modeling, encouragement, expectancies for success, provision of activity-related experiences, and parent–child coactivity). Fourth, parents' behaviors will positively predict changes in their children's ability self-concepts and values. Fifth, youth's ability self-concepts and values will positively predict changes in their own subsequent participation.

In relation to the direction of influence questions, based on prior literature, we have two specific hypotheses. First, although there will be reciprocal relations between parents' and their children's constructs, the direction of influence will largely flow from parents to youth in childhood. Second, although there will be reciprocal relations between parents' beliefs and behaviors, as well as youths' beliefs and behaviors, the direction of influence will largely flow from parents' beliefs to behaviors, and youth's beliefs to behaviors.

In terms of youth gender, we have two specific hypotheses. First, parents of daughters will hold higher beliefs and engage in more behaviors for reading and instrumental music than parents of sons. The opposite pattern will emerge for sports and math. Second, girls will have higher motivational beliefs and participation in reading and instrumental music as well as lower motivational beliefs and participation in sports and math than boys.

Because so little work has been done comparing different activity domains, we cannot base hypotheses on existing empirical literature. However, given that developing skills and interests in both sports and instrumental music in the United States depend more on parental efforts than do developing skills and interests in math and reading, we expect the consistency of evidence and the strength of the associations to be higher for parental influences in sports and instrumental music than in math and reading.

22

II. METHODS

Participants

The data are from the Childhood and Beyond Study (CAB), which has a cohort-sequential design. This school-based study includes families with children in 12 public schools in four school districts in Southeastern Michigan (Eccles, Harold, & Wigfield, 1993). These districts served largely European American working- and middle-class families. The study began in 1987 in two school districts with children in three cohorts in kindergarten, first grade, and third grade. During the second and third year of the study, students were added to the study because two additional school districts were added and because siblings were added. Each recruitment year, letters describing the study and permission slips were given to families by children's teachers. Overall, 75% of the families agreed to participate.

Three of the four school districts consisted of medium to large suburban communities. The fourth was a medium-sized university city. Each district was primarily European American (95%), and included a small minority population of African Americans, Native Americans, Asian Americans, and Hispanics. These school districts were explicitly selected so that family income and neighborhood resources would not be obstacles to children's activity participation and course-taking, allowing researchers to investigate the impact of other parent and child factors on these choices. For example, each district had resources in terms of gifted or enrichment programs, computer programs, and instrumental music.

The CAB study included 987 children. In addition, 723 of their mothers and 541 of their fathers also agreed to participate. In order to keep our sample as representative as possible of the full population in these 4 school districts, we used data from the 723 families with data from the mothers and their children for all analyses that did not involve father data. We used the sample of 541 for those analyses that included father data, because this is the full sample of those families in which the father participated. Given the relative scarcity of studies based on fathers using data collected directly from fathers, we wanted to include our sample of fathers in this monograph but we also wanted to report the data for the larger sample of 723 for those analyses involving only the mother and child data in order to increase the power and the representativeness of the sample for these analyses. We provide information on our treatment of missing data in Chapter 3.

The families were largely European American, spoke English, and had lived in the United States for several generations. As shown in Table 1, annual family income, which was created using data from Waves 1 through 4 (i.e., from 1987 to 1990), ranged from $10,000 to over $80,000 with a median of $40,000–$49,999. Ninety-eight percent (98%) of parents had received a high school degree and over 37% had received a bachelor's degree. Within each cohort of youth, the sample was split equally by gender.

Procedures

Data for this report came from multiple waves of CAB. Table 2 displays the overall design of CAB, including children's grade levels at each wave. For example, Wave 3 data were collected in 1989 when children were in grades 2, 3, and 5. Most waves were spaced 1 year apart, but there were two exceptions

TABLE 1

PARTICIPANT DEMOGRAPHIC INFORMATION

	Youngest Cohort		Middle Cohort		Oldest Cohort	
	Mothers	Fathers	Mothers	Fathers	Mothers	Fathers
Parent information						
European American	97%	95%	92%	92%	95%	94%
Parents' education[a]						
Less than high school	2%	3%	3%	1%	1%	1%
High school degree	22%	11%	18%	9%	20%	12%
Some college	40%	37%	42%	38%	39%	37%
Bachelor's degree	19%	31%	28%	28%	16%	32%
Advanced degree	15%	18%	10%	23%	13%	20%
Family income[a]						
Median	$40,000–$49,999		$40,000–$49,999		$50,000–$59,999	
Child information						
Age at Wave 1 [M (SD)]	6.42 (.37)		7.37 (.38)		9.37 (.37)	
Females	49%		50%		52%	
European American	94%		92%		90%	
Recruited at						
Wave 1: n (%)	148 (52%)		182 (60%)		152 (39%)	
Wave 2: n (%)	116 (40%)		111 (36%)		85 (21%)	
Wave 3: n (%)	23 (8%)		13 (4%)		157 (40%)	

[a]These indicators are based on data reported across Waves 1 through 4.

24

TABLE 2

Data Collection Schedule of the Youngest, Middle, and Oldest Cohorts

		Grade Level												
Spring of	Wave	K	1st	2nd	3rd	4th	5th	6th	7th	8th	9th	10th	11th	12th
1987	1	Young	Middle		Oldest									
1988	2		Young	Middle		Oldest								
1989	3			Young	Middle		Oldest							
1990	4				Young	Middle		Oldest						
1991														
1992														
1993														
1994	5								Young	Middle		Oldest		
1995	6									Young	Middle		Oldest	
1996	7										Young	Middle		Oldest
1997														
1998	8													Middle
1999	9													Young

to this rule. First, Wave 5 (grades 7, 8, and 10) occurred four years after Wave 4 (grades 3, 4, and 6) due to a funding gap. Second, Waves 8 and 9 occurred when children in the middle and youngest cohorts were in grade 12. Data used in this investigation were collected from children, parents, and teachers.

Data from all parents were collected in Waves 1, 2, 3, 4, and 6. However, we only used parent data from Waves 2 through 4 for the analyses reported in this monograph. Waves 1 and 6 parent data were not included because these waves did not include all of the constructs of interest. These waves also included a large amount of missing data because recruitment was not complete at Wave 1 and because of parent attrition at Wave 6. Self-administered parent questionnaires were mailed home with a stamped, return envelope in the spring of Waves 2 through 4. Children provided information during the spring of Waves 2 through 9. Questionnaires were administered in their school classroom under project staff supervision, except in Wave 6 when questionnaires were mailed to youth. During Waves 2 through 4, questionnaires were read aloud to the entire class. At Waves 5, 7, 8, and 9, the child questionnaires were self-administered in the classroom. Teachers reported information on children during Waves 1 through 4. Teacher data from Waves 1 through 3 were used in the analyses. These questionnaires were self-administered during the spring of each wave. Children also completed IQ and athletic ability assessments when they joined the study.

Parent-Reported Indicators

In this study, we used data from parent questionnaires, which included information about their demographic characteristics, beliefs, and behaviors. Parents' beliefs and behaviors were specific to the four domains included in this investigation: sports, instrumental music, math, and reading. Mothers and fathers separately reported information on all indicators.

Parents' Beliefs

Two parental beliefs were used in the current investigation at Waves 2 through 4: Perceptions of their child's ability and their valuing of a domain for their child. The specific items are listed in Table 3. *Parents' perceptions of their child's ability* were measured with three items in each domain at each wave. The reliability of this three-item scale was acceptable across parents, domains, and waves (Table 4). *Parents' valuing of a domain* was assessed with one item at Wave 2 and with two items in each domain at Waves 3 and 4.

Parents' Behaviors

There were five indicators of parents' behavior in each domain measured at Waves 2–4. Generally, the same items were used to measure each indicator

26

TABLE 3

ITEMS OF PARENTS' BELIEFS

Items
Parents' perception of their child's ability
1a. How good is this child at (sports/music/math/reading)? ($1 = $ *not at all good*, $7 = $ *very good*)
1b. Compared with other children, how much innate ability or talent does this child have in (sports/instrumental music/math/reading)? ($1 = $ *much less than*, $7 = $ *much more than*)
1c. How well do you think this child will do in each of these areas next year (for sports/music/math/reading)? ($1 = $ *not at all well*, $7 = $ *very well*)
Parents' valuing of a domain for their child
2a. How important is it to you that this child do well in (sports/music/math/reading) ($1 = $ *not at all important*, $7 = $ *very important*)
2b. How useful to do think each of these activities (sports/music/math/reading) will be to this child in the future? ($1 = $ *not at all useful*, $7 = $ *very useful*)[a]

[a]Item was not assessed at Wave 2.

across parents, domains, and waves (see Table 5 for a complete listing). Exceptions to this rule are noted in Table 5 and the text below. For instance, in sports, there was one additional item for parental coaching that was not assessed in the other three domains. The means and standard deviations are presented in Table 6. Similar response scales were used across waves unless noted otherwise in Table 5.

Parents' encouragement described the extent to which they "encouraged their child to participate" in each domain. Encouragement in all four domains was assessed at Waves 2 and 3. Sports and music encouragement also were measured at Wave 4. As shown in Table 5, encouragement was measured with a single item with the exception of music encouragement at Wave 3. The two music encouragement items were averaged to create the Wave 3 indicator of music encouragement.

Parent-child coactivity was measured with two items: how often parents: (1) participated in child's daily activities and (2) took child to community events/institutions related to each domain. Parents indicated how often they generally participated in their child's daily activities in the four domains. Coactivity in sports and music was assessed with a single item at all three waves as listed in Table 5. Math coactivity was measured with one item at Waves 2 and 3 and two items at Wave 4. At all waves, parents reported how often they did math and science activities with their child. The additional item at Wave 4 assessed the extent to which parents helped the child with his/her math and science homework. Reading coactivity was assessed with two items at Waves 2 and 3: (1) how often the parent read to the child and (2) how often the child read to the parent. There was not an indicator of parent–child coactivity in children's daily reading activities at Wave 4.

27

TABLE 4

Reliability, Means (Standard Deviations), and Gender Differences of Parents' Perception of Their Child's Ability and Value of a Domain

Indicator	Mothers					Fathers				
	α	Females	Males	r^a	r^b	α	Females	Males	r^a	r^b
Sports										
Ability—W2	.92	4.75 (1.24)	5.32 (1.29)	−.19***	−.12**	.92	4.50 (1.27)	5.15 (1.27)	−.20***	−.15***
Ability—W3	.89	4.87 (1.16)	5.24 (1.31)	−.15***	−.06	.90	4.54 (1.32)	5.09 (1.28)	−.13***	−.07
Ability—W4	.87	4.93 (1.23)	5.28 (1.24)	−.09*	−.00	.89	4.60 (1.29)	5.04 (1.28)	−.13***	−.07
Value—W2	n/a	4.05 (1.38)	4.47 (1.28)	−.12**	−.08*	n/a	4.07 (1.46)	4.63 (1.34)	−.15***	−.11**
Value—W3	.73	4.08 (1.30)	4.58 (1.31)	−.15***	−.12**	.77	3.80 (1.32)	4.30 (1.29)	−.13***	−.08*
Value—W4	.75	4.13 (1.34)	4.47 (1.34)	−.10**	−.07	.78	4.04 (1.31)	4.45 (1.26)	−.08*	−.05
Music										
Ability—W2	.86	4.73 (1.57)	4.01 (1.66)	.19***	.16***	.87	4.46 (1.45)	3.80 (1.41)	.16***	.11**
Ability—W3	.90	5.14 (1.40)	4.26 (1.65)	.21***	.18***	.91	4.88 (1.35)	3.88 (1.51)	.19***	.15***
Ability—W4	.90	5.05 (1.46)	4.30 (1.64)	.16***	.14***	.91	5.03 (1.37)	3.68 (1.67)	.19***	.13***
Value—W2	n/a	4.30 (1.60)	3.87 (1.57)	.12**	.11**	n/a	4.15 (1.44)	3.75 (1.61)	.07	.05
Value—W3	.84	4.38 (1.59)	3.80 (1.72)	.16***	.14***	.84	4.17 (1.46)	3.35 (1.56)	.14***	.09
Value—W4	.84	4.30 (1.65)	3.61 (1.70)	.16***	.13**	.84	4.31 (1.42)	3.23 (1.64)	.19***	.12**
Math										
Ability—W2	.90	5.62 (1.09)	5.81 (1.12)	−.07	−.05	.89	5.50 (1.02)	5.79 (.95)	−.11**	−.11**
Ability—W3	.88	5.65 (1.11)	5.75 (1.09)	−.06	−.05	.87	5.41 (1.08)	5.68 (.97)	−.12**	−.13***
Ability—W4	.86	5.69 (1.05)	5.75 (1.10)	−.05	−.05	.86	5.70 (.96)	5.71 (.96)	−.03	−.04
Value—W2	n/a	6.28 (.94)	6.42 (.80)	−.06	−.06	n/a	6.02 (1.02)	6.37 (.91)	−.10*	−.09*
Value—W3	.51	6.48 (.64)	6.63 (.49)	−.09*	−.08*	.70	6.23 (.85)	6.41 (.69)	−.05	−.06
Value—W4	.50	6.60 (.61)	6.66 (.51)	−.04	−.03	.74	6.42 (.65)	6.51 (.64)	−.05	−.06
Reading										
Ability—W2	.92	5.98 (1.07)	5.71 (1.29)	.11**	.08*	.86	5.89 (.97)	5.62 (1.03)	.07	.03
Ability—W3	.88	6.04 (1.06)	5.68 (1.12)	.12**	.08*	.91	5.99 (1.06)	5.60 (1.14)	.09*	.04
Ability—W4	.88	6.00 (1.04)	5.66 (1.11)	.09*	.05	.88	6.04 (.89)	5.55 (1.12)	.11**	.10*
Value—W2	n/a	6.49 (.87)	6.59 (.72)	−.04	−.03	n/a	6.44 (.70)	6.48 (.93)	−.01	−.01
Value—W3	.45	6.66 (.53)	6.68 (.45)	−.00	−.00	.67	6.57 (.70)	6.57 (.60)	.01	.02
Value—W4	.47	6.76 (.44)	6.74 (.43)	.03	.03	.76	6.67 (.54)	6.60 (.56)	.02	.01

Note. W, Wave. n/a, only one item was assessed in Wave 2. r refers to the effect size of differences between males and females where a minus sign denotes that males were higher.
*$p < .05$.
**$p < .01$.
***$p < .001$.
[a]Findings from regressions with child gender as the predictor.
[b]Findings from regressions with child gender, cohort, family income, parent education, and ability as predictors.

The second component of parent–child coactivity was how often parents took children to community events or institutions related to these domains. This type of community coactivity was measured at Waves 2–4 in sports, music, and reading, but not in math. Parent–child attendance at paid sporting events was measured with one item. Two items measured parent–child attendance at music concerts: (a) took child to a rock concert and (b) took child to a classical music concert. These two items were averaged to create a subscale of attendance at concerts. Parents also reported how often they took the child to the library at Wave 4. This reading coactivity item was not assessed at Waves 2 and 3.

TABLE 5

INDICATORS OF PARENTS' BEHAVIORS

	Sports			Music			Math			Reading		
Indicators	W2	W3	W4	W2	W3	W4	W2	W3	W4	W2	W3	W4
A. Encouragement												
Please indicate the extent to which you encourage the following activities for this child (1 = *strongly discourage*, 7 = *strongly encourage*)												
Playing competitive sports	x	x	x									
Taking music lessons				x	x	x						
Playing a musical instrument					x							
Doing math- or science-related activities at home							x	x				
Reading										x	x	
B. Coactivity: Daily activity												
Please indicate how often you do each of these things to get involved with this child's daily activities (1 = *never*, 7 = *almost every day for a long while*)												
Play sports with this child	x	x	x									
Play a musical instrument with this child				x	x	x						
Do math or science activities with this child							x	x	x			
Help this child do his/her math and science homework									x			
Read to this child										x	x	
Have this child read to you										x	x	
C. Coactivity: Community events												
Please indicate how often you have done each of the following activities in the past year (W2 and W3: 1 = *never*, 7 = *almost every day for a long while*, W4: 1 = *never*, 7 = *weekly*)												
Take child to paid sporting events	x	x	x									
Take child to classical music concerts				x	x	x						
Take child to rock music concerts				x	x	x						
Take child to the library												x

(Continued)

TABLE 5. (*Continued*)

Indicators	Sports			Music			Math			Reading		
	W2	W3	W4	W2	W3	W4	W2	W3	W4	W2	W3	W4
D. Provision of materials												
Check all that were bought or rented for this child in the past year (1 = *yes*, 0 = *no*)												
Sports equipment	x	x	x									
Sports books or magazines	x	x	x									
Musical instruments				x	x	x						
Music or dance books, supplies, clothing				x	x	x						
Math-related books, games, toys, or magazines							x	x	x			
General interest books										x	x	
General interest magazines										x	x	
General interest in books or magazines												x
E. Parents' participation												
Use the following scale to estimate the amount of time spent last week on each of the following activities (1 = *0 hours*, 8 = *>20 hours*)												
Organized competitive sports	x	x	x									
Playing sports with friends	x	x	x									
Doing athletic activities alone (like running)	x	x	x									
Playing musical instruments				x	x	x						
Math- and science-related activities							x	x	x			
Reading books, magazines, or newspapers for pleasure										x	x	x
F. Coaching												
Do you coach of one of your children's sports teams (1 = yes, 0 = no)	x	x	x									

Note. W, Wave. The response scale is the same at each wave unless noted otherwise.

TABLE 6

MEANS (STANDARD DEVIATIONS) AND GENDER DIFFERENCES OF PARENTS' BEHAVIORS

Indicator	Mothers				Fathers			
	Females	Males	r^a	r^b	Females	Males	r^a	r^b
Sports								
Encouragement—W2	4.33 (.87)	4.97 (1.17)	−.25***	−.19***	4.52 (1.02)	5.31 (1.14)	−.17***	−.14***
Encouragement—W3	3.42 (1.48)	4.16 (1.65)	−.16***	−.13***	3.69 (1.44)	4.68 (1.50)	−.21***	−.18***
Encouragement—W4	3.43 (1.55)	4.29 (1.68)	−.20***	−.17***	3.81 (1.52)	4.68 (1.53)	−.16***	−.14***
Daily coactivity—W2	2.52 (1.41)	2.98 (1.52)	−.12***	−.10*	3.08 (1.48)	3.94 (1.28)	−.19***	−.17***
Daily coactivity—W3	2.34 (1.25)	2.82 (1.53)	−.13***	−.12**	2.96 (1.28)	3.92 (1.47)	−.21***	−.17***
Daily coactivity—W4	2.34 (1.26)	2.51 (1.40)	−.04	−.03	2.80 (1.37)	3.83 (1.38)	−.14**	−.12**
Events—W2^c	.52 (.50)	.82 (.38)	−.23***	−.20***	.63 (.48)	.80 (.39)	−.16***	−.13***
Events—W3^c	.65 (.47)	.81 (.39)	−.17***	−.13***	.69 (.46)	.89 (.31)	−.12**	−.11**
Events—W4	2.25 (1.03)	2.75 (1.05)	−.19***	−.16***	2.38 (1.11)	2.92 (1.03)	−.08*	−.07
Provision—W2	.71 (.62)	1.36 (.62)	−.40***	−.38***	.73 (.61)	1.33 (.63)	−.28***	−.25***
Provision—W3	.84 (.58)	1.45 (.61)	−.35***	−.32***	.87 (.59)	1.42 (.61)	−.26***	−.21***
Provision—W4	.77 (.63)	1.46 (.65)	−.39***	−.35***	.89 (.68)	1.41 (.70)	−.18***	−.16***
Modeling—W2	1.67 (.64)	1.80 (.69)	−.06	−.05	2.08 (.94)	2.07 (.87)	.05	.05
Modeling—W3	.74 (.71)	.78 (.75)	−.02	−.01	1.12 (.92)	1.06 (.89)	.03	.05
Modeling—W4	.77 (.84)	.70 (.73)	.02	.02	1.22 (.97)	1.12 (.94)	.01	.03
Coaching—W2^c	n/a	n/a			.14 (.35)	.27 (.45)	−.14***	−.10**
Coaching—W3^c	n/a	n/a			.14 (.35)	.36 (.48)	−.15***	−.12**
Coaching—W4^c	n/a	n/a			.16 (.36)	.31 (.46)	−.09*	−.07
Music								
Encouragement—W2	4.82 (1.21)	4.56 (1.08)	.09*	.06	4.70 (1.14)	4.34 (.96)	.07	.04
Encouragement—W3	4.33 (1.96)	3.69 (1.94)	.14***	.11**	4.23 (1.83)	3.43 (1.70)	.13***	.10**
Encouragement—W4	4.33 (1.91)	3.42 (1.84)	.17***	.14***	4.28 (1.65)	3.17 (1.54)	.14***	.09*
Daily coactivity—W2^c	.34 (.47)	.29 (.45)	.05	.03	.23 (.42)	.17 (.38)	.05	.05

(Continued)

31

TABLE 6. (*Continued*)

Indicator	Mothers				Fathers			
	Females	Males	r^a	r^b	Females	Males	r^a	r^b
Daily coactivity—W3[c]	.37 (.47)	.29 (.45)	.05	.03	.23 (.42)	.20 (.40)	.01	.01
Daily coactivity—W4[c]	.30 (.46)	.22 (.42)	.05	.03	.19 (.39)	.17 (.37)	.02	.01
Events—W2	.36 (.48)	.27 (.44)	.06	.03	.28 (.45)	.19 (.39)	.06	.08*
Events—W3	.39 (.49)	.36 (.48)	.06	.04	.35 (.48)	.27 (.44)	.05	.06
Events—W4	1.48 (.54)	1.34 (.49)	.09*	.07	1.30 (.48)	1.24 (.42)	.00	.02
Provision—W2	.79 (.69)	.46 (.67)	.20***	.20***	.83 (.71)	.48 (.68)	.17***	.16***
Provision—W3	1.96 (.99)	1.43 (1.04)	.19***	.16***	1.93 (1.00)	1.46 (1.08)	.13**	.11**
Provision—W4	.97 (.71)	.54 (.72)	.20***	.19***	1.09 (.75)	.50 (.68)	.18***	.17***
Modeling—W2[c]	.15 (.36)	.19 (.39)	−.04	−.08*	.09 (.29)	.09 (.29)	.05	.06
Modeling—W3[c]	.17 (.38)	.17 (.38)	.01	.02	.10 (.30)	.11 (.31)	−.00	−.01
Modeling—W4[c]	.17 (.38)	.16 (.37)	.02	.03	.09 (.29)	.14 (.34)	−.02	−.02
Math								
Encouragement—W2	4.76 (.89)	5.08 (1.10)	−.11**	−.10**	4.82 (1.06)	4.99 (1.07)	−.02	−.01
Encouragement—W3	4.09 (1.59)	4.39 (1.55)	−.07	−.06	4.06 (1.52)	4.30 (1.45)	−.04	−.03
Daily coactivity—W2	3.41 (1.35)	3.39 (1.29)	.03	.03	3.24 (1.12)	3.16 (1.22)	.02	.01
Daily coactivity—W3	3.44 (1.41)	3.31 (1.35)	.03	.04	3.21 (1.16)	3.26 (1.21)	−.01	−.01
Daily coactivity—W4	3.33 (1.28)	3.20 (1.23)	.06	.05	3.23 (1.15)	3.10 (1.00)	.04	.03
Provision—W2	.66 (.47)	.60 (.49)	.06	.07	.69 (.46)	.59 (.49)	.04	.06
Provision—W3	.54 (.50)	.53 (.50)	.02	.03	.48 (.50)	.49 (.50)	−.02	−.02
Provision—W4	.37 (.48)	.32 (.47)	.05	.06	.38 (.49)	.35 (.48)	.01	.01
Modeling—W2	2.48 (1.42)	2.51 (1.52)	−.01	−.00	2.35 (1.47)	2.36 (1.50)	−.05	−.05
Modeling—W3	1.32 (1.42)	1.49 (1.53)	−.03	−.02	1.68 (1.83)	1.51 (1.74)	.03	.02
Modeling—W4	1.23 (1.37)	1.34 (1.54)	−.03	−.03	1.57 (1.81)	1.28 (1.32)	.08*	.07
Reading								
Encouragement—W2	6.57 (.66)	6.35 (.82)	.16***	.16***	6.20 (.87)	5.98 (.95)	.04	.02

(*Continued*)

TABLE 6. (*Continued*)

Indicator	Mothers				Fathers			
	Females	Males	r^a	r^b	Females	Males	r^a	r^b
Encouragement—W3	6.14 (1.15)	6.01 (1.10)	.05	.05	6.01 (1.08)	5.40 (1.27)	.12**	.10**
Daily coactivity—W2	4.01 (1.36)	3.88 (1.35)	.03	.06	3.24 (1.30)	3.07 (1.33)	.01	.01
Daily coactivity—W3	3.35 (1.44)	3.37 (1.36)	−.01	−.06	2.73 (1.24)	2.61 (1.18)	.03	.03
Events—W4	5.00 (1.24)	4.66 (1.20)	.08*	.08*	3.80 (1.50)	3.64 (1.41)	.05	.04
Provision—W2	1.59 (.65)	1.52 (.68)	.04	.04	1.62 (.61)	1.54 (.67)	.06	.06
Provision—W3	1.60 (.58)	1.53 (.67)	.06	.06	1.58 (.61)	1.51 (.73)	.01	.01
Provision—W4	.84 (.36)	.86 (.34)	−.02	−.01	.82 (.39)	.77 (.42)	.04	.02
Modeling—W2	4.11 (1.32)	4.09 (1.37)	.00	.00	3.69 (1.20)	3.75 (1.18)	.00	.00
Modeling—W3	3.15 (1.30)	3.09 (1.43)	.03	.03	2.84 (1.31)	2.84 (1.19)	.01	.02
Modeling—W4	3.38 (1.29)	3.25 (1.45)	.00	.01	3.06 (1.23)	2.98 (1.15)	.01	.03

Note. W, wave. *r* refers to the effect size of differences between males and females where a minus sign denotes that males were higher. n/a coaching for mothers was not included in the analyses.

*$p < .05$.

**$p < .01$.

***$p < .001$.

[a]Findings from regressions with child gender as the predictor.

[b]Findings from regressions with child gender, cohort, family income, parent education, and ability as predictors.

[c]This indicator was dichotomized.

Parents' provision of activity-related materials assessed whether activity-related materials were bought or rented for their child in the past year. For instance, parents reported if they bought or rented ($1 = yes$, $0 = no$): (a) sports equipment or (b) sports books or magazines in the last year. The specific items for each domain are listed in Table 5. Within each domain, the items were summed to create indicators of parents' provision of materials. In the case of sports, the range of the sport provision variable was 0–2 at Waves 2–4. The music items had the same range as those for sports. Math provision of materials ranged from 0 to 1 at Wave 2–4. Reading materials ranged from 0 to 2 at Waves 2 and 3 and 0–1 at Wave 4. In addition, fathers did not report provision of activity-related materials at Wave 2. Thus, we used mothers' report of this item for Wave 2 in the father models.

Parents' modeling or participation in activities indicated how much time they spent at home or after work on several activities during the previous week at Waves 2–4. These included playing three types of sport activities, playing a musical instrument, participating in math- and science-related activities, and reading for pleasure (Table 5). The three indicators of parents' sport activities were averaged to create a scale. All other items were single indicators.

Coaching assessed if parents coached their children's sports team in the last year ($1 = yes$, $0 = no$). Because so few mothers coached sports teams (e.g., $n = 17$ at Wave 3), we dropped mothers' data on coaching from the analyses.

Child-Reported Indicators

The focus of this study is children's beliefs and behaviors in sports, instrumental music, math, and reading. Comparable measures were collected across these four domains. Specifically, children reported their self-concept of ability, value, and participation in each of these domains after and during school (e.g., elective classes).

Self-Concept of Ability

Children's self-concept of ability represents children's beliefs about their abilities or the extent to which they believe they are good in a particular domain. In this investigation, we used children's self-concept of ability in each of the four domains reported at Waves 2 (grades 1, 2, and 4) through 5 (grades 7, 8, and 10). Children's self-concept of ability was measured with the same four items in each domain and at each wave as listed in Table 7. The only exception was that one item was not measured at Wave 2 for music (i.e., "if you were to list the students..."). The scale reliabilities (Cronbach's alpha) and descriptive statistics by gender are noted in Table 8. These scales have excellent face, convergent, and discriminant validity, as well as strong psychometric properties (Eccles, Wigfield, et al., 1993; Jacobs et al., 2002).

34

TABLE 7

Indicators of Youths' Self-Concept of Ability and Value

Youths' self-concept of ability
    1a. How good at (sports/music/math/reading) are you? ($1 = $ *not very good,* $7 = $ *very good*)
    1b. If you were to list all the students from best to worst in (sports/music/math/reading) where are you? ($1 = $ *one of the worst,* $7 = $ *one of the best*)
    1c. Compared to other subjects how good are you at (sports/playing a musical instrument/math/reading)? ($1 = $ *a lot worse,* $7 = $ *a lot better*)
    1d. How good would you be at learning something new in (sports/to play a new musical instrument/math/reading)? ($1 = $ *not very good,* $7 = $ *very good*)
Youths' value
    2. Youths' ratings of importance
        2a. Compared to other activities how useful is learning (sports/to play a musical instrument/math/reading)? ($1 = $ *not as useful,* $7 = $ *a lot more useful*)[a]
        2b. For me being good in (sports/music/math/reading) is ($1 = $ *unimportant,* $7 = $ *important*)
    3. Youths' ratings of interest
        3a. I find working on (sports/a musical instrument/math assignments/reading assignments) ($1 = $ *boring,* $7 = $ *interesting*)
        3b. How much do you like (sports/playing a musical instrument/math/reading)? ($1 = $ *a little,* $7 = $ *a lot*)

[a]This item was not assessed at Wave 2.

Task Value

Children's perceptions of task value incorporate aspects of importance (i.e., attainment and utility value) and interest (i.e., intrinsic value). The importance of each domain was assessed with questions about how much children believe a particular domain is important to them and how useful it is to them now and in the future. Two indicators of importance were measured for each domain at Waves 2 (grades 1, 2, and 4) through 5 (grades 7, 8, and 10). These are the first two items in Table 7. At Wave 2, one of the two importance items was not used. This item required children to compare a domain to other domains (i.e., the item in Table 7 that starts with "compared to other activities"). This item was not included at Wave 2 because such comparisons about the utility of a domain were too difficult for young children. The second component of task value is children's interest. Two questions addressed children's interest in each domain at Waves 2 through 5 (see Table 7). The scales had adequate reliability and excellent convergent and discriminate validity (Jacobs et al., 2002). The scale reliability (Cronbach's alpha) and descriptive statistics for importance and interest are presented in Table 8.

Activity Participation and Courses

Several indicators of children's participation in the four domains are available in CAB. We included indicators from Waves 2 to 9. Youth can

TABLE 8

Reliability (Cronbach's alpha), Means (Standard Deviations), and Gender Differences of Females' and Males' Self-Concept of Ability and Value

| Indicator | | Self-Concept of Ability | | | | | Value | | | |
	α	Females	Males	r^a	r^b	α	Females	Males	r^a	r^b
Sports										
Wave 2	.84	4.94 (1.30)	6.01 (1.13)	−.36***	−.31***	.68	5.78 (1.41)	6.33 (1.19)	−.18***	−.14***
Wave 3	.83	4.80 (1.19)	5.97 (1.04)	−.44***	−.41***	.84	4.98 (1.30)	5.80 (1.07)	−.31***	−.26***
Wave 4	.89	4.71 (1.28)	5.89 (1.16)	−.38***	−.32***	.88	4.63 (1.47)	5.62 (1.22)	−.32***	−.25***
Wave 5	.92	4.66 (1.41)	5.49 (1.32)	−.26***	−.20***	.91	4.73 (1.55)	5.43 (1.50)	−.20***	−.15***
Music										
Wave 2	.75	5.01 (1.48)	4.34 (1.74)	.18***	.20***	.81	5.57 (1.66)	4.61 (2.07)	.22***	.21***
Wave 3	.82	5.04 (1.22)	4.47 (1.61)	.20***	.18***	.88	4.68 (1.51)	3.84 (1.83)	.23***	.21***
Wave 4	.89	4.28 (1.55)	3.66 (1.81)	.18***	.16***	.91	4.08 (1.57)	3.40 (1.81)	.20***	.17***
Wave 5	.93	4.31 (1.71)	3.65 (1.84)	.17***	.16***	.95	3.76 (1.94)	3.31 (1.96)	.11**	.09*
Math										
Wave 2	.64	5.18 (1.13)	5.54 (1.07)	−.15***	−.15***	.65	5.46 (1.47)	5.18 (1.68)	.08*	.08*
Wave 3	.75	5.01 (1.07)	5.48 (1.07)	−.21***	−.21***	.75	5.00 (1.17)	5.15 (1.28)	−.06	−.06
Wave 4	.81	5.00 (1.14)	5.49 (1.11)	−.19***	−.19***	.81	4.88 (1.13)	5.01 (1.21)	−.05	−.05
Wave 5	.88	4.79 (1.26)	4.95 (1.27)	−.03	−.03	.88	4.41 (1.17)	4.35 (1.21)	.04	.03
Reading										
Wave 2	.78	5.67 (1.12)	5.70 (1.14)	−.01	−.03	.67	5.77 (1.35)	5.15 (1.70)	.17***	.16***
Wave 3	.81	5.55 (1.08)	5.27 (1.25)	.11**	.10**	.78	5.40 (1.07)	4.90 (1.35)	.19***	.19***
Wave 4	.83	5.44 (1.13)	5.25 (1.12)	.09*	.07	.76	5.23 (1.02)	4.92 (1.21)	.14***	.13***
Wave 5	.90	5.01 (1.20)	4.65 (1.23)	.12**	.10**	.84	4.55 (1.17)	4.14 (1.23)	.14***	.11**

Note. r refers to the effect size of differences between males and females where a minus sign denotes that males were higher.
*$p < .05$.
**$p < .01$.
***$p < .001$.
[a]Findings from regressions with child gender as the predictor.
[b]Findings from regressions with child gender, cohort, family income, parent education, and ability as predictors.

participate in these domains through (a) informal activities, such as a neighborhood pick-up sport game, (b) organized activities, such as participating on a little league baseball team, and (c) elective coursework. Activities also vary in terms of whether they are community or school based. For instance, children may have opportunities to participate on organized teams in their community and on organized school sports teams. Youth make choices and can get involved in these domains through settings that take place during the school hours (e.g., elective courses) and after school hours. In this study, we included a variety of participation indicators that span these various distinctions. As expected, the available opportunities and choices vary by the four domains and across development.

For the high school indicators, we calculated the average across high school due to the design of the study. Participants were assessed a different number of times during Waves 6 through 9. For example, the oldest cohort was assessed twice during these waves whereas the middle and youngest cohorts were assessed three times. As a result of the different number of assessments, we used data from Waves 6 through 9 to create the average across these years. A complete listing of the items in all four domains is presented in Table 9. The means and standard deviations are presented in Table 10.

Children can participate in *sports activities* through organized and informal avenues. During Waves 2 through 5, children reported on how much time they spent in organized sports (Table 9). During the high school years (i.e., Waves 6–9), we used four indicators of sport participation. These included: (a) time spent in organized sports, (b) time spent in other informal sports, (c) number of organized school-based sports youth participated in, and (d) number of organized community-based sports youth participated in. Each of these indicators was averaged across the high school years. For example, time spent in organized sports was the average amount of time they spent in organized sports per year throughout high school. The number of sport teams was the average number of sport teams per year throughout high school.

Children have opportunities to engage in *instrumental music activities* in and outside of school. At Waves 2 (grades 1, 2, and 4) through 5 (grades 7, 8, and 10), children reported how much time they practiced a musical instrument (Table 9). This indicator of music participation focuses on instrumental music and not choral or other forms of music, which do not require equipment and may often occur in churches or other venues. Music practice focused on time spent practicing outside of school. During the high school years, we had two indicators of music participation. Youth reported how much time they practiced a musical instrument and whether they participated in a school or community band each year. The high school indicators were based on data reported when adolescents were in grades 9 through 12, which included Waves 6 through 9 depending on the cohort. Time practicing was the average amount of time they practiced each year

TABLE 9

INDICATORS OF YOUTHS' PARTICIPATION

Indicator	W2	W3	W4	W5	W6	W7	W8	W9
Sports								
A. Time in organized sports								
How often do you play sports on organized teams where someone keeps score? (W2: 0 = *Never*, 4 = *Everyday*; W3: 0 = *Never*, 7 = *Almost every day for a lot of time*; W4: 0 = *Never or Almost never*, 5 = *Almost every day for a lot of time*)	x	x	x					
Time spent each week taking part in organized sports? (W5–W9: 0 = *none*, 7 = *21 or more hours*)				x	x	x	x	x
B. Time in other sports								
Time spent each week doing other athletic or sports activities? (1 = *none*, 8 = *21 or more hours*)					x	x	x	x
C. Number of sport teams at school								
Do you (did you) compete in any of the following school teams (varsity, junior varsity, or other organized school program) outside of Physical Education? Baseball, gymnastics, softball, football, ice hockey, volleyball, tennis, basketball, cheerleading, wrestling, track/cross country, swimming/diving, soccer, ice skating, field hockey, other					x	x	x	x
D. Number of sports in the community								
Do you (did you) participate **regularly and often** in any of the following sports outside of school? Baseball, gymnastics, dancing, softball, basketball, track, soccer, swimming, rollerblading, skateboarding, weightlifting, aerobics, football, martial arts, ice skating, hockey, skiing, wrestling, tennis, other					x	x	x	x
Music								
A. Time								
How often do you practice an instrument? (W2: 0 = *Never*, 4 = *Everyday*; W3: 0 = *Never*, 7 = *Almost every day for a lot of time*; W4: 0 = *Never or Almost never*, 5 = *Almost every day for a lot of time*; W5–W9: 0 = *none*, 7 = *21 or more hours*)	x	x	x	x	x	x	x	x

(Continued)

TABLE 9. (*Continued*)

Indicator	W2	W3	W4	W5	W6	W7	W8	W9
B. Band or orchestra								
Which of the following activities or clubs at school did you do in the school year?					x	x	x	x
Band or orchestra (yes/no)								
Do you participate in any of the following clubs or activities outside of school? Band (yes no)								
Math								
A. Time								
How often do you do math games (i.e., flash cards, playing with calculators, doing math on computer)? (W2: 0 = *Never*, 4 = *Everyday*; W3:0 = *Never*, 7 = *Almost every day for a lot of time*, W4: 0 = *Never or Almost never*, 5 = *Almost every day for a lot of time*)	x	x	x					
B. Math/Science clubs at school								
Which of the following activities or clubs at school did you do in the school year? (Check): math club, science fair, environmental group, chess club, computer club					x	x	x	x
C. Math classes—drawn from their record data					x	x	x	x
Reading								
A. Time								
How often do you read comic books, magazines, newspapers or other books that are not for your schoolwork? (W2: 0 = *Never*, 4 = *Everyday*; W3: 0 = *Never*, 7 = *Almost every day for a lot of time*, W4: 0 = *Never or Almost never*, 5 = *Almost every day for a lot of time*)	x	x	x					
Time spent each week reading for fun? (1 = *none*, 8 = *21 or more hours*)				x	x	x	x	x
B. Literary clubs								
Which of the following activities or clubs at school did you do in the school year? (Check): foreign language club, literary magazine					x	x	x	x
C. English courses—drawn from their record data					x	x	x	x

Note. W, Wave. The response scale is the same at each wave unless noted otherwise.

TABLE 10

Means (Standard Deviations) and Gender Differences of Females' and Males' Participation

Indicator	Females	Males	r^a	r^b
Sports				
Time in organized sports				
Wave 2	1.21 (1.39)	2.23 (1.18)	−.29***	−.26***
Wave 3	1.97 (1.96)	3.57 (2.00)	−.35***	−.31***
Wave 4	2.79 (1.73)	4.40 (1.77)	−.38***	−.33***
Wave 5	3.50 (2.07)	4.02 (2.21)	−.12**	−.06
High school	3.06 (2.05)	3.42 (2.16)	−.07	−.03
Time in other sports				
High school	2.92 (1.32)	3.70 (1.69)	−.21***	−.18***
Number of school sport teams				
High school	.82 (.83)	.96 (1.18)	−.06	−.02
Number of community sports				
High school	2.05 (2.01)	3.06 (2.61)	−.19***	−.17***
Music				
Time practicing				
Wave 2	1.45 (1.61)	1.17 (1.42)	.07*	.08*
Wave 3	2.78 (2.26)	1.94 (2.19)	.18***	.16***
Wave 4	2.65 (1.73)	1.97 (1.57)	.20***	.17***
Wave 5	1.54 (1.86)	1.24 (1.81)	.07*	.05
High school	1.12 (1.51)	1.35 (1.84)	−.04	−.05
Band				
High school	.26 (.44)	.22 (.42)	.04	.03
Math				
Time on math activities				
Wave 2	1.56 (1.27)	1.55 (1.34)	.01	.00
Wave 3	2.75 (1.69)	2.43 (1.93)	.08*	.08*
Wave 4	2.88 (1.62)	3.06 (1.76)	−.05	−.05
Number of AP math courses				
High school	.47 (.62)	.44 (.66)	.01	.01
Reading				
Time reading				
Wave 2	2.98 (1.19)	2.64 (1.30)	.11**	.10**
Wave 3	4.37 (1.64)	4.01 (1.82)	.11**	.10**
Wave 4	4.25 (1.67)	3.70 (1.69)	.14***	.13***
Wave 5	3.04 (1.64)	2.44 (1.49)	.16***	.17***
High school	2.72 (1.09)	2.55 (1.29)	.09*	.08*
Literature clubs				
High school	.36 (.48)	.17 (.38)	.17***	.17***
English courses				
High school	1.99 (.48)	1.99 (.60)	.01	.05

Note. r refers to the effect size of differences between males and females where a minus sign denotes that males were higher.

*$p < .05$.

**$p < .01$.

***$p < .001$.

[a]Findings from regressions with child gender as the predictor.

[b]Findings from regressions with child gender, cohort, family income, parent education, and ability as predictors.

across high school. School band participation indicated whether they participated in a school or community band at any point in high school. This indicator was dichotomized because approximately 75% of the sample did not participate in a school or community band during high school.

Youth also have a variety of avenues through which they can participate in *math-related activities*. Youths' opportunities to engage in math-related pursuits shift across development. During childhood, children can engage in math pursuits after school in formal and informal activity settings. However, as children age into adolescence, few participate in *informal* math activities after school beyond completing their homework (Simpkins, Davis-Kean, et al., 2006). As shown in Table 9, time spent in math-related activities was measured in Waves 2 through 4.

During the high school years, adolescents are able to select in or out of math pursuits through their participation in school clubs associated with those domains and their advanced courses at school. We assessed adolescents' participation in a variety of clubs associated with math. However, because 91% of the sample did not participate in any one of these clubs throughout high school, this indicator was dropped from analyses. Adolescents' math coursework was collected from their high school record data (i.e., when students were in grades 9–12). We computed the average number of AP math courses per year throughout high school. AP math courses included four sets of classes that the four school districts designated as honors/AP courses: (a) Honors Algebra, Enriched Algebra, Accelerated Algebra (I and II), Algebra HS, (b) Pre-Calculus, Accelerated Analysis, (c) advanced math enrichment (math honors general)/Honors Math 3, 4, 5, and 6, and (d) AP Calculus, AP math general.

Youth can engage in *reading activities* through a variety of avenues. At Waves 2 (grades 1, 2, and 4) through 5 (grades 7, 8, and 10), youth reported how much time they spent reading for fun, which is an informal reading activity (Table 9). We used three indicators of reading-related pursuits when adolescents were in high school: (a) time spent reading per year, (b) the percentage of years they participated in school clubs related to reading, and (c) English and literature coursework. For each of these items, we examined adolescents' responses across grades 9–12. First, time spent reading was the average amount of time they spent reading each year across grades 9–12. Second, we created an indicator of participation in the school foreign language club and/or literary magazine by taking the average number of clubs they participated in from grades 9–12. Because 73% of the sample never participated in either of these two clubs at any time in high school, this indicator was dichotomized. Third, the average number of English and literature courses per year was computed based on their record data from grades 9–12. Following procedures outlined in Durik et al. (2006), we included a variety of courses related to English and literature: advanced

English courses, writing courses (e.g., creative writing, composition), literature courses, and applied English courses (e.g., school newspaper, debate). We calculated the average number of English/literature courses taken each year across grades 9–12.

Exogenous Indicators Used as Controls

In the Eccles's models illustrated in Figures 1a and 1b, various exogenous constructs are listed in the boxes in the far left side of each model. We assume these indicators serve as a starting place for the cascade of processes that make up the socialization and enactment of motivated behavioral choice. However, to keep our statistical model as simple as possible, we have included these predictors as control variables rather than as constructs central to the SEMs. This decision is in keeping with the classic treatment within the fields of sociology, economics, and quantitative non-experimental developmental science of constructs assumed to be selection factors that can bias estimates of potentially causal relationships among the endogenous constructs in one's structural model. Including these exogenous constructs as controls allows one to partial out the influence of these constructs on the "outcomes" of interest and thus provides a conservative estimate of the magnitude of the possible causal association of parents' beliefs and behaviors to their children's developing beliefs and achievement-related behavioral choices. However, given that we see these exogenous constructs as theoretically important in their own right, we also present their correlations with all of our endogenous constructs as part of our descriptive analyses.

Parents' Education

Parents indicated their highest level of educational attainment on a list of pre-coded responses (1 = *grade school*, 9 = *Ph.D.*). The highest level of education within a parental pair was used to characterize parents' education (Shumow & Lomax, 2002).

Family Annual Income

Parents described their annual income on a scale listing income brackets in $10,000 increments (minimum = none, maximum = over $80,000). Mothers' and fathers' incomes were summed to create the family annual income.

Assessment Indicators

When children entered the study, they completed the Bruininks-Oseretsky Test of Motor Proficiency (Bruininks, 1978) and the Slosson Intelligence Test (1991 edition; Slosson, Nicholson, & Hibpshman, 1991). The Bruininks-Oseretsky Test of Motor Proficiency has been widely used to assess the proficiency of individuals' gross and fine motor skills (Hattie &

Edwards, 1987). This measure was included in all analyses on sports as an indicator of physical aptitude. Children's overall cognitive skills were measured with the Slosson Intelligence Test—Revised. This measure was included as an indicator and control for the children's starting cognitive aptitude in all analyses.

Teacher Reported Indicators

Teachers completed a questionnaire on each child who participated in the study at Waves 1–3. Teachers assessed children's natural ability or talent in each of the four domains with one item: "Compared to other children, how much <u>innate ability</u> or <u>talent</u> does this child have in each of the following?" (1 = *very little*, 7 = *a lot*). Teachers' ratings from Waves 1 through 3 were averaged to create an indicator of children's natural ability in each domain. We included these ratings as an additional control for the children's natural aptitude in each specific domain in all models. We also report the correlation of these ratings with our several endogenous constructs because we assume that these aptitudes influence parents' perceptions of their children's abilities and thus serve as a starting point for the cascade of developmental processes inherent in the Eccles's models illustrated in Figures 1a and 1b. Of the sample used in the mother models and youth only models ($N = 723$), the rate of missing data was 25% at Wave 2, 17% at Wave 3, and 28% at Wave 4, but only 1 participant was missing teacher rated data at all three waves.

In all models except one set of models in Chapter 4, teachers' rating of children's natural ability was used as a control variable. In the one set of models in Chapter 4, teachers' rating of children's natural ability was one of the focal variables in the cross-lagged models. We present more detailed information on the plan of analysis in the next chapter. However, it is important to note here in this methods chapter that teachers' rating was the average across the 3 years when it was used as a control variable. When it was used as a focal variable in the cross-lagged models in Chapter 4, we used the rating from Waves 2 and 3 as separate indicators to compute all of the paths across Waves 2 and 3 in the cross-lagged models.

III. MISSING DATA, DESCRIPTIVE STATISTICS, AND OVERVIEW OF THE ANALYSES

In this chapter, we provide some information about the data and an overview of the plan of analysis. First, we discuss missing data in the study. Second, we present the descriptive statistics, mean-level gender differences, and bivariate correlations between the control variables and the indicators in the models. Third, we present an overview of the structural equation models that were used to examine the relations in Chapters 4 through 7.

Missing Data

All participants were tracked and asked to participate at each wave. A combination of mailed surveys and telephone interviews (coupled with a variety of tracking strategies, including parent or friend contacts, the State Motor Vehicle Department records, social security numbers, and forwarding address information available from the post office) was used to minimize attrition. The most common source of attrition was moving out of the data collection area. The missing data rates in this study are comparable to rates in other longitudinal studies. The rate of missing data for each participant was as follows: Wave 2 was 24% for mothers, 36% for fathers, 16% for youth; Wave 3 was 31% for mothers, 35% for fathers, 7% for youth; Wave 4 was 37% for mothers, 48% for fathers, 14% for youth; Wave 5 was 31% for youth; Wave 6 was 49% for youth; and high school was 36% for youth.

Parent Missing Data

To examine missing data from parents, we tested differences in family demographics and youth indicators between families based on whether or not the parent participated. These comparisons were computed separately for mothers and fathers as the rate of missing data varied for the two parents. For mothers, we compared families in which the mother participated ($n = 723$) with families in which the mother did not participate ($n = 264$). For fathers, we compared families in which the father participated ($n = 541$) with families in which the father did not participate ($n = 486$). These analyses provide information on whether there were systematic differences between families in which the parent participated and families with missing parent data. Continuous variables were tested with t tests; categorical variables were examined with chi-square tests. Everything was converted to the effect size r. Only a handful of the differences were statistically significant and they were all small in size.

There were no significant differences between these two groups of mothers and fathers in terms of youth gender or cohort. Parents' education ($r = .17$) and family income ($r = .17$) were higher if the father participated compared to families in which the father did not participate. Of the 32 youth beliefs, 4 beliefs had small effect sizes. Youths' reading self-concept of ability at Wave 5 (Fathers: $r = .12$) as well as their music value and self-concept of ability at Wave 5 were higher for youth whose parent participated compared to youth whose parent did not participate (Mothers: $r = .11$ and .15, Fathers: $r = .12$ and .14, respectively); in contrast, music self-concept of ability at Wave 2 was lower for youth whose parent participated compared to youth whose parent did not participate (Mothers: $r = .11$, Fathers: $r = .12$). Of the 25 indicators of youth participation, 3 indicators evidenced small effect sizes. Youth whose parent participated had a higher number of English ($r = .14$) and math classes (Mothers: $r = .14$, Fathers: $r = .11$) in high school, and spent more time in instrumental music at Wave 5 (Mothers: $r = .16$, Fathers: $r = .12$) than youth whose parent did not participate. Two of the four teacher ratings of children's natural ability were higher for youth whose parent participated than for their peers: teacher ratings of children's natural math and reading ability (Math, Mothers: $r = .11$, Fathers: $r = .12$; Reading, Mothers: $r = .11$ and Fathers: $r = .10$, respectively). Finally, there was no difference in physical aptitude, but youth whose parent participated had a higher IQ score than youth whose parent did not participate (Mothers: $r = .22$, Fathers: $r = .17$).

Youth Missing Data

Of the 723 youth who had maternal data, we examined how many of the youth left the study. We created an early attrition group (participants who left the study during the elementary school years) and a late attrition group (participants who left the study during the high school years). We found that 13% of the sample was in the early attrition group (left during the elementary school years), 32% of the sample was in the late attrition group (left during the middle school or high school years), 15% of the sample had data missing at random, and 39% of the sample had complete data at all measurement points. We compared differences in the indicators across these four groups (i.e., complete data, early attrition, late attrition, and missing randomly) with ANOVA or chi-square tests depending on the outcome. All four groups were compared on demographic indicators, and indicators from Waves 2 through 3. Three of the four groups were compared on the Wave 4, Wave 5, and high school indicators because the early attrition group left the study before these indicators were collected. In all, 143 tests were calculated.

For 81% of the indicators (116 out of 143 tests), there were no significant differences among the four groups. Twenty-seven of the tests were statistically significant with small effect sizes (eta^2: small $\geq$ .01, medium $\geq$ .06, large $\geq$.14; phi: small $\geq$ .10, medium $\geq$ .30, large $\geq$.50; Cohen, 1988). The means and effect sizes for indicators with significant differences are presented in Table 11. Eight out of 10 indicators of youths' demographic characteristics and ability evidenced small differences across groups. Youth with complete data were more likely to be female, had families with higher parents' education and higher family income, had higher IQ score, and higher teacher ratings of natural ability in math, reading, and sports, as compared to youth in at least one of the other missing data groups (see Table 11 for more details).

There were nine significant differences among the 76 indicators of mothers' beliefs and behaviors across the four attrition groups. For example, mothers of youth with complete data rated their youth higher in ability than did mothers of youth in the late attrition group on five of the indicators. In addition, there were four significant differences in maternal behavior in music and reading domains across the four groups. The pattern of these differences was not consistent across these four behaviors and the effect sizes were small in size (see Table 11 for details). Finally, 10 of the 57 indicators of youths' beliefs and participation significantly differed across groups. Three of the motivational beliefs and seven of the participation indicators were statistically significant with small effect sizes (see Table 11). For example, youth with complete data spent more time reading at Wave 2 and 4 and took more AP math courses in high school as compared to any of the other attrition groups.

Mean-Level Gender Differences

Plan of Analysis

Means and standard deviations of parents' beliefs and participation as well as youths' beliefs and behaviors are presented in Tables 4, 6, 8, and 10 (respectively). Mean level differences between males and females were tested with multiple imputation through SAS with regression analysis to incorporate cases with missing data (Enders, 2010). Ten datasets were imputed. Two sets of regression analyses were computed. In the first regression, only child gender was used to predict each indicator. In the second regression, several exogenous indicators were also included as controls to test whether the gender differences persisted. The exogenous control variables included

46

TABLE 11

STATISTICALLY SIGNIFICANT DIFFERENCES BASED ON YOUTH ATTRITION

Indicator	M(SD)/%				Effect Size
	Complete Data	Missing Randomly	Early Attrition	Late Attrition	
Demographic characteristics					
Female	59%	43%	45%	42%	.08[a]
Cohort (youngest/middle)	30%/32%	32%/34%	37%/40%	25%/29%	.09[a]
Parent education	6.11 (1.84)[b]	5.42 (1.73)[b]	5.60 (1.97)	5.84 (1.85)	.02
Family income	5.93 (1.78)[b]	5.54 (2.05)	5.06 (2.00)[bc]	5.87 (2.13)[c]	.02
Youths' ability					
IQ	119.48 (16.20)[bd]	118.79 (16.26)[c]	113.33 (15.61)[d]	113.33 (14.99)[bc]	.03
Physical	48.31 (9.84)[b]	45.92 (9.79)[c]	45.05 (10.54)[d]	51.52 (10.68)[bcd]	.05
Math (teacher rated)	5.36 (1.09)[b]	5.24 (1.03)	5.09 (1.23)	5.00 (1.16)[b]	.02
Reading (teacher rated)	5.45 (1.09)[b]	5.36 (1.12)[c]	5.18 (1.34)	5.00 (1.16)[bc]	.02
Mothers' perception of their children's ability					
Sports W2	4.87 (1.26)[b]	5.16 (1.16)	4.81 (1.49)	5.26 (1.29)[b]	.02
Math W4	5.89 (1.03)[b]	5.62 (1.03)	5.49 (1.12)	5.97 (.94)[b]	.03
Reading W2	6.10 (.97)[b]	5.77 (1.28)	5.80 (1.34)	5.59 (1.35)[b]	.03
Reading W3	6.02 (1.07)[b]	5.84 (1.05)	5.80 (.97)	5.61 (1.16)[b]	.03
Reading W4	6.01 (1.01)[b]	5.75 (1.14)	—	5.56 (1.14)[b]	.03
Mothers' behavior					
Music events W3	.35 (.48)	.51 (.50)[b]	.17 (.39)[b]	.37 (.48)	.02
Music modeling W4	1.28 (.87)[b]	1.32 (.80)	1.70 (1.19)[b]	1.34 (.74)	.02
Reading encouragement W2+	6.53 (.71)	6.44 (.76)	6.62 (.59)	6.31 (.81)	.02
Reading provision W4	.89 (.31)[b]	.91 (.28)[c]	—	.76 (.43)[bc]	.03
Youths' self-concept of ability					
Sport W2	5.30 (1.39)[b]	5.30 (1.33)	5.73 (1.14)	5.65 (1.28)[b]	.02
Reading W4	5.48 (1.07)[b]	5.09 (1.22)[b]	—	5.28 (1.15)	.02

(Continued)

TABLE 11. (*Continued*)

Indicator	Complete Data	Missing Randomly	Early Attrition	Late Attrition	Effect Size
		$M(SD)$ / %			
Math W5	4.93 (1.29)[b]	5.06 (1.16)[c]	—	4.56 (1.25)[bc]	.02
Youths' participation					
Reading time W2	2.97 (1.16)[b]	2.76 (1.23)	2.52 (1.44)[b]	2.75 (1.27)	.01
Reading time W4	4.21 (1.66)[b]	4.03 (1.72)	—	3.66 (1.68)[b]	.02
English classes in HS[+]	2.03 (.44)	2.04 (.60)	—	1.86 (.66)	.01
Literature clubs in HS	33%	16%	—	20%	.09[a]
Sport time W4[+]	3.85 (1.36)	4.15 (1.36)	—	4.15 (1.42)	.01
Sport time W5	3.67 (2.17)[b]	4.37 (2.18)[bc]	—	3.47 (2.01)[c]	.02
Math classes in HS	.54 (.67)[b]	.39 (.58)	—	.30 (.56)[b]	.03

Note. [a]Effect sizes are phi (small $\geq$ .10, medium $\geq$ .30, large $\geq$ .50). All other effect sizes are partial eta^2 (small $\geq$ .01, medium $\geq$ .06, large $\geq$ .14). [bcd]The same superscripts within the same row are significantly different. [+]None of the pairwise comparisons were statistically significant. — These cells were not included because early attrition youth had already left the study when these data were collected. The percentages are calculated within each attrition group.

parents' education, family income, cohort, children's IQ score, teacher ratings of children's natural ability in each domain, and children's physical aptitude (in the sport models).

Parents' Beliefs

As shown in Table 4, there were more consistent gender differences in parents' sports and instrumental music beliefs than in their math and reading beliefs even after controls for child aptitude in each domain were entered. In sports, at all three time points, parents of girls placed lower value on sports and had lower perceptions of their child's ability than did parents of boys. In instrumental music, parents of girls placed higher value on music and thought their children were more skilled at music than parents of boys at all three time points. In addition, parents of girls rated their child's reading ability higher than did parents of boys, though there were no gender differences in parents' reading values at any wave. All of these differences were typically small in size (i.e., $r = .10$) after accounting for all of the control variables.

Parents' Behaviors

The domain with the most consistent gender differences in parents' reports of their own behaviors was sports—ranging from small to medium in size even after including all of the exogenous control variables (Table 6). Parallel to parents' beliefs, both mothers and fathers of girls engaged in fewer sport-related behaviors (i.e., encouragement, daily coactivity, events, and provision of opportunities) than did parents of boys. In addition, there were small differences in parents' music behaviors based on child gender. Parents of girls reported providing slightly more reading encouragement and provision of opportunities in the home than did parents of boys. Although aligned with our expectations, only 1 of the 22 differences emerged in math and 3 of the 24 differences emerged in reading. Mothers of boys provided more encouragement in math at Wave 2 than did mothers of girls. In contrast, parents of girls reported providing more encouragement than parents of boys, and mothers of girls went to the library together more often than mothers of boys. Although all four of these differences remained after including the exogenous control variables, they were small in size.

Youths' Motivational Beliefs

As shown in previous studies, youths' self-concept of ability and value declined over time in each domain (Table 8). Furthermore, the gender differences found here parallel those found in previous research. Girls had lower self-concepts of abilities in sports and math as well as higher self-concepts of abilities in music and reading than boys. Similar patterns emerged for youths' values, except that there were few gender differences in youths' value of math. These differences were small in all domains except sports, in which several of the differences were moderate in size.

Youths' Participation

Gender differences in participation varied across domains. Girls reported spending moderately less time in sports than boys (Table 10). Girls also participated in a slightly smaller number of high school community sports, though there was no gender difference in school sport teams. In contrast, girls reported spending more time practicing music and reading than did boys. Girls also had higher participation rates in high school literature clubs than boys. After controlling for indicators of ability, these differences in music and reading were small in size. There were few significant mean-level differences between girls and boys for high school courses or time spent in math. The one exception was that girls spent slightly more time on math activities outside of school at Wave 3 than did boys.

Correlations of Other Exogenous Constructs With Our Endogenous Constructs

The correlations between our 11 exogenous constructs and our parent and child/adolescent endogenous indicators are summarized in Tables S1 to S6 in the online material. We highlight the main patterns here for all exogenous constructs except child gender, which was summarized in the previous section and are all in the gender-stereotyped direction and consistently significant. In fact, the child's gender is the most consistent correlate of each of our endogenous constructs, suggesting the continuing power of children's gender in socialization processes. As noted above in the section on mean-level differences, most of these gender associations remained significant even when other covariates linked to independent indicators of natural ability were controlled.

Parents' Beliefs

Most interestingly, family income and parents' education show only very weak and mostly nonsignificant associations with these parental beliefs (Tables A and B in the online material). In contrast, as we would expect, parents' estimates of their children's ability in each domain were significantly and fairly highly related to the corresponding independent indicator we had for each domain (i.e., teachers' rating of children's natural ability); these associations were large for math and reading ($rs > .49$ in all cases). Furthermore, the teachers' rating the child's natural ability in math was almost as highly correlated with the parents' ratings of their children's reading ability as with the parents' ratings of the their children's math ability. Additionally, the children's scores on the Slosson IQ Test were moderately correlated (i.e., $rs \geq .30$) with the parents' ratings of their children's ability for both math and reading. Finally, with the exception of parents' valuing of sports for their children and fathers' valuing of music, the indicators of

50

teachers' ratings of children's natural abilities in each domain were only weakly related to the parents' valuing of each domain for their child.

Parents' Behaviors

In contrast to the patterns for parents' beliefs, parents' behaviors were only weakly related to all of the exogenous constructs except gender in the sport and instrumental music domains (Tables S3 and S4 in the online material). The exceptions were that teachers' ratings of children's natural ability positively predicted parents' sport behaviors and fathers' music behaviors. In addition, co-reading for both parents and provision of math materials for mothers was higher for the youngest cohort compared to the oldest cohort. Again, and even more surprisingly, neither family income nor parents' education correlated very highly with parents' behaviors, with the exception of mothers' provision of music materials and taking children to music events.

Youths' Beliefs

As was true for the parents' beliefs, there was moderate correspondence between teachers' ratings of the children's natural ability in each domain and children's own ability self-concepts in the corresponding domain (Table S5 in the online material). This correspondence was moderate in sports ($rs > .39$ for 3 of the 4 sports scores), small to moderate in math and reading ($rs > .30$ for 2 out the 4 math scores, and $rs > .20$ for all reading scores), and small in instrumental music ($rs = .07$–$.13$). Teachers' ratings of the children's natural ability in sports also correlated significantly with children's valuing of sports. This relation was typically close to zero in the other domains. No other associations other than those associated with child gender showed a consistent pattern.

Youths' Participation

Being a girl correlated negatively with several indicators of sport participation particularly in grades K–9 and with time spent practicing instrumental music during the late elementary school years (Table S6 in the online material). Being a girl also correlated weakly with amount of time spent reading during the elementary school years and with being in a literature club in high school. Teachers' rating of the children's natural ability for sports and reading moderately predicted children's participation in the corresponding domain throughout childhood and adolescence. Finally, children's scores on the Slosson IQ test correlated with the number of high school math courses taken ($r = .42$), participation in reading and literature (rs range from .09 to .21), and playing a musical instrument during the secondary school years ($rs = .18$ and .17).

Overview of the Analyses in the Monograph

We present the plan of analysis in two places in this document. First, we provide a general overview of the analysis that is applicable to all chapters in this section. Second, we provide additional details specific to the models in a chapter in each results chapter. The central goal of this study was to test the relations posited in the Eccles's expectancy-value models. Consistent with a cascade perspective on development, we broke our analyses down into a series of 2-wave chunks that would allow us to do cross-lagged analyses in order to investigate the most probable directions of influence operating at each point along the cascade, looking first at the most fundamental socialization step—the link between the beliefs of parents and indicators of their children's abilities, beliefs, and participation. Essentially, we begin this study by asking: Does the model begin with parents' beliefs or does it begin with the child? We then move to the more specific sets of relations of beliefs and behaviors within parents, across parents and children, and finally within children.

At each step in the model, our goal was to test the direction of influence. An overview of the analytic plan is presented in Figure 2. We isolate each cross-lagged model depicted in Figure 2 in a separate chapter. Chapter 4 addresses whether the model begins with parent or child effects across Waves 2 (grades 1, 2, and 4) and 3 (grades 2, 3, and 5). Chapter 5 describes the relations between parents' beliefs and their own behaviors at Wave 2 (grades 1, 2, and 4) and at Wave 3 (grades 2, 3, and 5). Chapter 6 describes the relations between parents' behaviors and children's beliefs at Wave 3 (grades 2, 3, and 5) and at Wave 4 (grades 3, 4, and 6). Chapter 7 includes models testing the relations

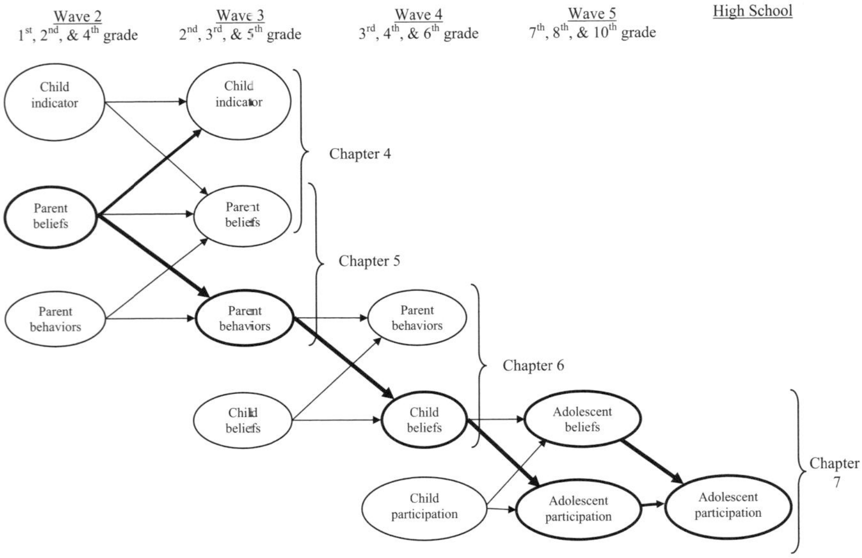

FIGURE 2.—Overall analytic model. The bolded paths show the direction of influence theorized in the Eccles's models.

52

between youths' beliefs at Wave 4 (grades 3, 4, and 6) and Wave 5 (grades 7, 8, and 10) and youths' participation at Wave 4, Wave 5, and high school.

These specific waves were selected for each model for multiple reasons. Most importantly they were selected so the proposed ordering of the cascading developmental sequence of influences was captured in the sequence of waves represented in each analysis—with the earliest steps in cascade represented by the earliest waves of data. This ordering is logically consistent with our view of the order of causal steps in the socialization and enactment sequence and makes use of time as a tool to help us interpret our findings. We did not use Wave 1 data because only 49% of the families were recruited in Wave 1 and not all questions were in Likert-type scales at this wave. Furthermore, because we needed to test three cross-lagged models with parent data across three waves (i.e., Waves 2 through 4), we decided to analyze the first two sets of cross-lagged models on Waves 2 and 3 (i.e., the results in Chapters 4 and 5) and the last cross-lagged model with parent data at Waves 3 and 4 (i.e., the results in Chapter 6).

What is also evident in our plan for the cross-lagged analyses is that our analyses were largely driven by wave and not cohort (or grade level). This was a decision based on several factors. As evident in Table 2, typically only one or two cohorts were assessed at any single grade level. Restructuring the data from wave to grade would have resulted in a sizeable drop in our sample size. Second, because some of the measures changed from wave to wave, we were unable to collapse measures across grade. Such analyses are possible if you have *both* measures collected at least at one time point. That was not the case here. Third, for a cross-lagged analysis, we wanted the time between each wave to be consistent across youth, which was true when we organized the analyses by wave. Therefore, we designed the models based on wave (rather than grade). Other analyses based on the same data, but driven by different questions, namely the developmental progression of these phenomena over time, were organized by grade level (Fredricks & Eccles, 2002; Jacobs et al., 2002; Simpkins et al., 2010).

All models were structural equation models estimated in AMOS v19. These models were estimated with full information maximum likelihood (FIML) to incorporate cases with missing data (Enders, 2010). We used several indicators of model fit, including the Comparative Fit Index (CFI; Bentler, 1990), the Root Mean Square Error of Approximation (RMSEA; Steiger, 1990), and chi-square. A CFI $\geq$ .95 and a RMSEA $\leq$ .06 are indicative of a model that fit the data well (Hu & Bentler, 1999). A CFI between .90 and .95 and a RMSEA between .06 and .10 indicate that the model fit the data adequately.

Separate models were estimated for each of the four domains (i.e., instrumental music, sports, math, and reading), each parent (i.e., mothers and fathers), and each parent or youth belief (i.e., perceptions of ability and value). We estimated separate models for mothers and fathers because (a) more mothers participated in the study ($n = 723$) than fathers ($n = 541$), (b) we wanted to use as large a sample as possible for both sets of analyses, and (c) we were not interested in comparing mothers and fathers or estimating mothers' versus fathers' relative contribution, which is what is assessed in GLM models that include both parents. The results of our previous studies that included both mothers and fathers in the same analyses suggested that fathers had relatively little unique influence on their children (Eccles [Parsons] et al., 1982). Such a conclusion is inconsistent with the results of more qualitative studies that suggest a much more important role for fathers. They are also inconsistent with our factor work that finds that mothers' and fathers' reports of their perceptions of their children often load on the same factor—a finding that suggests mothers and fathers, on average, have quite similar views of their children and quite similar socialization goals. If this is true, then putting both mothers' and fathers' data into the same GLM analysis is likely to underestimate the coefficient for one of the two parents due to multicollinearity. We wanted to avoid this statistical problem primarily because so little is known about fathers.

We also estimated separate models for individuals' perceptions of ability and value to avoid statistical problems associated with multicollinearity. We know from our previous work that individual's perceptions of their abilities in and the value they attach to being good at different domains are significantly and often fairly highly correlated even though they factor onto different scales (Eccles & Wigfield, 1995), making multicollinearity a concern. The fact that these two major motivational beliefs are the key components of different theoretical traditions within the field of motivation led us to the conclusion that it was best to run the models separately for these two constructs so that our findings would be maximally useful to both traditions. More specifically, competence-related beliefs are the cornerstone of self-efficacy, self-worth, self-concept, and self-determination theories. In contrast, value beliefs are related more closely to intrinsic motivation and interest theories. Combining these indicators into a single construct would make it virtually impossible for researchers in these fields to compare the findings of this study with prior research in their area.

Measurement Models

Because we were interested in testing longitudinal cross-lagged models for boys and girls, we had to establish that the measurement models were invariant across time and across child gender (Little, 2013; Millsap, 2011). Each latent variable, with the exception of parents' value, had more than three manifest indicators as recommended for identification (Little, 2013; Millsap, 2011). Each latent variable was identified by fixing one of the

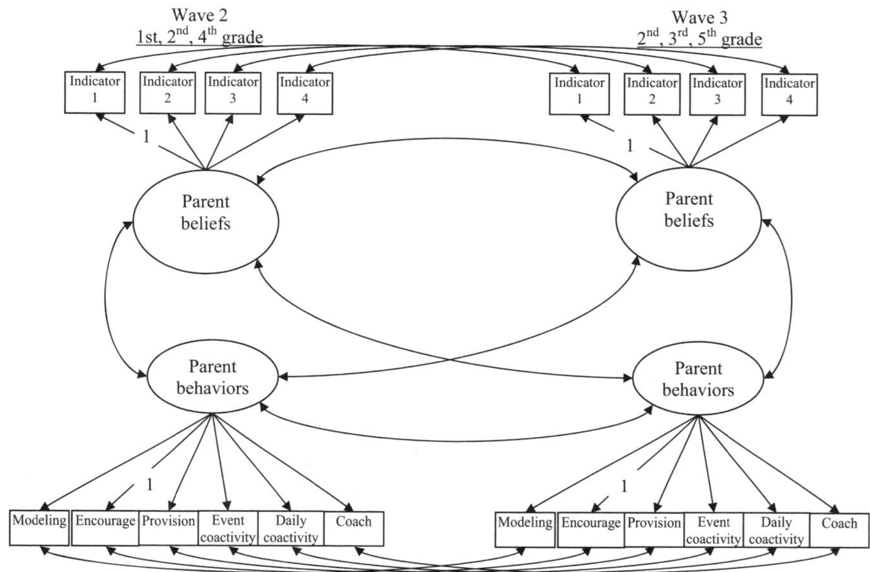

FIGURE 3.—Example of the measurement model of parents' beliefs and parents' behaviors.

loadings to 1.0. These measurement models were different from the full cross-lagged structural models in that they are simply measurement models. An example measurement model is shown in Figure 3. The measurement models did not include control variables, stability or cross-lagged paths, or unique factors for the latent variables. Instead, these measurement models included the latent variables with their manifest (or measured) indicators as well as the covariances among the latent variables and the covariances among the unique factors for the manifest variables.

Following recommendations on estimating cross-lagged models in SEM, we correlated the unique factors of the same measured indicator at the two waves (Little, 2013; Little, Preacher, Selig, & Card, 2007). For example, the covariance between mothers' modeling of sport behaviors at Waves 2 and 3 were estimated. We included two additional covariances among the unique factors for youths' value. Youth value was comprised of two interest items and two importance items. In the expectancy-value model, interest and importance are two aspects of value. As such, we expected the two interest items to be related and the two importance items to be related. We estimated (a) the covariance among the unique factors for the two interest items within each wave, and (b) the covariance among the unique factors for the two importance items within each wave. Thus, for youths' value, we estimated cross-wave covariances among the same indicator over time and within-wave covariances among the interest items and among the importance items. The only exception to this rule was that we did not include the within wave covariances for the interest items in the reading and math models as the models would not converge with these two additional covariances in the model.

Our goal was to examine the relations among the latent variables. We were not focused on the means (such as, whether beliefs declined over time). Other publications based on this dataset have addressed such questions. Because our goal was to examine the relations among the latent variables, we only needed to establish weak measurement invariance across time and across gender. Weak measurement invariance is when the loadings are similar across time and gender (Millsap, 2011).

Traditionally, scholars have used the change in chi-square across two models to indicate whether the loadings are invariant. However, the chi-square statistic and the change in chi-square test are influenced by sample size. When sample size is large as is true in this study, the change in chi-square test can be statistically significant when the change in the model is relatively small. Although experts agree that there are problems with the chi-square, there is less agreement on the alternative criterion. Because adding constraints often worsens fit of the model, researchers need to make sure that the loss of fit is meaningful and important (Little, 2013; Millsap, 2011; Thompson & Green, 2013). Experts have recommended that scholars use the criterion of ΔCFI $\geq$ .010 to understand if the measurement model is similar across groups or time (i.e., invariant). Although this criterion has only been tested in one study to date (Cheung & Rensvold, 2002), it has been endorsed by experts to examine invariance (Little, 2013; Thompson & Green, 2013). A second CFI criterion of .002 has also been put forward (Meade, Johnson, & Braddy, 2008); however, the criterion of .010 has appeal in part because it has been used more often by statistics experts and has practical meaning to researchers. Imagine we had an unconstrained model where the CFI = .995. It would seem like having a constrained model with a CFI = .993 and a ΔCFI = .002 is not a large difference, but a constrained model with a CFI = .985 and a ΔCFI = .010 might raise some concern. We present the change in chi-square, CFI, and RMSEA in all of our nested models for readers who are interested in these various statistics. As can be seen in the tables presenting the overall model statistics for measurement invariance, typically models that evidenced a ΔCFI $\geq$ .010 also had a ΔX^2 with a p-value < .001. It was infrequent when a model evidenced a ΔCFI $\geq$ .010, but did not have a ΔX^2 with a p-value < .001 or vice versa. Given that we tested measurement invariance in 88 models, we used the criteria of ΔCFI $\geq$ .010 to provide an objective indicator of measurement invariance.

Most published work on invariance addresses invariance across one aspect, such as across time or across groups. Few published studies address invariance across two aspects simultaneously. Little (2013) recommended that unless researchers have greater concerns about one aspect (e.g., time or

56

gender in this case), invariance across the two aspects should be tested simultaneously rather than sequentially. We did not have greater concerns for one aspect nor a priori expectations about invariance across time and gender. As a result, we first used an initial omnibus test examining invariance across time and gender simultaneously.

The specific steps to our invariance testing are presented in Figure 4. To test invariance across time and gender simultaneously, we examined the difference between two models. The first model was a multi-group model in which nothing was constrained across time and gender (except for the loading fixed to 1.0 to identify each latent variable). The second model was a multi-group model in which the factor loadings were constrained across time and gender. Thus, for any one loading, four separate loadings were estimated in the first model; but, only one loading was estimated in the second model. For example, take fathers' coaching as an indicator of fathers' sport behavior. In the first model, a loading for coaching was estimated at Wave 2 for girls, Wave 2 for boys, Wave 3 for girls, and Wave 3 for boys. In the second model, all four of these loadings were constrained to be equal so that only one loading was estimated. All loadings were constrained in this manner. Sometimes, there were indicators that were only measured at one of the two waves. In this case, this loading was not constrained across time in the second model (because it was not measured at both time points). This loading was still constrained across gender in the second model. Other than this type of situation, all of the loadings were constrained across both time and gender in the second model.

If the omnibus test evidenced invariance across time and gender (i.e., $\Delta \text{CFI} < .010$), we constrained the paths across both aspects and continued with the full cross-lagged structural models. If the omnibus test suggested that the model was not invariant across time and gender (i.e., $\Delta \text{CFI} \geq .010$), we followed up with a series of invariance tests (Figure 4). First, we examined if the model was invariant across time separately from whether it was invariant across gender to understand each of these aspects separately. We compared each of these two models to the fully unconstrained model. If one of these models also evidenced a $\Delta \text{CFI} \geq .010$ suggesting the loadings were not invariant, we conducted another series of follow-up tests to examine if each loading was invariant.

Experts often use the modification indices to identify which loadings may be invariant. However, AMOS does not provide modification indices when estimating models with missing data. Thus, we computed a series of models to help identify which loadings might not be invariant. In most cases, the models were either invariant across time or across gender. Only two models emerged that were not invariant across *both* time and gender. Given that there were only two instances of this in the whole monograph, we discuss those two models in their respective chapters. Here, we describe our steps in examining which

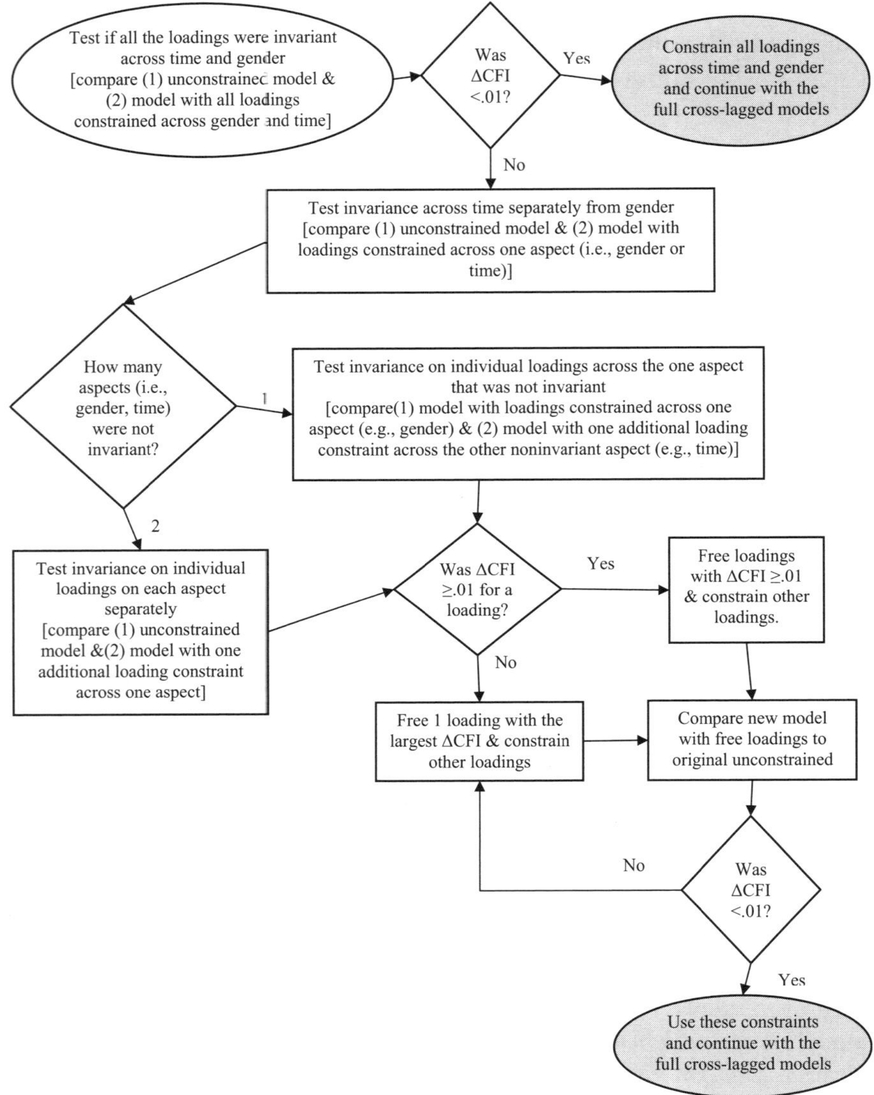

FIGURE 4.—Steps in testing weak measurement invariance across time and gender.

specific loadings were not invariant in one aspect when the other aspect was constrained. If a model was invariant across time but not across gender, the baseline model for our follow-up tests was the model with invariance constraints across time. Then, we estimated models in which we added a gender constraint on the loading of one manifest variables (i.e., constraining

58

the loading for girls to equal the loading for boys) to test if that single loading was invariant across gender. If a model was invariant across gender but not across time, the baseline model for our follow-up tests was the model with invariance constraints across gender. Then, we estimated models in which we added one time constraint on the loadings of two manifest variables (i.e., constraining the loadings of the two indicators over time to be equal) to test if the loadings for the one indicator were invariant over time. In this step of the analysis, each loading was tested in a separate model to help identify which specific loadings may not be invariant. As in our previous model comparisons, we used the criterion of $\Delta CFI \geq .010$ to determine if a loading was invariant. We constrained all loadings across gender or time if the $\Delta CFI < .010$. Then, we estimated the new final model where we freed individual loadings across gender or time if a $\Delta CFI \geq .010$ was evident in the individual tests. If there was not any one individual loading that had $\Delta CFI \geq .010$, we freed the one loading with the largest ΔCFI.

Because each loading was tested separately in the previous step, we conducted one final comparison. We compared our new final, constrained model (with some loadings that were freed) to the original unconstrained model. If the ΔCFI between these two models was greater than or equal to .010, we freed a single loading with the largest ΔCFI even if the ΔCFI might be less than our criteria of .010. This step was repeated until the ΔCFI between our final model and the original unconstrained model was less than .010.

As noted in texts on invariance (Little, 2013; Millsap, 2011), we needed full or partial weak invariance to test the relations in the full structural model. Weak measurement invariance across time was necessary to estimate the full cross-lagged models. Weak measurement invariance across gender was necessary to test whether the structural portion of the model was invariant across gender. If the measurement model was invariant across gender but not time, we did not estimate the full cross-lagged model nor test gender as a moderator of the relations in the structural portion of the model. If the measurement model was invariant across time but not gender, we estimated the full cross-lagged structural model but we did not test gender as a moderator.

Full Cross-Lagged Structural Models

We tested the direction of influence in every model by estimating full cross-lagged models over two waves of data. For example, in Chapter 5, we estimated the cross-lagged model of parents' behaviors and children's beliefs over Waves 3 and 4. The model included parenting behaviors at Waves 3 and 4 as well as child beliefs at Waves 3 and 4. As shown in Figure 7, the stability of each latent variable from Waves 3 to 4 and the cross-lagged paths across these waves were estimated. By including these stability and cross-lagged paths, we

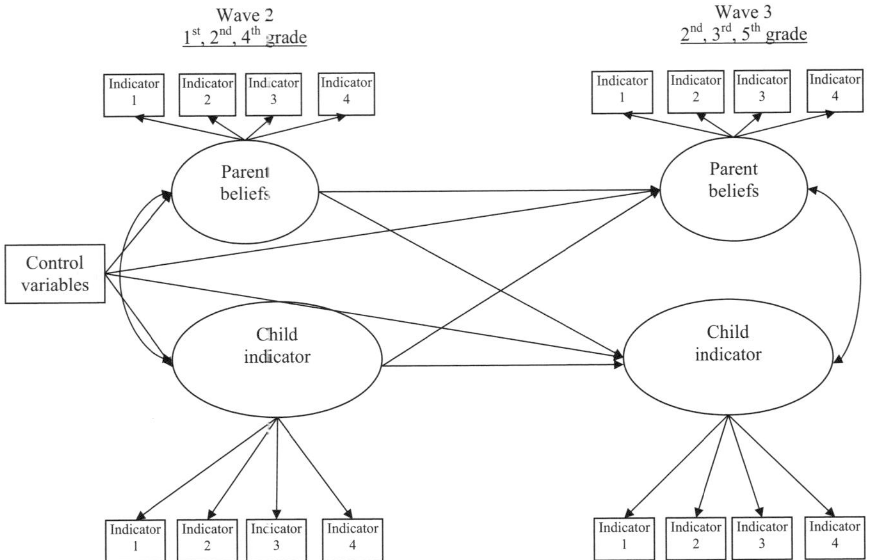

FIGURE 5.—Cross-lagged model of parents' beliefs and child factors.

could examine whether parents' behaviors at Wave 3 predicted changes in children's beliefs over time as well as whether children's beliefs at Wave 3 predicted changes in parents' behaviors over time.

Figures 5–8 show the predictive paths of the full cross-lagged structural models. The additional aspects of the models that are not shown in these overarching figures include (a) the unique factors associated with each latent variable, (b) the unique factors associated with each manifest variable, (c) the covariances among the unique factors of the manifest variables, and (d) the covariances among the control variables. The full list of indicators for each latent variable is presented in the Methods section, and Tables 3, 5, and 7.

Exogenous Control Variables

Several family- and child-level control variables were also included in each model. They were parents' education, family income, teachers' ratings of children's natural ability, children's gender, and children's cohort. Our selection of control variables was based on theory and previous research noting the importance of these indicators in the processes addressed in this monograph. These indicators predicted parents' and youths' beliefs and behaviors at every wave. For example, in the model testing the relations between parents' beliefs and parents' behaviors across Waves 2 and 3, the control variables predicted the four latent variables of parents' beliefs and parents' behaviors at Waves 2 and 3 (see Chapter 5). Although we initially had

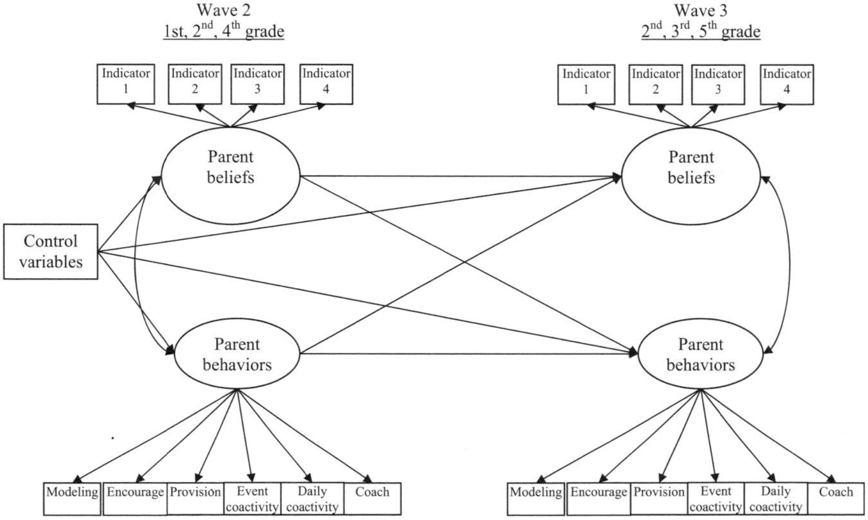

FIGURE 6.—Cross-lagged model of parents' beliefs and parents' behaviors.

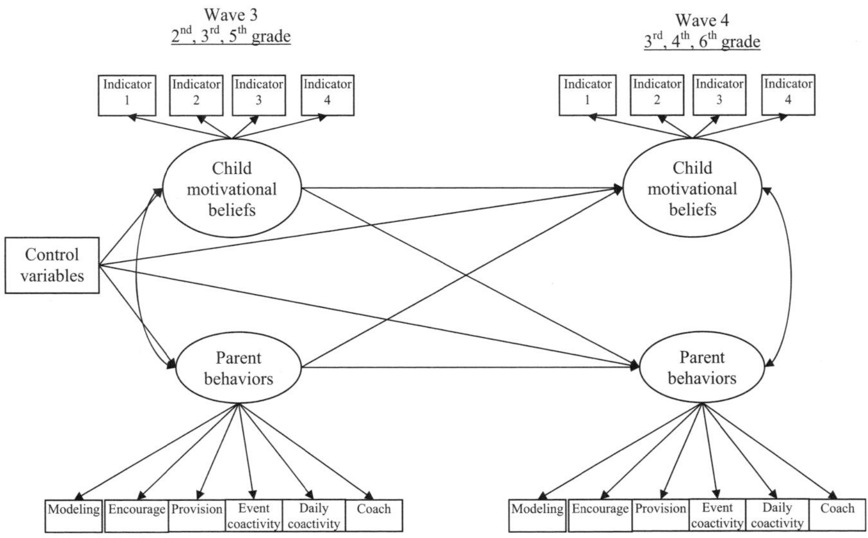

FIGURE 7.—Cross-lagged model of parents' behaviors and children's beliefs.

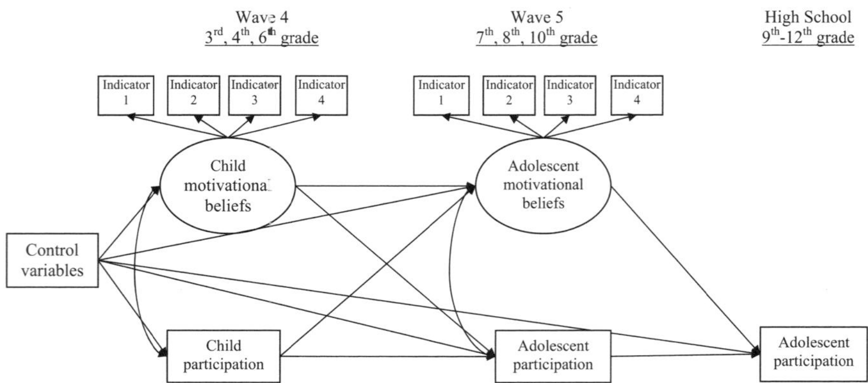

FIGURE 8.—Cross-lagged model of youths' beliefs and youths' participation.

each control variable predict each latent variable of parents' and youths' beliefs and behaviors, this type of analysis can lead to over controlling (Little, 2013). Following recommendations, we dropped paths when a control variable did not significantly predict a particular latent variable at the $p < .10$ level. If a control variable did not significantly predict any of the latent variables representing parents' and youths' beliefs and behaviors in a particular model, it was dropped from that model.

Controlling for these indicators in our analyses at each wave is important so that we can understand the relative contribution of the focal latent variables while controlling for these selection effects. For example, children's Slosson IQ score was included as a control variable in all models. By controlling for this score, we are controlling for the possibility that children with high verbal and day-to-day knowledge (what is measured on the Slosson) are also likely to have parents who support children in these domains and to have high self and task beliefs themselves as well as high rates of participation in these domains. This is the strongest correlational design we can use to adjust for selection effects with non-experimental data. However, the inclusion of these controls at each wave, along with controlling for the stability of each focal parent and youth latent variable across the two waves, makes our analyses of the relative contribution to the change in parents and youth very conservative. The specific findings concerning the control variables (i.e., coefficients) are not presented in the text, but are available from the authors.

Gender Moderation

As noted earlier, one central goal of this study was to examine whether the relations among parents' and youths' beliefs and behaviors varied by child

62

gender. As we noted in the introduction, mean-level gender differences are a separate issue from gender moderation. The same is true for testing measurement invariance for child gender and child gender as a moderator of the relations among the constructs. Measurement invariance examines the extent to which the constructs have similar meaning across girls and boys. Even if the constructs have similar meaning (i.e., they are invariant), it is still possible that the constructs have different correlates. Thus, it is necessary to examine if gender moderates the relations among the constructs. In our cross-lagged models, we tested whether the relations within each time point (i.e., the covariances) and the predictive relations across time (i.e., the stability and cross-lagged paths) varied by child gender.

To test for this invariance in the structural model, we tested the difference between two nested models through a multi-group analysis: (a) a model in which the loadings were constrained across time and gender (based on the previous measurement invariance findings) and (b) a model in which the loadings were constrained across time and gender, and the focal paths were constrained to be equal across girls and boys. The six focal paths included the stability paths, the cross-lagged paths, and the within-wave covariances. All of these paths address the relations among the focal latent variables. Other paths or covariances (e.g., paths from the control variables to the focal latent variables or the covariances among the control variables) were not constrained across gender.

In order to determine if there may be gender differences in the structural portion of the model, we first examined whether the change in model chi-square (based on the change in df) was significant at $p < .001$ due to the effect of large sample sizes on the chi-square statistic (Little, 2013). If this overall test was statistically significant, we computed a series of follow-up tests in which we tested each individual path or covariance to identify the path(s) and covariance(s) that differed across girls and boys.

Presentation of the Results

Given the number of analyses, we present some of the findings in the text and some are available through the supplemental material online. The goodness-of-fit indicators and the standardized path estimates are presented in the text. The online material includes four pieces of information. First, the model fit for measurement invariance across time and gender are presented in the online material as these tests are necessary but not the central questions of this monograph. Second, the unstandardized and standardized path estimates are presented in the supplemental materials. Third, we present the gender moderation in the online material as only one test was statistically significant. Fourth, we also include in the supplemental material the loadings for the parental behaviors as some of the loadings for parents' reading behaviors were not statistically significant (detailed information on this issue is presented in Chapter 5). The loadings for other latent variables are available from the first author.

SUPPORTING INFORMATION

Additional supporting information may be found in the online version of this article at the publisher's website.

IV. CHILD FACTORS AND PARENT BELIEF MODELS

Our goal in this chapter is to summarize the findings from a series of cross-lagged models between child factors (i.e., ability self-concepts, task value, participation, and teachers' rating of the child's natural abilities in each domain) and parent beliefs in each domain measured at Wave 2 (grades 1, 2, and 4) and one year later at Wave 3 (grades, 2, 3, and 5). These models were designed to compare the extent to which the sequence of processes described in the Eccles's expectancy-value model starts with parents or with children. In other words, do parents shape children as theorized in the model, do children influence parents (Bell, 1979), or both? For the most part, we predict that parents' beliefs, particularly their perceptions of their children's abilities, will influence changes in their children's ability self-concepts and task valuing over time more than vice versa because the children's self-concepts are still developing and children's capacity to draw inferences about their abilities from their own performance is limited during the early elementary school years (Parsons & Ruble, 1978; Stipek & MacIver, 1989). We make a similar prediction for the association between parents' beliefs and children's participation in each domain for two reasons: (1) Parents' beliefs should directly influence the extent to which they actively encourage and support their children's participation in each domain; and (2) Parents' beliefs should indirectly influence their children's participation through the impact of these beliefs on the children's ability self-concepts and task valuing.

We also predict that the relative size of these predictions from parents to their children will be stronger in the leisure domains than in math due to the greater likelihood that children have more of their socialization experiences with their parents in leisure domains than in math. Whether this will also be true for reading is not clear because reading is an activity that is often done with one's parents in some homes.

In contrast, we predict that the teachers' rating of each child's natural ability will be more likely to influence changes in the parents' ratings of their children's abilities over time to a greater extent than vice versa, particularly in the areas of math and reading. Teachers provide parents with new information about their child's performance in school that should influence changes in the parents' views of their children's academic abilities over time. Such a pattern of results is consistent with the Eccles and her colleagues' model in which the young children's aptitudes influence the parents' perceptions of the associated abilities, which in turn influence children's developing domain-specific ability self-concepts through the interpretative messages parents provide to their children about their aptitudes and performances, particularly during the elementary school years when children's own ability to interpret their experiences is still developing. In other words, parents are assumed to influence their children's developing ability self-concepts at least in part through their role as interpreters of experience and reality, particularly during the elementary school years.

Data Analysis Plan

Sixty-four separate structural equation models were estimated to test the relations between child factors and parent beliefs across the four domains (i.e., sports, instrumental music, math, and reading), two parents (i.e., mothers and fathers), four child factors (i.e., ability self-concept, value, participation, and teachers' ratings of child natural ability), and the two parent beliefs (i.e., perceptions of their child's domain-specific abilities and the task value the parents attach to each domain). Parents' beliefs were included as latent variables in the models with one exception: Parents' value at Wave 2 was a single-item indicator and thus was included as a measured variable in all models.

A conceptual representation of the cross-lagged model with these constructs is shown in Figure 5 (p. 50). Each model included two stability coefficients, two cross-lagged paths, and two within-wave covariances among the two latent variables. In each model, we first tested whether the relations between the child factors and parents' beliefs varied by child gender with the three steps outlined in the overview of the plan of analysis in Chapter 3.

There was one difference between the models with teachers' rating of the child's natural ability and the models with three other child indicators (i.e., children's ability self-concept, value, and participation). In the models with children's ability self-concept, value, and participation, teachers' rating of children's natural ability averaged across Waves 1–3 was included as a control variable. In the models where teachers' rating of the child's natural ability was included as one of the two central indicators in the cross-lagged analyses, the indicators of teachers' rating of the child's natural ability were single indicators at Waves 2 and 3. Obviously, teachers' rating of the child's natural ability could not be included as a control variable in the models with the cross-lagged relations between teachers' rating of the child's natural ability and

66

parental beliefs. Thus, that one control variable was removed from all the models with teachers' rating of the child's natural ability as one of the two central indicators in the main cross-lagged relations. All of the other control variables were used in all models.

Results

Measurement Invariance

Before presenting the results of the specific paths and covariances, we present the results on measurement invariance across time and gender (model fit for the unconstrained models is presented in Tables S7–S10 in the online material). Fifty-eight of the 64 models evidenced full weak measurement invariance across time and gender when we tested time and gender simultaneously. In other words, in 90% of the models, the loadings for parents' beliefs and children's indicators were similar over time and were similar for girls and boys.

Six of the 64 models had a ΔCFI $\geq$ .010 across the two nested models, suggesting that each of these models included loading(s) that were different (i.e., were not invariant) across time, gender, or across both time and gender. The six models were (a) mothers' sport value and children's sport ability self-concept, (b) fathers' perception of their children's sport ability and children's sport ability self-concept, (c) fathers' sport value and children's sport ability self-concept, (d) mothers' music value and children's music ability self-concept, (e) fathers' reading value and teachers' rating of children's natural reading ability, and (f) fathers' reading value and children's participation.

In each of the three sport models, the loading for one indicator of children's sport ability self-concept was different for girls compared to boys. Therefore, in each of these three sport models, we freed the loading for this item across gender (but constrained it over time). All other loadings in these models were similar across gender and time, and constrained to be equal.

We want to take a moment here to point out that the model with fathers' perception of their children's sport ability and children's ability self-concept is the first model in this monograph where we freed a loading that did not meet our criterion of ΔCFI $\geq$ .010. We noted in the analysis plan presented in Chapter 3 that we used ΔCFI $\geq$ .010 as a marker indicating if the loading(s) were significantly different across gender or time. When we ran the omnibus test including multiple loadings and the ΔCFI $\geq$ .010, there were usually one or two loadings that were driving the differences found in the omnibus test. However, sometimes the omnibus test suggested the loadings were significantly different across gender/time (i.e., ΔCFI $\geq$ .010), but none of the tests for the individual loadings were significant (i.e., ΔCFIs $<$ .010). As shown in Table S7, in the model of fathers' perception of their child's sport ability and children's ability self-concept, the omnibus test was significant suggesting that some loadings differed across child gender (i.e., ΔCFI = .013). However, none of the tests on the individual loadings were significant according to our ΔCFI criterion—suggesting that each individual loading was similar across child gender. We had to reconcile these conflicting findings before we could estimate our full cross-lagged model. Unless we freed at least one loading, the omnibus test would still suggest the loadings differed across girls and boys. Of the individual loadings, the item asking children to compare themselves to other students had the largest change in CFI (i.e., ΔCFI = .007). After we freed that loading to be estimated separately for girls and boys, the omnibus test suggested the remaining loadings were similar across girls and boys (i.e., ΔCFI = .005, which is less than .010). We constrained all other loadings to be equal across time and gender. We proceeded with estimating the full cross-lagged structural models and testing gender moderation as only one loading varied in each of these models.

As shown in Table S8, some of the loadings were not invariant over time in the model with mothers' music value and children's music ability self-concept. Follow-up tests suggested that two of the four loadings for children's music ability self-concept were different at Wave 2 compared to Wave 3. Music ability self-concept included four indicators. The loading for one of these indicators was set to 1.0 to identify the latent variable. Therefore, two of the remaining three indicators had different loadings over time. The lack of invariance suggests that the structure of children's music ability self-concept (i.e., the loadings) changed over time. As a result, any comparisons of children's music ability self-concepts in this model over time would be like comparing "apples and oranges" so to speak and is discouraged. Thus, our analysis of the model with mothers' music value and children's music ability self-concept stopped here. We did *not* continue and estimate the full cross-lagged model.

Two of the reading models with fathers' reading value (i.e., teachers' ratings of children's natural ability and participation) had loadings that were not invariant (i.e., different) across gender. Each of these models included only one freely estimated loading. Children's natural ability and participation were single-item indicators at both waves. Fathers' value was a single indicator at Wave 2 and had only two measured indicators at Wave 3. The only invariance test for these models was to examine if the one loading in each model was similar (i.e., invariant) across girls and boys (Table S10). It was not similar suggesting that the loading for fathers' value was different for fathers of girls compared to fathers of boys and should be estimated separately for each group. Because fathers' value had a different structure (i.e., loadings) across girls and boys, we could not make comparisons across girls and boys using fathers' value.

Thus, we could not test whether gender moderated the relations between fathers' value of reading and children's ability or participation. However, we could continue and estimate the full cross-lagged model (just not include the step on gender moderation).

Final Models

All of the 64 models fit the data well according to the RMSEA (i.e., RMSEA < .05; Table 12 and Tables S11–S14 in the online material). According to the CFI, 58 of the 64 models fit the data well (i.e., CFI = .950–1.000), and the remaining 6 models that fit the data adequately (i.e., CFI = .900 to .949). We summarize the general patterns across the four domains, the various child constructs (i.e., ability self-concept, value, participation, and natural ability), girls and boys, and mothers and fathers. We also note where differences occurred by domain, child gender, and parent. The standardized path estimates are presented in Tables 13 through 16 for sports, instrumental music, math, and reading (respectively). The estimates are organized by the model and then by the type of predictive path within each model: cross-lagged paths, stability paths, and within-wave covariances. The unstandardized estimates, standard errors, and standardized path estimates are in Tables S15–S18 in the online supplemental materials.

There were a few general patterns of findings for the cross-lagged paths that are worth highlighting (Tables 13–16). First, with the exception of instrumental music, parents' valuing of a domain was often not a significant predictor of their children's constructs nor were they often predicted by their children's constructs. In contrast, parents' beliefs about their child's abilities often predicted significant changes in children's beliefs, participation, and teachers' ratings of the child's natural ability over time. As predicted, children whose parents rated their ability the highest showed the largest gains in their own domain-specific ability self-concepts and free time participation in the domain. Interestingly, these same children also showed the highest gains in their teachers' ratings of their natural ability over time.

Second, as predicted, the children's ability self-concepts, subjective task value and participation at Wave 2 did not predict changes in their parents' beliefs from Wave 2 to Wave 3. For instance, as expected, children's participation and children's ability self-concepts rarely ever predicted their parents' beliefs in sports, math, or reading. In instrumental music, however, all five models tested with parental values of music and children's music ability self-concepts, value, and participation had significant child effects. Specifically, mothers' and fathers' valuing of music increased over time if their child had high scores for their music ability self-concept, their perceived value of instrumental music, and their participation in instrumental music. (Note: one of the models was not tested due to lack of measurement invariance). These paths were small to moderate in size (β = .13 to .36, ps < .05).

TABLE 12

Model Fit Indexes for the Models With Child Factors and Parents' Beliefs

Model	Mothers				Fathers			
	df	X^2	CFI	RMSEA	df	X^2	CFI	RMSEA
Sports								
Parent perception of their children's ability								
Child ability self-concept	265	443.34***	.962	.031	258	371.43***	.966	.029
Child value	273	340.29**	.984	.018	247	305.58**	.980	.021
Child participation	106	99.90	1.000	.000	94	112.68	.990	.020
Teacher rating of child natural ability	106	95.58	1.000	.000	84	94.67	.994	.016
Parent sport value								
Child ability self-concept	179	307.97***	.949	.032	171	240.53***	.963	.028
Child value	162	203.01*	.980	.019	124	163.95**	.971	.025
Child participation	41	52.85	.981	.020	53	68.80	.977	.024
Teacher rating of child natural ability	53	51.22	1.000	.000	39	36.23	1.000	.000
Music								
Parent perception of their children's ability								
Child ability self-concept	243	308.59**	.984	.019	229	383.89***	.938	.036
Child value	223	389.06***	.951	.032	219	290.59***	.975	.025
Child participation	104	131.49*	.988	.019	88	150.76***	.958	.037
Teacher rating of child natural ability	74	78.13	.998	.009	92	131.56**	.973	.029
Parent music value								
Child ability self-concept	n/a				144	279.86***	.913	.043
Child value	144	199.09**	.979	.023	138	183.88**	.976	.025
Child participation	45	32.11	1.000	.045	45	60.37	.973	.026
Teacher rating of child natural ability	29	25.58	1.000	.000	33	40.50	.981	.021
Math								
Parent perception of their children's ability								
Child ability self-concept	291	464.09***	.958	.029	285	374.61***	.968	.025
Child value	231	364.93***	.961	.028	255	331.76***	.970	.024
Child participation	110	129.67*	.992	.016	102	104.55	.999	.007
Teacher rating of child natural ability	58	87.75**	.987	.027	94	99.39	.997	.011
Parent math value								
Child ability self-concept	130	189.89***	.965	.025	160	218.53***	.958	.027
Child value	108	173.92***	.947	.029	100	121.21	.978	.020
Child participation	29	37.48	.976	.020	59	75.75	.973	.023
Teacher rating of child natural ability	35	40.01	.992	.014	37	36.99	1.000	.000
Reading								
Parent perception of their children's ability								
Child ability self-concept	265	421.78***	.966	.029	271	441.85***	.946	.035
Child value	199	232.86*	.991	.015	228	307.34***	.969	.026
Child participation	72	109.64**	.987	.027	110	181.53***	.965	.036
Teacher rating of child natural ability	86	121.47**	.988	.024	86	164.08***	.960	.042
Parent reading value								
Child ability self-concept	196	277.96***	.968	.024	182	274.99***	.947	.031
Child value	112	120.59	.993	.010	132	151.91	.982	.017
Child participation	41	45.68	.992	.013	40	42.57	.996	.011
Teacher rating of child natural ability	41	36.98	1.000	.000	39	45.76	.991	.018

Note. n/a = This model was not estimated as the measurement model was not invariant over time.
*$p < .05$.
**$p < .01$.
***$p < .001$.

TABLE 13

Standardized Path Estimates for the Models With Child Factors and Parents' Beliefs in Sports

| Path | Models With Parent Perception of Their Child's Ability and | | | | Models With Parent Value and | | | |
| | Mothers | | Fathers | | Mothers | | Fathers | |
	Girls	Boys	Girls	Boys	Girls	Boys	Girls	Boys
Child ability self-concept								
Cross-lagged paths								
W2 parent beliefs → W3 child self-c	.13**	.15**	.17***	.23***	.07	.08	.14**	.17**
W2 child self-c → W3 parent beliefs	.01	.01	.00	.00	.04	.03	−.06	−.04
Stability paths								
W2 parent beliefs → W3 parent beliefs	.76***	.76***	.73***	.68***	.51***	.48***	.59***	.55***
W2 child self-c → W3 child self-c	.43***	.41***	.42***	.38***	.45***	.43***	.44***	.40***
Within wave covariances								
W2 parent beliefs ↔ W2 child self-c	.20***	.24***	.10*	.19*	.04	.05	.08	.13
W3 parent beliefs ↔ W3 child self-c	.15*	.17*	.14*	.24*	.27***	.31***	.16*	.24*
Child value								
Cross-lagged paths								
W2 parent beliefs → W3 child value	.03	.07	.03	.07	.01	.02	.07	.11
W2 child value → W3 parent beliefs	.08	.06	.14**	.12**	.12	.10	.10	.08
Stability paths								
W2 parent beliefs → W3 parent beliefs	.71***	.67***	.71***	.66***	.56***	.49***	.67***	.64***
W2 child value → W3 child value	.24***	.40***	.28***	.55***	.27***	.45***	.48***	.66***
Within wave covariances								
W2 parent beliefs ↔ W2 child value	.26***	.27***	.21***	.30***	.06	.07	.18**	.27**
W3 parent beliefs ↔ W3 child value	.14**	.27**	.10*	.33*	.18***	.32***	.08	.16
Child participation								
Cross-lagged paths								

(Continued)

TABLE 13. (*Continued*)

Path	Models With Parent Perception of Their Child's Ability and				Models With Parent Value and			
	Mothers		Fathers		Mothers		Fathers	
	Girls	Boys	Girls	Boys	Girls	Boys	Girls	Boys
W2 parent beliefs → W3 child time	.21***	.22***	.13**	.13**	.09	.09	.10	.09
W2 child time → W3 parent beliefs	.00	.00	.08	.06	.06	.05	.10	.09
Stability paths								
W2 parent beliefs → W3 parent beliefs	.73***	.71***	.72***	.68***	.53***	.51***	.67***	.66***
W2 child time → W3 child time	.19***	.16***	.23***	.19***	.22***	.19***	.19***	.16***
Within wave covariances								
W2 parent beliefs ↔ W2 child time	.09*	.09*	.08	.11	.12**	.14**	.13*	.16*
W3 parent beliefs ↔ W3 child time	.17**	.17**	.19**	.23**	.16**	.16**	.12	.12
Teacher rating of child natural ability								
Cross-lagged paths								
W2 parent beliefs → W3 teacher rating	.22***	.23***	.23***	.21***	.10	.09	.07	.06
W2 teacher rating → W3 parent beliefs	.11*	.10*	.18***	.19***	.17**	.18**	.16*	.18*
Stability paths								
W2 parent beliefs → W3 parent beliefs	.72***	.72***	.72***	.69***	.52***	.49***	.65***	.62***
W2 teacher rating → W3 teacher rating	.22***	.21***	.25***	.24***	.31***	.31***	.27***	.27***
Within wave covariances								
W2 parent beliefs ↔ W2 teacher rating	.41***	.41***	.34***	.40***	.16***	.19***	.29***	.33***
W3 parent beliefs ↔ W3 teacher rating	.19**	.20**	.21*	.24*	.02	.02	.03	.04

*$p < .05$.
**$p < .01$.
***$p < .001$.

TABLE 14

STANDARDIZED PATH ESTIMATES FOR THE MODELS WITH CHILD FACTORS AND PARENTS' BELIEFS IN MUSIC

| | Models With Parent Perception of Their Child's and | | | | Models With Parent Value and | | | |
| | Mothers | | Fathers | | Mothers | | Fathers | |
Path	Girls	Boys	Girls	Boys	Girls	Boys	Girls	Boys
Child ability self-concept								
Cross-lagged paths								
W2 parent beliefs → W3 child self-c	.18**	.17**	.32***	.22***	n/a	n/a	.24*	.16*
W2 child self-c → W3 parent beliefs	.03	.04	.06	.08	n/a	n/a	.15*	.20*
Stability paths								
W2 parent beliefs → W3 parent beliefs	63***	.64***	.59***	.54***	n/a	n/a	−.03	−.03
W2 child self-c → W3 child self-c	.33***	.34***	.36***	.33***	n/a	n/a	.48***	.44***
Within wave covariances								
W2 parent beliefs ↔ W2 child self-c	.20**	.15**	.27***	.23***	n/a	n/a	−.03	−.03
W3 parent beliefs ↔ W3 child self-c	.40***	.29***	.47***	.30***	n/a	n/a	.37***	.23***
Child value								
Cross-lagged paths								
W2 parent beliefs → W3 child value	.24***	.21***	.21**	.16**	.01	.01	.17	.13
W2 child value → W3 parent beliefs	.06	.07	.07	.09	.13*	.15*	.33***	.36***
Stability paths								
W2 parent beliefs → W3 parent beliefs	.63***	.63***	.56***	.51***	.38***	.29***	.14	.14
W2 child value → W3 child value	.35***	.32***	.28***	.33***	.34***	.35***	.15*	.20*
Within wave covariances								
W2 parent beliefs ↔ W2 child value	.23***	.18***	.22**	.16**	.05	.04	−.08	−.06
W3 parent beliefs ↔ W3 child value	.35***	.24***	.30**	.21**	.39***	.26***	.24**	.17**

(Continued)

TABLE 14. (*Continued*)

Path	Models With Parent Perception of Their Child's and				Models With Parent Value and			
	Mothers		Fathers		Mothers		Fathers	
	Girls	Boys	Girls	Boys	Girls	Boys	Girls	Boys
Child participation								
Cross-lagged paths								
W2 parent beliefs → W3 child time	.19***	.25***	.19***	.22***	.06	.06	.14*	.13*
W2 child time → W3 parent beliefs	.07	.05	−.03	−.03	.32***	.25***	.29***	.25***
Stability paths								
W2 parent beliefs → W3 parent beliefs	.63***	.65***	.61***	.62***	.41***	.31***	.10	.09
W2 child time → W3 child time	.21***	.21***	.18***	.18***	.29***	.27***	.26***	.23***
Within wave covariances								
W2 parent beliefs ↔ W2 child time	.32***	.29***	.37***	.37***	−.01	−.02	.09	.11
W3 parent beliefs ↔ W3 child time	.38***	.36***	.40***	.40***	.30***	.25***	.18**	.17**
Teacher rating of child natural ability								
Cross-lagged paths								
W2 parent beliefs → W3 teacher rating	.02	.02	.14	.14	.03	.03	.14	.14
W2 teacher rating → W3 parent beliefs	−.05	−.04	.05	.04	.01	.01	.15	.12
Stability paths								
W2 parent ability → W3 parent beliefs	.66***	.64***	.62***	.55***	.31***	.31***	.05	.04
W2 teacher rating → W3 teacher rating	.18**	.18**	.11	.10	.19**	.19**	.15	.13
Within wave covariances								
W2 parent beliefs ↔ W2 teacher rating	.19**	.17**	.20**	.23**	−.09	−.10	−.09	−.12
W3 parent beliefs ↔ W3 teacher rating	−.00	−.00	.07	.06	.05	.05	.12	.12

Note. n/a = This model was not estimated as the measurement model was not invariant over time.
*p < .05.
**p < .01.
***p < .001.

TABLE 15

STANDARDIZED PATH ESTIMATES FOR THE MODELS WITH CHILD FACTORS AND PARENTS' BELIEFS IN MATH

	Models With Parent Perception of Their Child's and				Models With Parent Value and			
	Mothers		Fathers		Mothers		Fathers	
Path	Girls	Boys	Girls	Boys	Girls	Boys	Girls	Boys
Child ability self-concept								
Cross-lagged paths								
W2 parent beliefs → W3 child self-c	.07	.08	−.03	−.03	.06	.06	.01	.01
W2 child self-c → W3 parent beliefs	.08	.08	−.03	−.04	−.12	−.12	.04	.04
Stability paths								
W2 parent beliefs → W3 parent beliefs	.52***	.62***	.62***	.65***	.62***	.58***	.63***	.65***
W2 child self-c → W3 child self-c	.42***	.40***	.45***	.45***	.42***	.44***	.43***	.44***
Within wave covariances								
W2 parent beliefs ↔ W2 child self-c	.28***	.27***	.33***	.36***	.07	.06	.04	.04
W3 parent beliefs ↔ W3 child self-c	.22***	.28***	.26***	.35***	.10	.09	.07	.07
Child value								
Cross-lagged paths								
W2 parent beliefs → W3 child value	.12*	.12*	.08	.08	.00	.00	.04	.04
W2 child value → W3 parent beliefs	.09*	.10*	−.08	−.09	−.02	−.02	.04	.04
Stability paths								
W2 parent beliefs → W3 parent beliefs	.53***	.63***	.64***	.69***	.61***	.57***	.63***	.64***
W2 child value → W3 child value	.37***	.38***	.45***	.46***	.41***	.39***	.47***	.48***
Within wave covariances								
W2 parent beliefs ↔ W2 child value	.17**	.14**	.29***	.28***	.12*	.14*	.02	.02
W3 parent beliefs ↔ W3 child value	.24***	.27***	.12	.16	.17*	.16*	.26*	.25*

(Continued)

TABLE 15. (*Continued*)

| | Models With Parent Perception of Their Child's and | | | | Models With Parent Value and | | | |
| | Mothers | | Fathers | | Mothers | | Fathers | |
Path	Girls	Boys	Girls	Boys	Girls	Boys	Girls	Boys
Child participation								
Cross-lagged paths								
W2 parent beliefs → W3 child time	.04	.03	.01	.01	−.01	−.01	.09	.09
W2 child time → W3 parent beliefs	.03	.04	−.05	−.05	.09	.08	.03	.03
Stability paths								
W2 parent beliefs → W3 parent beliefs	.54***	.64***	.61***	.65***	.58***	.54***	.63***	.67***
W2 child time → W3 child time	.06	.05	.08	.08	.05	.06	.11*	.10*
Within wave covariances								
W2 parent beliefs ↔ W2 child time	−.04	−.03	−.05	−.05	−.02	−.02	−.14*	−.12*
W3 parent beliefs ↔ W3 child time	.08	.09	−.03	−.05	.16*	.16*	.16	.16
Teacher rating of child natural ability								
Cross-lagged paths								
W2 parent beliefs → W3 teacher rating	.19***	.19***	.22***	.18***	.01	.01	.03	.02
W2 teacher rating → W3 parent beliefs	.18***	.21***	.16***	.21***	.07	.06	.08	.09
Stability paths								
W2 parent beliefs → W3 parent beliefs	.56***	.64***	.64***	.67***	.58***	.56***	.61***	.64***
W2 teacher rating → W3 teacher rating	.42***	.46***	.38***	.42***	.54***	.49***	.45***	.50***
Within wave covariances								
W2 parent beliefs ↔ W2 teacher rating	.40***	.35***	.42***	.44***	−.02	−.02	.16*	.13*
W3 parent beliefs ↔ W3 teacher rating	.26***	.32***	.28***	.34***	.01	.01	.08	.08

*$p < .05$.
**$p < .01$.
***$p < .001$.

TABLE 16

STANDARDIZED PATH ESTIMATES FOR THE MODELS WITH CHILD FACTORS AND PARENTS' BELIEFS IN READING

| | Models With Parent Perception of Their Child's and | | | | Models With Parent Value and | | | |
| | Mothers | | Fathers | | Mothers | | Fathers | |
Path	Girls	Boys	Girls	Boys	Girls	Boys	Girls	Boys
Child ability self-concept								
Cross-lagged paths								
W2 parent beliefs → W3 child self-c	.20***	.20***	.25***	.24***	−.08	−.06	.07	.08
W2 child self-c → W3 parent beliefs	−.08*	−.07*	−.08	−.08	.05	.06	.06	.08
Stability paths								
W2 parent beliefs → W3 parent beliefs	.70***	.77***	.83***	.87***	.59***	.58***	.33***	.56***
W2 child self-c → W3 child self-c	.40***	.34***	.42***	.37***	.42***	.37***	.45***	.43***
Within wave covariances								
W2 parent beliefs ↔ W2 child self-c	.22***	.20***	.25***	.24***	.06	.07	−.02	−.01
W3 parent beliefs ↔ W3 child self-c	.23**	.18**	.27**	.23**	.17	.17	.17*	.22*
Child value								
Cross-lagged paths								
W2 parent beliefs → W3 child value	.18**	.17**	.06	.06	−.02	−.01	.06	.07
W2 child value → W3 parent beliefs	−.01	−.02	.06	.07	.00	−.01	.04	.06
Stability paths								
W2 parent beliefs → W3 parent beliefs	.68***	.76***	.70***	.75***	.57***	.57***	.34***	.56***
W2 child value → W3 child value	.39***	.41***	.46***	.50***	.41***	.43***	.47***	.52***
Within wave covariances								
W2 parent beliefs ↔ W2 child value	.18**	.13**	.17*	.14*	.10	.09	.09	.05
W3 parent beliefs ↔ W3 child value	.04	.03	.25**	.22**	.10	.10	−.10	−.12

(*Continued*)

TABLE 16. (*Continued*)

Path	Models With Parent Perception of Their Child's and				Models With Parent Value and			
	Mothers		Fathers		Mothers		Fathers	
	Girls	Boys	Girls	Boys	Girls	Boys	Girls	Boys
Child participation								
Cross-lagged paths								
W2 parent beliefs → W3 child time	−.01	−.01	.22***	.22***	−.06	−.04	−.05[a]	.17[a,*]
W2 child time → W3 parent beliefs	.03	.03	.01	.01	.04	.05	−.03[a]	−.02[a]
Stability paths								
W2 parent beliefs → W3 parent beliefs	.67***	.76***	.72***	.78***	.57***	.58***	.48[a,***]	.44[a,*]
W2 child time → W3 child time	.24***	.24***	.32***	.30***	.24***	.23***	.34[a,***]	.23[a,***]
Within wave covariances								
W2 parent beliefs ↔ W2 child time	.07	.06	.05	.05	−.01	−.01	−.17[a,*]	−.05[a]
W3 parent beliefs ↔ W3 child time	.18*	.14*	.10	.09	.04	.04	−.11[a]	.02[a]
Teacher rating of child natural ability								
Cross-lagged paths								
W2 parent beliefs → W3 teacher rating	.18***	.19***	.27***	.27***	−.05	−.04	.11[a]	−.03[a]
W2 teacher rating → W3 parent beliefs	.20***	.18***	.09	.09	.01	.01	.12[a]	.08[a]
Stability paths								
W2 parent beliefs → W3 parent beliefs	.71***	.72***	.77***	.77***	.56***	.56***	.51[a,***]	.48[a,***]
W2 teacher rating → W3 teacher rating	.51***	.50***	.46***	.45***	.58***	.60***	.49[a,***]	.56[a,***]
Within wave covariances								
W2 parent beliefs ↔ W2 teacher rating	.52***	.47***	.45***	.41***	.04	.04	.06[a]	.14[a]
W3 parent beliefs ↔ W3 teacher rating	.20**	.16**	.20*	.18*	−.05	−.06	.22[a]	−.18[a]

*$p < .05$.
**$p < .01$.
***$p < .001$.
[a]These paths were not tested for gender differences because the loadings were not invariant across gender.

Third, as predicted, teachers' ratings of children's natural ability predicted changes in both parents' confidence in their children's sport and math ability as well as mothers' confidence in their child's reading abilities. Teacher's rating of each child's natural ability also predicted changes in both parents' valuing of sports. Interestingly, and contrary to our prediction, parents' confidence in their children's ability also predicted increases in teachers' ratings of children's natural ability in sports, math, and reading. There is consistent support for reciprocal influence between teachers' ratings of children's natural ability and parents' estimates of children's domain-specific abilities in sports, math, and reading.

Fourth, most of the support for parent to child pathways involved the association of parents' estimates of their children's abilities with increases over time in their children's domain-specific self-concepts and activity participation. Only fathers' valuing of an activity had any significant paths and, contrary to what we had expected, none of these were to their children's valuing of a domain. Also contrary to what we had predicted, the only parent beliefs that predicted increases in the children's valuing of a domain were parents' estimates of their child's ability in instrumental music and mothers' ratings of their child's ability in reading. Thus, children's valuing of activities was not predicted by their parents' valuing of similar activities for them.

Fifth, as predicted, there were more significant cross-lagged paths from parent to child in the leisure domains than in the math domain. For example, parents' confidence in their children's sport and instrumental music ability consistently predicted small to moderate changes in children's sport and music beliefs and participation ($\beta = .12$ to $.32$, $ps < .05$). Within the academic domains, there were more significant paths from parent to child in reading as compared to math, most of which involved the parents' estimates of their children's reading ability and the children's own perceptions of their reading ability. In contrast, the only significant path from child to parent in the math domain was that children's valuing of math at Wave 2 predicted small increases in their mothers' estimates of their children's math ability at Wave 3. There was also a significant relation between parents' confidence in their children's math ability and their children's valuing of math.

In the majority of models across the four domains, the parent and child constructs were moderately to highly stable from Wave 2 (grades 1, 2, and 4) to Wave 3. That included parents' value, parents' perception of their child's ability, children's ability self-concept, task valuing, and participation, as well as the teachers' ratings of the child's natural ability. There were two consistent exceptions to this pattern: Neither fathers' music valuing nor children's participation in math were stable over time. Furthermore, in all domains, parents' beliefs showed greater cross-time stability than their children's beliefs. This is particularly true for sports and reading. Parents' ratings of their children's abilities were more stable in all domains than were teachers' ratings of each child's natural ability. This is particularly true for sports and instrumental music. The lower stability for teachers' ratings is not surprising, because children changed teachers each year. Finally, the stability of children's out-of-school participation is much lower than the stability of the other three child indicators, particularly in the math domain. Interestingly, children's participation in reading showed the highest stability across time.

Gender Moderation

As shown in Tables S11 through S14 in the online material, none of the 62 tests for gender moderation in the structural portion of the model were statistically significant at the $p < .001$ level. In other words, the six paths and covariances tested in each model were similar across boys and girls. These paths and covariances in each model were constrained across gender. The paths presented in Tables 13 through 16 in the text and in Tables S15 through S18 in the online material include these constraints.

Please note that we only tested gender moderation in 62 of the 64 models as the loadings were not invariant over time (i.e., were different at Wave 2 and Wave 3) in one of the instrumental music models and the loadings were not invariant over gender in one of the reading models. It is important to note that the standardized paths may be different for boys and girls even when the path was constrained to be equal across groups. Different standardized paths can arise if the variance within boys is different than the variance within girls.

Exogenous Control Variables

Before we conclude the overview of the results for this chapter, we would like to provide information on the relations between the exogenous control variables and the other parent and child variables ($ps < .05$). Teachers' ratings of children's natural abilities consistently and positively predicted youths' ability self-concept at Waves 2 and 3 ($\beta = .12$ to $.47$), mothers' perceptions of their children's abilities at Waves 2 and 3 ($\beta = .16$ to $.57$), and fathers' value at Wave 2 ($\beta = .17$ to $.32$). One exception to this pattern was instrumental music. Teachers' ratings of children's natural music ability often did not predict any of the music indicators at hand. Children's IQ positively predicted teachers' ratings of children's natural ability at Wave 2 ($\beta = .11$ to $.49$), and mother's perception of their children's ability in instrumental music, math, and reading ($\beta = .16$ to $.45$). In addition, IQ also predicted higher participation in math and reading ($\beta = .14$ to $.18$), as well as higher parental value at Wave 2 ($\beta = .25–.40$). One exception to this pattern was sports, in which children's IQ negatively predicted teachers' ratings of children's natural sport ability at Wave 2 ($\beta = -.21$ to $-.17$), and parents' perception of their children's sport ability at Wave 2 ($\beta = -.24$ to $-.14$). The cohort differences typically suggested that children in the youngest and middle cohorts had higher values ($\beta = .15$ to $.37$) and ability self-concepts ($\beta = .14$ to $.37$), but lower participation than children in the oldest cohort ($\beta = -.36$ to $-.12$). There were not many differences by cohort in parents' beliefs although, in some models, mothers' beliefs were lower for the youngest and middle cohorts compared to the oldest cohort ($\beta = -.34$ to $-.14$). Parent education and family income were not strong predictors of parents' beliefs or the child indicators.

Discussion

In sports, instrumental music, and reading, we found consistent evidence supporting the hypothesis that parents act as expectancy socializers for their children (Eccles, 1993). Consistent with social constructivist perspectives, the Eccles's expectancy-value model assumes that individual differences in self- and task-perceptions come from individuals' interpretation of reality, and parents play a critical role in this interpretative process (Eccles, 1993; Frome & Eccles, 1998). The strongest evidence for the positive association between parents' beliefs and children's beliefs and participation emerged in the leisure domains. Because organized sports and instrumental music opportunities often occur outside of school during the elementary school years, parents need to provide such opportunities for their child in these activity domains. These findings are consistent with prior studies linking parents' beliefs to children's motivation in the sport domain (Bois et al., 2002; Fredricks & Eccles, 2002, 2005) and contribute to a very limited research base in instrumental music (Klinedinst, 1991).

Interestingly, and contrary to our predictions, we found much less support for the role of parents in the socialization of children's beliefs and behaviors in math than in the other three domains. One possible explanation for this discrepancy is that math largely occurs in school and there was little math homework during the elementary school years for this population. In this sample, the children reported very low rates of involvement in math in the after-school hours. As a result, there may have been fewer opportunities for parents to have an influence in this domain. In contrast, although reading is also covered in school, parents and children often read at home together during the preschool and early elementary school years. However, it is important to note that our math findings contrast with prior research linking mothers' ratings of children's ability to older children's perceptions of their ability in math (Fredricks & Eccles, 2002; Frome & Eccles, 1998). Thus, parents may play a more important role in supporting their children's ability self-concepts and interest in math when math becomes more salient and difficult in the secondary school years.

It is also important to note that the strength of the pathways from parents' beliefs to their children's participation was weaker in the reading domain than in the two leisure domains. In fact, contrary to our predictions, mothers' confidence in their children's reading abilities did not predict changes in out-of-school reading over time (it does, however, for fathers). Why might this be true? Perhaps mothers engage their children in out-of-school reading for two quite different reasons: to enhance already good reading skills or to remediate reading problems. In the first case, we would expect a positive association between mothers' estimates of their children's reading ability and the amount of out-of-school time the children spend reading. In the second case, we would expect a negative association between mothers' estimates of their children's reading abilities and the time the children spend reading at home. These two cases could cancel each other out at the population level.

The majority of developmental researchers assume there is a reciprocal feedback process between parent and child, with parents shaping children as well as parents being shaped by children. According to the results of our cross-lagged models and consistent with our predictions, during the elementary school years, the direction of influence regarding children's developing ability self-concepts and activity participation largely flows from parents to children rather than vice versa in instrumental music and reading. This is also true for children's valuing of instrumental music and reading.

However, also as we had predicted, we found consistent evidence that children's characteristics (in this case the teacher's estimates of each child's natural ability) predicted changes in parents' estimates of their children's abilities in sports, math, and reading. Either one or both parents' confidence in their child's domain-specific abilities in these three domains increased over time if their child's teachers rated their child's natural abilities high. These findings are consistent with the idea that teachers give parents' messages about their children's ability through grades and other types of feedback that parents likely use to help them form their own perceptions of their children's competencies in different domains. This was not true in the domain of instrumental music perhaps because teachers have little opportunity to either observe the children's instrumental music skills or communicate their perceptions to the parents.

What is equally interesting is that parents' confidence in their children's abilities also predicted, in a reciprocal fashion, changes over time in the teachers' ratings of each child's natural ability in sports and reading. Why might this be true? We know that parents' (either one or both) confidence in their children's abilities predicts increases in participation in sports and reading. It seems likely that increases in participation in these domains will lead to increases in their children's skill levels, which, in turn, could lead the Wave 3 teacher to perceive these children as having more natural ability than the children whose parents see them as less able in sport and reading. If so, this would be a good example of parent expectancy effects leading to a self-fulfilling prophecy in these two domains. But why would not this also be true for math? Neither parents' confidence in the children's math ability nor the value they place on math for their child predicted increases in their child's participation in math. The most likely explanation for this discrepancy is that parents in this sample had much less opportunity to do math with their children at home than sports or reading. If so, then we expect to find stronger evidence of a parental self-fulfilling prophecy effect for math today given that there are more opportunities and more pressure on parents to engage their children in math activities out of school.

Setting aside the analyses involving the teacher perceptions of the children's natural ability, the strongest evidence for reciprocal influences and child to parent effects is in the domain of instrumental music. In this case, parents' estimates of their children's instrumental music abilities predicted increases over time in children's instrumental music ability self-concepts and value, and the children's Wave 2 instrumental music value and participation also predicted increases in the value their parents attached to instrumental music for them. This suggests that children's interests may have a greater influence on their parents' provision of opportunities for them to engage in instrumental music than they have in the other three domains studied. We have three pieces of evidence that suggest this might be true for fathers. First, the amount of time children spent doing instrumental music at Wave 2 predicted increases in the value their fathers placed on instrumental music at Wave 3. Second, the value that the children placed on instrumental music at Wave 2 predicted increases in their parents', especially their fathers', valuing of instrumental music for them. Third, the value fathers placed on instrumental music at Wave 2 predicted increases in their children's participation in instrumental music at Wave 3.

We see some evidence of indirect reciprocal influences in the sport domain, though the strength of these associations was smaller than music. In this case, parents' confidence in their children's abilities at Wave 2 predicted increases in their children's participation in sports at Wave 3. Furthermore, both children's valuing of sports and their confidence in their sport ability at Wave 2 predicted increases in their fathers' confidence in the child's sport ability at Wave 3. This pattern suggests that children's interest in sports may influence their opportunities to participate in sports through its impact on their parents' confidence in their child's sport ability. Why might this pattern be true for both sports and instrumental music but not for either math or reading and why is the pattern stronger for instrumental music than for sports? We suspect it reflects differences in when parents in this country think it is most appropriate to begin to provide opportunities for their children to engage in these different domains. Middle-class parents are eager to engage with their children in reading from very early in their children's lives. Similarly, although somewhat later, middle-class communities in the United States offer many opportunities for 5-year-olds to get involved in organized sport activities. In contrast, the opportunities for instrumental music are fewer and more likely to be offered to children after they have begun elementary school. Parents of elementary school-aged children in the United States may also be waiting for more evidence that their children will enjoy instrumental music classes before trying to get them involved. We expect that these domain differences are culturally grounded and likely to vary across nations and cultural subgroups within each nation.

The final pattern that needs discussion is the fact that parents' confidence in their children's abilities were more predictive of changes in their children's beliefs and participation than were parents' valuing of each domain for their child. Because we included teachers' ratings of the each child's natural ability in each domain as a covariate (with the exception of the models with teachers' rating of children's natural ability as a focal indicator in the cross-lagged models), we know this pattern is not an artifact of the relatively high association between parents' estimates of their children's abilities and an independently assessed indicator of their child's ability in each domain. Why then might parents' perceptions of their children's abilities have stronger predictive effects on changes in children's beliefs and participation than the value parents attach to each domain? It might reflect differences in the psychometrics of these two beliefs. Inspection of Table 4 (p. 28) suggests this might be true for math and reading given that the means are higher and the standard deviations are lower for the valuing items than for the perceived ability items and there are fewer items on the valuing scale than on the perceived ability scales leading to lower internal consistency reliabilities for the valuing scales. It could also be that parents have more stable beliefs about their children's abilities than about the value of particular domains for their child. If so, these beliefs could exert a stronger effect over time because they remain more stable. Inspection of Tables 13 to 16 provides some support for this suggestion in that the stability coefficients were usually larger for the perceived ability scales than for the task valuing scales. Finally, it could be that parents' perceptions of their children's abilities are a stronger predictor of their parenting practices than are the values they attach to each domain for their child. We address this hypothesis in Chapter 5.

SUPPORTING INFORMATION

Additional supporting information may be found in the online version of this article at the publisher's website.

V. PARENT BELIEF AND BEHAVIOR MODELS

In this chapter, we summarize our findings for the link between parents' beliefs and parents' behaviors. As in most social cognitive theories of behavior, Eccles and her colleagues (1983) assume that individuals' beliefs drive their behaviors. However, there is a long tradition within the social psychology of the link between attitudes and behaviors in which scholars question this assumption. Thus, we test for both of these possibilities.

It is important to note that Eccles and her colleagues hypothesize that two types of beliefs can influence parents' behaviors: general beliefs and child-specific beliefs. In this monograph, we focus on the link between child-specific beliefs and a composite indicator of different ways that parents try to influence their children's achievement-related task- and self-beliefs as well as participation. We chose this focus for two reasons: (1) The social psychological literature on attitudes and behaviors suggests that the belief to behavior link will be strongest the more similar the beliefs and behaviors are to each other, and (2) we needed to reduce the length and complexity of this monograph to what we consider to be its most important, new contributions. As reviewed in Chapter 1, others have investigated the link between such general beliefs as gender-role beliefs and parents' valuing of different types of competencies and activities for sons versus daughters. Far fewer researchers have looked at the link between child-specific beliefs and patterns of domain-specific parenting behaviors.

In general, we predict that parents' child-specific beliefs will predict changes in their behaviors over time. Second, given the more consistent relations between parents' beliefs and the child outcomes in the leisure domains reviewed in Chapter 4, we predict a more consistent pattern of associations between parents' beliefs and parents' behaviors in the leisure domains.

Data Analysis Plan

To test these hypotheses and to more generally investigate these associations, we tested the cross-lagged relations between parents' beliefs and parents' behaviors measured at Wave 2 (i.e., grades, 1, 2, and 4) and one year later at Wave 3 (i.e., grades 2, 3, and 5). Sixteen separate structural equation models were estimated to test the relations between parents' beliefs and behaviors across the four domains (i.e., sports, instrumental music, math, and reading), two parents (i.e., mothers and fathers), and the two parent beliefs (i.e., beliefs about children's domain-specific abilities and the value of each domain). For example, in the sport domain, models were run to examine: (1) maternal beliefs about her child's sport ability and maternal sport support-related behaviors, (2) maternal valuing of sport and maternal sport support-related behaviors, (3) paternal beliefs about his child's sport ability and paternal sport support-related behaviors, and (4) paternal valuing of sport and paternal sport support-related behaviors. A conceptual version of the cross-lagged model is shown in Figure 6 (p. 61). Figure 6 differs from Figure 3 in that Figure 6 is a predictive model with controls and includes predictive paths whereas Figure 3 is simply the measurement model.

Parents' beliefs and behaviors were included as latent variables with one exception. Parents' value of each domain at Wave 2 was measured with a single item and included as a measured indicator in the models. The specific indicators of parents' beliefs and behaviors measured at each wave and for each domain varied slightly (see Tables 3 and 5 in Chapter 2 for the specific items). Each model included the basic cross-lagged model with two stability coefficients, two cross-lagged paths, and two within-wave covariances among parents' beliefs and behaviors.

Before we discuss the results for the models, we need to discuss parents' behavior in the domain of reading. Parents' reading behaviors operated differently than the parenting behaviors in the three other domains. In sports, math, and instrumental music, all parent behaviors significantly loaded onto a single latent variable suggesting that they were related indicators of an overall construct. In reading, however, some of the parenting behaviors did not significantly load onto the latent variable (see Tables S19 and S20 in the online material for the loadings of parents' behaviors). Some of the parenting behaviors, such as parental encouragement of reading, were highly skewed with nearly all parents rating their encouragement of reading above the midpoint of the scale. In addition, the bivariate relations among parents' reading behaviors evidenced only low to modest relations, with some of these associations not reaching statistical significance (correlations ranged from .01 to .27). Experts have noted that such low correlations can impact the extent to which indicators load on a single latent variable (Millsap & Olivera-Aguilar, 2012). Thus, we were not empirically justified in creating a latent parenting variable in reading.

Although these behaviors did not load onto a single latent variable, theoretical and empirical evidence suggests each behavior supports children's reading motivation and participation. Items that have these properties are called cause indicators (Bradley, 2004). Cause indicators may not be highly associated with each other, but comprise a single scale because they theoretically all cause or predict the same outcome. One of the most widely used cause indicators is the HOME scale (Bradley, 2004).

We used an approach similar to that used with the HOME subscales as well as by risk and resiliency researchers to create a parenting variable for reading (Rutter, 1988; Sameroff et al., 1998). Using the same set of parental indicators, we created an index of the number of promotive reading factors in the home. For each variable, parents were given a score of 1 or 0, depending on whether they were above or below a certain cutoff point on the variable. As shown in Table 17, the cutoff point was at a value that corresponded to the top 25% or the lower 75% of the distribution for that variable. Researchers have used similar coding methods in previous work with this data (Fredricks & Eccles, 2005; Fredricks et al., 2005; Simpkins, Fredricks, et al., 2006). A higher

TABLE 17

CUTOFFS FOR READING PROMOTIVE VARIABLES AT WAVES 2, 3, and 4

Parent Variable	0	1
Wave 2		
Mother modeling	0–5	6–8
Mother coactivity	1–5	5.50–6
Mother encouragement	4–6	7
Mother provision of opportunities	0 or 1	2
Father modeling	0–4	5–7
Father coactivity	0	1
Father encouragement	1–5	6–7
Wave 3		
Mother modeling	0–4	5–7
Mother coactivity	0–4.5	5–7
Mother encouragement	2–6	7
Mother provision of opportunities	0–1	2
Father modeling	0–3	4–7
Father coactivity	1–3.5	4–7
Father encouragement	2–6	7
Father provision of opportunities	0–1	2
Wave 4		
Mother modeling	0–3	4–7
Mother coactivity	1–3.5	4–7
Mother events	2–6	7
Father modeling	0–3	4–7
Father coactivity	0	1
Father events	1–4	5–7

Note. Father provision of opportunities was not measured at Wave 2.

score signified that parents engaged in more behaviors to support children's reading.

The number of reading promotive factors was used as a measured indicator of parents' behaviors at each wave. For the other three domains, latent variables of parents' behaviors at both waves were used. Other than this difference, all of the models were the same across domains.

Results

Measurement Invariance

Before presenting results of the cross-lagged models, we describe the findings from the tests of measurement invariance. All of the unconditional models fit the data well (i.e., CFI $\geq$ .95, RMSEA $\leq$ .05) or adequately (i.e., CFI $\geq$ .90, RMSEA $\leq$ .08) with the exception of the model with fathers' sport value, which did not fit the data well according to the criterion for evaluating CFI (i.e., .877), but fit the data well according to the RMSEA (i.e., .043). The significance tests of measurement invariance are shown in Table S21 in the online material.

All models evidenced full or partial weak measurement invariant across time and gender. Full weak measurement invariance is when all loadings in

TABLE 18

MODEL FIT INDEXES FOR THE MODELS WITH PARENTS' BELIEFS AND BEHAVIORS

	Mothers				Fathers			
Model	df	X^2	CFI	RMSEA	df	X^2	CFI	RMSEA
Sports								
Perception of their child's ability	344	440.00***	.971	.020	493	674.57***	.940	.027
Value	219	317.48***	.922	.025	316	510.50***	.870	.035
Music								
Perception of their child's ability	339	598.13***	.924	.033	289	432.09***	.932	.031
Value	235	446.02***	.901	.025	193	280.79***	.922	.030
Math								
Perception of their child's ability	241	457.12***	.928	.036	287	327.40*	.980	.017
Value	153	218.78***	.935	.024	158	181.64	.964	.017
Reading								
Perception of their child's ability	116	151.87	.988	.021	116	214.58***	.952	.041
Value	45	34.56	1.000	.000	33	32.48	1.000	.000

$^*p < .05.$
$^{**}p < .01.$
$^{***}p < .001.$

88

the model were similar across time and child gender. Partial weak measurement invariance is when some but not all loadings are similar across time and child gender. Ten of the sixteen models evidenced full weak invariance across time and gender when tested simultaneously. This means that in those 10 models, the loadings were similar across Waves 2 and 3 as well as across parents of girls and parents of boys. Thus, we constrained these loadings to be the same across time and gender in the subsequent full cross-lagged models.

The remaining six models evidenced partial weak measurement invariance. Five of these six models emerged in the leisure domains; only one of these models was in an academic domain. Most of the differences in the loadings emerged for one or two parental behaviors. The loadings for parents' beliefs were typically invariant (i.e., similar) across Waves 2 and 3 as well as across parents of girls and parents of boys. Furthermore, the differences largely emerged across gender for fathers, but across time for mothers. Below we discuss the details of these tests organized by parent gender given these different patterns.

The loadings for mothers' modeling and coactivity were different across Waves 2 and 3 (i.e., not invariant across time) in some of the instrumental music and math models. The loadings for mothers' modeling of music, coactivity with her child in music, and coactivity with her child in math were significantly different at Waves 2 and 3. Thus, we freed these loadings in the respective model so that they were estimated separately at each time point.

Three of the four models with fathers' data in sports and instrumental music had loadings that varied. In all cases except one, the findings suggested that a behavior loaded differently depending on whether it was a father of a girl or a father of a boy. In the father sport models, the loadings for fathers' coaching, modeling, and expectations for child's success next year (i.e., item 1c in Table 3) were different for fathers of girls compared to fathers of boys in one or both sport models. In all cases, we freed the loading so that the loading was estimated separately for fathers of girls versus fathers of boys.

The model with fathers' valuing of instrumental music is one of the two models in the entire monograph that had loadings that varied across *both* time and gender. In this case, we ran separate follow-up tests for gender and time. These tests suggested that the loadings for provision and coactivity varied across child gender, and the loading for coactivity also varied over time (as shown in Table S21). It should be noted that two of these three loadings met our criterion for measurement invariance, namely the ΔCFI < .010, as discussed in Chapter 3. However, we had to free a third additional loading with the highest ΔCFI so that the new final model had a ΔCFI < .010 compared to the original unconstrained model (see Figure 4 [p. 58] for invariance steps).

Despite a handful of differences, the majority of our latent variables had a similar structure across time and across parents of girls and parents of boys. Thus, it is possible and makes sense to examine the relations among these constructs over time and across parents of girls and parents of boys. We, therefore, continued with our cross-lagged models and tested gender moderation in the structural portion of the model. In the models moving forward, we freed the loadings noted in Table S21 and in the text above, but constrained all other loadings to be equal across time and gender.

Final Models

As shown in Table 18 (and Table S22 in the online material), the models fit the data well (i.e., CFI $\geq$ .95, RMSEA $\leq$ .05) or adequately (i.e., CFI $\geq$ .90, RMSEA $\leq$ .08), with the exception of the father sport value model where the CFI was below adequate (i.e., CFI $= .870$) but the RMSEA suggested the model fit the data well (i.e., RMSEA $= .035$). Table 19 includes the standardized path estimates and Table S23 in the online material includes the unstandardized estimates. Unless noted, the findings were similar across the ability self-concept and value models, child gender, and mothers and fathers.

Some of the patterns differed across the academic and leisure domains. In math and reading, parents' behavior never predicted changes in parents' beliefs. In contrast, this same relation was statistically significant in seven of the eight sport and instrumental music models. Parents who exhibited higher sport or music behaviors at Wave 2 showed increases in both their perception of their children's competence and the value the parents' attached to that domain one year later. These paths were generally moderate to strong in size ($\beta = .17$–$.73$, $ps < .05$).

The other cross-lagged path in these models tested the extent to which parents' beliefs predicted changes in parents' behaviors over time. Parents' beliefs predicted small to moderate changes in parents' behaviors in 6 of the 16 models ($\beta = .07$–$.25$, $ps < .05$). Specifically, parents' perceptions of their children's ability predicted small increases in mothers' reading and sport behavior, and fathers' math behavior ($\beta = .07$–$.24$, $ps < .05$). Parents' valuing of a domain predicted small increases in mothers' and fathers' sport behavior and fathers' reading behavior ($\beta = .15$–$.22$, $ps < .05$).

There were a few consistent differences in this path from parents' beliefs to their behaviors across domains. First, three of the six significant cross-lagged paths from parents' beliefs to behaviors emerged in sports. Second, none of these cross-lagged paths were significant in instrumental music. Finally, we had only very limited evidence of parents' beliefs predicting changes in their behavior in math (1 path) and reading (2 paths).

In the majority of models, parents' beliefs and behaviors were moderately to highly stable across the two waves. These estimates are presented in the

TABLE 19

Standardized Path Estimates for the Models With Parents' Beliefs and Behaviors

Path	Mothers		Fathers		Mothers		Fathers	
	Girls	Boys	Girls	Boys	Girls	Boys	Girls	Boys
	Sports				Music			
Perception of their child's ability								
Cross-lagged paths								
W2 parent percept. → W3 parent behaviors	.24**	.23**	.15	.13	.03	.04	.12	.13
W2 parent behaviors → W3 parent percept.	.21**	.20**	.11	.13	.20*	.17*	.39**	.40**
Stability paths								
W2 parent percept. → W3 parent percept.	.64***	.62***	.64***	.62***	.53***	.53***	.36**	.34**
W2 parent behaviors → W3 parent behaviors	.65***	.55***	.81***	.84***	.72***	.72***	.48**	.55**
Within wave covariances								
W2 parent percept. ↔ W2 parent behaviors	.38***	.40***	.63***	.51***	.69***	.71***	.76***	.64***
W3 parent percept. ↔ W3 parent behaviors	.47***	.42***	.50**	.64**	.80***	.70***	.63***	.60***
Value								
Cross-lagged paths								
W2 parent value → W3 parent behaviors	.22*	.19*	.18*	.13*	.11	.10	−.09	−.09
W2 parent behaviors → W3 parent value	.31***	.38***	.37***	.50***	.64***	.62***	.71***	.73***
Stability paths								
W2 parent value → W3 parent value	.38***	.37***	.45***	.43***	.26**	.22**	−.09	−.08
W2 parent behaviors → W3 parent behaviors	.59***	.62***	.81***	.87***	.77***	.80***	.71***	.72***
Within wave covariances								
W2 parent value ↔ W2 parent behaviors	.42***	.45***	.67***	.52***	.05	.05	.10	.10
W3 parent value ↔ W3 parent behaviors	.68***	.74***	.61**	.63**	.62***	.51***	.43*	.39*

(Continued)

TABLE 19

(*Continued*)

Path	Mothers		Fathers		Mothers		Fathers	
	Girls	Boys	Girls	Boys	Girls	Boys	Girls	Boys
	Math				Reading			
Perception of their child's ability								
Cross-lagged paths								
W2 parent percept. → W3 parent behaviors	.04	.05	.25*	.22*	.07*	.09*	.12	.15
W2 parent behaviors → W3 parent percept.	.05	.05	−.09	−.11	.02	.02	.03	.03
Stability paths								
W2 parent percept. → W3 parent percept.	.70***	.81***	.66***	.70***	.66***	.73***	.72***	.77***
W2 parent behaviors → W3 parent behaviors	.89***	.85***	.75***	.79***	.48***	.49***	.41***	.40***
Within wave covariances								
W2 parent percept. ↔ W2 parent behaviors	.11	.10	.37***	.37***	.15**	.14**	.27***	.30***
W3 parent percept. ↔ W3 parent behaviors	−.25	−.24	.46*	.56*	.10	.09	.07	.08
Value								
Cross-lagged paths								
W2 parent value → W3 parent behaviors	−.01	−.01	.09	.08	.11	.04	.15*	.15*
W2 parent behaviors → W3 parent value	.03	.03	.04	.05	.04	.13	.12	.12
Stability paths								
W2 parent value → W3 parent value	.57***	.61***	.63***	.64***	.58***	.56***	.51***	.56***
W2 parent behaviors → W3 parent behaviors	.88***	.84***	.83***	.90***	.48***	.49***	.41***	.40***
Within wave covariances								
W2 parent value ↔ W2 parent behaviors	.10	.11	.19*	.16*	.16***	.20***	.25***	.29***
W3 parent value ↔ W3 parent behaviors	.18	.17	.24	.22	.08	.10	.01	.01

*$p < .05$.
**$p < .01$.
***$p < .001$.

middle two rows listed under each model in Table 19. The stability of parents' perception of their children's ability and parents' valuing of each domain were typically moderate to strong across the four domains ($\beta = .22–.81$, $ps < .001$) with just one exception. Furthermore, parenting behavior showed strong stability from Waves 2 to 3 in all four domains ($\beta = .40–.90$, $ps < .001$), making it difficult for our analyses to reveal significant cross-lagged predictive relations from parents' beliefs to changing parents' behavior.

Perhaps even more interesting, the within-wave associations of parents' beliefs and their parenting behaviors varied considerably across wave and domain. Contrary to the Eccles and her colleagues' model, these associations were not significant for mothers' estimates of their child's ability in math at Wave 2, for fathers' estimates of their child's ability in reading at Wave 3, and for both parents' valuing of reading at Wave 3. In addition, the relation between mothers' estimates of their child's math ability was negatively related to their behaviors in math at Wave 3 suggesting a compensatory relation in the upper elementary and early middle school grades.

These within-wave patterns were different in the leisure domains. All of these associations were statistically significant and very strong with one exception: Parents' valuing of instrumental music was not significantly related to supportive parents at Wave 2. Interestingly, in the instrumental music domain, the Wave 2 parent valuing to Wave 3 parenting behaviors path was not statistically significant. Furthermore, the stability of parents' valuing across time was small but significant only for mothers, whereas the stability of parents' instrumental music supportive behaviors was very high. Taken together, this pattern of coefficients suggests that the parents' valuing of instrumental music is coming into line with their behavior over this time period—when their children are in the middle to late childhood/very early adolescent period.

Gender Moderation

All tests for gender moderation were not statistically significant at $p < .001$ level (Table S22 online). These findings suggest that the relations among parents' beliefs and behaviors were similar across parents of girls and parents of boys in all domains. The paths presented in Table 19 and Table S23 includes these gender equality constraints.

Exogenous Control Variables

Before we discuss the findings of this chapter, we want to briefly present the findings between the exogenous control variables and parents' beliefs and behaviors ($ps < .05$). These findings are not presented in a table, but are available from the authors. Teachers' ratings of children's natural abilities positively predicted parents' beliefs about their children's abilities at Waves 2 and 3 ($\beta = .12–.55$). Teachers' ratings of children's natural abilities were not consistent predictors of parents' value of a domain or parents' behaviors.

Children's IQ typically only predicted parents' beliefs about their children's abilities at Wave 2 ($\beta = .11–.22$). These relations were positive, except in sports where IQ predicted lower parental beliefs ($\beta = -.15$). There were not many consistent cohort differences. Two consistent patterns were that parents of children in the youngest and middle cohorts exhibited fewer behaviors at Wave 2 in instrumental music ($\beta = -.39$ to $-.23$), but exhibited more behaviors in math and reading than parents of children in the oldest cohort ($\beta = .19–.34$). Parents' education and family income were not strong, consistent predictors of the indicators in sports, and math, reading. In instrumental music, parents' education positively predicted parents' beliefs and behaviors ($\beta = .14–.29$).

Discussion

According to the Eccles's model of parent socialization, the direction of influence should largely flow from parents' beliefs to parents' behaviors (Eccles, 1993). The evidence for this prediction was quite mixed and not particularly strong even when the paths were significant. The most consistent support was in the domain of sports with six of the eight possible cross-lag coefficients reaching statistical significance. Only the path from fathers' estimates of their children's sport ability to parenting was not significant, which could reflect the very high stability of fathers' sport-related parenting over these two waves. Thus, our findings do support the hypothesized path from parents' child-specific beliefs to parenting behaviors in the sport domain when their children are in the elementary school age period. The same cannot be said for instrumental music, math, and reading.

For example, none of the belief to behavior paths was significant for instrumental music even though there was little difference in the stability of the beliefs and behaviors across the two leisure domains and those differences that emerged showed less stability in instrumental music than in sports. Thus, this domain difference does not reflect differences in the psychometric properties of the scales across these two domains. Interestingly, the strength of the within-time covariance of parents' valuing of instrumental music and parenting behavior was nonsignificant at Wave 2 but highly significant at Wave 3, suggesting that synchronous relations between parents' beliefs and behaviors are changing rather dramatically over this time period. This finding may reflect the fact that each of the school districts introduced instrumental music at the third grade. At Wave 3, children were in the second, third, and fifth grades, meaning that more parents at Wave 3 would have the opportunity to observe their children's growing competence and interest in instrumental music. This shift could lead to a stronger linkage between parents' beliefs and parents' behaviors at Wave 3 while at the same time reducing the likely cross-time association between beliefs and behaviors.

In fact, the cross-time stability for both parents' estimates of their children's abilities in and the valuing parents have for instrumental music was the lowest of the four domains.

Why would we find stronger associations from beliefs to behaviors in sports than in instrumental music, reading, and math? First, the nature of the link between parents' beliefs particularly about their children's abilities and the parents' behaviors might be more varied in the academic than in the leisure domains. Parents' behavioral responses to their perceptions of their children's abilities likely vary depending on the value they attach to competencies in various domains. In the Eccles et al. framework, we assume that parents will provide more behavioral support for their child in those domains in which they feel their children have the greatest aptitude because they would like to further enrich their children's growing competence in these domains. However, if the parents and/or the society highly value a particular competency, then parents might respond to an assessment of their children's low ability with increased efforts to help remediate a perceived deficit in a very important skill domain. Math and reading certainly fit this category for most middle-class American parents. Thus, both relatively high and relatively low estimates of one's child's ability in these two domains could lead to increased support. Although similar curvilinear relations might emerge in leisure domains, many parents might just give up in these domains and find a different leisure pursuit at which their child might be more competent. The option of shifting focus is not as viable in reading and math during the elementary school years. Alternatively, parents' beliefs may have weaker links to their behaviors in academic versus leisure because some parents may assume that schools are addressing their children's academic needs. When the onus lies more squarely on parents, as in the case of leisure, there might be a stronger correspondence between parental beliefs and behaviors. Either case still supports the expectancy-value model. However, the linear approach we used to test the data would not detect such nonlinear relations. Pattern centered approaches with quantitative data or qualitative data may be more optimal to reveal such patterns.

In contrast to the mixed evidence supporting the hypothesis that parents' beliefs lead to changes in parents' behaviors, there was quite strong support for the association of parenting behaviors with changes in both parents' estimates of their children's sport ability and with the value both parents attached to both sports and instrumental music. The strength of these paths was often twice as large as the path from parents' beliefs to behaviors. Interestingly there was no such evidence of parents' behaviors leading to change in parents' beliefs over time in neither math nor reading. Why might the processes underlying the substantial cross-lag predictive association from parents' socialization behaviors to parents' beliefs manifest themselves more strongly in the leisure domains than in the academic domains?

One explanation is that the sources of information influencing parents' beliefs differ across these four domains. For example, parents likely have more sources of information to inform their beliefs in the academic domains than the leisure domains because they get substantial information in the early elementary years about their children's performance in math and reading from the school and their children's teachers. In academics, parents' beliefs about their child's abilities may be less strongly related to their personal assessment of their children at home precisely because they are likely to integrate (and perhaps heavily weigh) the information they receive from schools in reading and math into their perceptions of their children's ability in these domains.

In contrast, because instrumental music and sports are not taught in school, parents need to do more to support their children's skill acquisition. As a result, they have more opportunities to watch their skills develop over time in these domains than they do in math or reading. It is also possible that those parents who are putting a great deal of effort into helping their child in sports and instrumental music could be justifying the amount of effort they are putting in by raising both their estimates of their children's competencies and the value they attach to these competences.

Finally, it is also likely that measurement issues influenced domain differences in the parent behavior to parent beliefs cross-lag links. The lack of evidence could reflect, at least in part, the fact that these scores are positively skewed in the academic domains compared to the leisure domains (e.g., mean value was 6.4 in math, 7.0 in reading, 3.2 in instrumental music, and 4.5 in sports). The stabilities across time in parents' ratings of their children's math and reading ability are also quite high, as well as being more stable than the parents' ratings of their children's abilities in sports and instrumental music. Given both the ceiling effect and the high rate of stability leaves little room for behavior at Wave 2 to predict changes in these beliefs from Wave 2 to Wave 3.

Finally, it is also likely that the timing of the data collection influences the nature of the cross-lagged associations between parents' beliefs and behaviors. The time frame of data collection is critical to understanding the directionality of belief–behavior links. It is quite possible that the parents' beliefs at time one predicted their parenting at that time or shortly thereafter. If, as we show in Chapter 6, these behaviors lead to gradual increases in their children's competence or interest in a particular domain between Wave 2 and Wave 3, then it would appear that Wave 2 behaviors led to changes in Wave 3 beliefs, but the mechanism would not be through the parents inferring their beliefs from their behaviors as proposed by Bem (1970). Rather, the mechanism would be consistent with that proposed by Eccles et al. in Figure 1a, namely, that parents' beliefs influence their behaviors which, in turn, influence the children's developing ability and interest, which, in turn, influence the parents' subsequent perceptions of their children's competencies and values. This is a true example of reciprocal influences playing out over time in a quite logical fashion. Distinguishing between these possible mechanisms requires much more frequent measurement of parents' and children's relevant achievement-related beliefs along with their behaviors and activity engagement than our yearly assessments of these constructs.

SUPPORTING INFORMATION

Additional supporting information may be found in the online version of this article at the publisher's website.

VI. PARENT BEHAVIOR AND CHILD BELIEF MODELS

In this chapter, we move on to the next step in the cascade of influences outlined in Figure 1b, namely, the cross-lagged relations between parents' behaviors and children's beliefs over time. A conceptual model with the loadings and predictive paths is shown in Figure 7 (p. 61).

Eccles and her colleagues assume that parents' behaviors would influence their children's achievement-related behaviors, at least in part, through their influence on their children's achievement-related ability self-concepts and perceived value of the various domains. Thus, we predict positive associations between parents' behaviors in all domains with changes in their children's beliefs from Wave 3 (i.e., grades, 2, 3, and 5) to Wave 4 (i.e., grades 3, 4, and 6).

It is of course also possible that children's achievement-related beliefs can influence their parents' behaviors. Parents are likely to be sensitive to the value their children place on developing their skills and participating in various activities, particularly in the leisure domains in which parents have considerable leeway in their socialization behaviors. To the extent that this is true, their children's valuing of both sports and instrumental music should predict changes over time in parenting behaviors in these two domains. In addition, to the extent that children's valuing is influenced by their own ability self-concepts as shown by Jacobs et al. (2002), it is likely that children's confidence in sports and instrumental music will influence their parents' behaviors over time as well.

Whether this is also true for reading and math is a more open question. As we noted in Chapter 5, parents can quite reasonably respond in two ways to their perceptions of their children's abilities in these two domains precisely because these two domains are so highly valued by the society at large and their children have to participate in these two domains in school even if they do not like and/or are not particularly skilled at reading and math. More specifically, parents can engage in increased socialization efforts in reading and math either because they want to further enrich and encourage their high performing children's competencies and interests in math and reading or because they want to support their struggling children's skill acquisition in these domains.

Data Analysis Plan

To test the cross-lagged relations between parents' behaviors and children's beliefs over time, we examined full cross-lagged models that included parents' behaviors and children's beliefs at Waves 3 and 4. We used Wave 3 and Wave 4 because this represents the next phase in the cascading flow of processes from exogenous influences on parents' beliefs to the influence of parents' behaviors on their children's beliefs. A total of 16 structural equation models were estimated to test the relations between parents' behaviors and their children's beliefs across the four domains, mothers and fathers, and children's domain-specific ability self-concept and task values. As in Chapter 5, parents' reading behavior was not included as a latent variable in these models. The number of reading promotive factors was used as a measured variable for parents' behaviors at both waves (see Table 17 for the cutoff scores, Chapter 5 for a detailed description, and Tables S24 and S25 in the online material for the factor loadings). Also as in Chapter 5, latent variables of parents' behaviors were used in math, sports, and instrumental music. Other than this difference, all of the models were comparable across the four domains. As in the previous chapters, we first tested for weak measurement invariance across time and gender. Following the tests of measurement invariance, we present the findings for the final models, gender moderation of the relations among the latent variables, and the relations with the exogenous control variables.

Results

Measurement Invariance

The model-level statistics testing weak measurement invariance across gender and time are presented in Table S26 in the online material. All of the models for instrumental music, math, and reading evidenced full weak measurement invariance simultaneously across time and gender, which suggests that the structure of the latent variables for parents' behaviors and children's beliefs was similar across Waves 3 and 4 as well as across girls and boys. Because the loadings for the latent variables were similar in each of these models, all of the loadings were set to be equal across time and gender in the full cross-lagged models.

In contrast, all of the sport models evidenced partial weak measurement invariance, suggesting that some of the loadings for the latent variables differed across time or child gender. There were two consistent findings across the sport models. First, the child ability self-concept item about learning something new in sports had a significantly different loading across girls and boys in both the mother and the father models (i.e., item 1d in Table 7 [p. 61]). Second, fathers' participation in community sporting events with their children had a different loading at Wave 3 compared to Wave 4 in the two father sport models (i.e., it was not invariant over time). In each of the sport models, only one or two of the individual loadings on a latent variable varied across child gender or across time. Furthermore, in each of these cases, the individual loading varied across only one aspect, namely, time or child gender, and not both aspects. Therefore, we estimated the loading separately across the one aspect that was significantly different, but at the same time set the other aspect to be equal. For example, fathers' co-participation in sporting events was similar for fathers of girls and fathers of boys, but varied across Wave 3 and Wave 4. Therefore, we set the loading to be equal for fathers of girls and fathers of boys, but to be estimated separately for Waves 3 and 4. All other loadings were constrained across time and gender simultaneously in the full cross-lagged models. In the next paragraph, we provide specifics on the tests for each of the four sport models.

The measurement invariance findings of the sport models require further discussion. In many cases, the omnibus or overall test examining invariance in all of the loadings across time and gender simultaneously suggested that the loadings were not the same over time and/or gender. However, our follow-up tests that were used to isolate which individual loadings varied often suggested that each individual loading was similar over time and/or gender. In other words, the omnibus tests suggested that there were significant differences in the loadings (i.e., ΔCFIs $\geq$ .010), but the individual follow-up tests suggested those differences were not significant (i.e., ΔCFIs $<$ .010). Unless we freed some of the individual loadings in these models or allowed them to be estimated separately by child gender or time, the omnibus test would still say that the loadings were significantly different. As noted in Figure 4 (p. 58), in these cases, we freed the individual loading with the largest ΔCFI because that loading is likely to have the largest differences over time and/or gender compared to the other individual loadings. We continued to free one loading at a time until the comparison between the final model with some freed loadings and the original unconstrained model met our criterion of ΔCFI $<$ .010.

In both of the models with mothers' sport data, the majority of loadings were similar across child gender and time (i.e., invariant). However, there were 1 to 2 individual loadings in each model that significantly varied. For example, in the model with mothers' behavior and children's sport value, the loading for mothers' coactivity was different for mothers of girls compared to mothers of boys.

Parallel to the models with mother data, the majority of loadings in the models with father sport data were similar across child gender and time (i.e., they were invariant). In both of the father sport models, attending community sporting events with their children had a significantly different loading across time. Therefore, we freed this loading and estimated it separately at Wave 3 and Wave 4. This was the only change we needed to make in the model with children's value to meet our criterion for invariance (i.e., ΔCFI < .010). However, the results suggested that more loadings significantly differed in the model with children's self-concept of sport ability. The child-reported item on learning something new in sports was different across girls and boys, which was the same finding in the model with mothers' data. By freely estimating this loading for girls and for boys, we met our criterion for our omnibus test suggesting the remaining loadings were similar across child gender and time. In moving to our full cross-lagged models, we freely estimated the loadings across gender or time noted above. All other loadings in the sport models were constrained to be equal across child gender and time.

Final Models

Most of the math and reading models fit the data well according to both the CFI and RMSEA (Tables 20 and S27). All other models fit the data adequately with one exception: The model with fathers' behaviors and children's music value had mixed fit. The CFI = .869, which was not adequate, but the RMSEA (.043) suggested the data fit the model well. In general, the findings were similar across domain, children's ability self-concept and value, girls and boys, and mothers and fathers (Tables 21 and S28 in the online material). Thus, we summarize the general patterns unless a difference emerged.

There were three patterns worth highlighting in the cross-lagged paths (Table 21). First, in all models, children's ability self-concepts and value at Wave 3 never significantly predicted changes in parents' behavior over time, and the majority of these paths did not meet the criterion for even a small effect size (i.e., the $\beta \leq .10$). In contrast, in 9 out of 16 models, parents' behavior predicted changes in children's motivational beliefs over time.

Second, the paths from parents' behaviors at Wave 3 to the changes in their children's beliefs from Waves 3 to 4 were moderate in instrumental music ($\beta = .19–.58$, $ps < .05$), but small to moderate in the other domains ($\beta = .13–.29$, $ps < .05$). In fact, the paths for instrumental music were often more than twice the size of the equivalent paths in the other domains for fathers.

Third, all of the significant paths from parents' behavior to children's beliefs in the academic domains emerged for fathers but not for mothers even though the main direction of influence was the same for mothers and fathers. Fathers' behavior predicted small changes in their children's math ability self-concept, math task value, and reading task value.

TABLE 20

MODEL FIT INDEXES FOR THE MODELS WITH PARENTS' BEHAVIOR AND CHILDREN'S BELIEFS

	Mothers				Fathers			
Model	*df*	X^2	CFI	RMSEA	*df*	X^2	CFI	RMSEA
Sports								
Self-concept of ability	457	687.15***	.940	.026	554	751.52***	.941	.026
Value	428	686.63***	.927	.029	553	730.22***	.944	.024
Music								
Self-concept of ability	417	853.60***	.904	.038	372	610.39***	.924	.035
Value	451	735.72***	.941	.030	273	537.54***	.869	.043
Math								
Self-concept of ability	305	422.58***	.958	.023	258	325.27**	.959	.023
Value	262	346.38***	.964	.021	381	662.66***	.916	.038
Reading								
Self-concept of ability	140	227.85***	.968	.030	135	175.35*	.979	.024
Value	151	200.26**	.975	.021	137	173.51*	.973	.023

*$p < .05$.
**$p < .01$.
***$p < .001$.

Across the four domains, children's beliefs and their parents' behaviors were moderately to highly stable from Waves 3 to 4 (see Table 21 in the text and Table S28 of the online material). Two standardized stability paths were over 1.00: the stability of mothers' sport behavior in the model with boys' value, and the stability of fathers' music behavior in the model with girls' value. Jöreskog (1999) noted that it is possible to obtain standardized path estimates close to and over 1. In fact, he stated that "a standardized coefficient of 1.04, 1.40, or even 2.30 does not necessarily imply that something is wrong, although, as will be seen, it might suggest that there is a high degree of multicollinearity in the data" (p. 1).

Gender Moderation

The tests for gender moderation in the relations among parents' behaviors and children's beliefs (shown in Figure 7 [p. 61]) are presented in Table S27 online. The overall tests suggested that 1 of the 16 models included a path that varied across gender. Specifically, the covariance between mothers' behavior and children's reading ability self-concept within Wave 4 was negative for boys, but positive for girls. Because this was true in only 1 out of 16 tests, we conclude that it likely reflects a chance finding.

Exogenous Control Variables

We conclude our summary of the results with a brief discussion of the relations between the exogenous control variables and parents' behaviors and children's beliefs ($ps < .05$). Child physical abilities, family income, and

TABLE 21

Standardized Path Estimates for the Models With Parents' Behavior and Children's Beliefs

| | Sports | | | | Music | | | |
| | Mothers | | Fathers | | Mothers | | Fathers | |
Path	Girls	Boys	Girls	Boys	Girls	Boys	Girls	Boys
Self-concept of ability								
Cross-lagged paths								
W3 parent behaviors → W4 child beliefs	.08	.11	.13**	.19**	.30***	.35***	.58***	.48***
W3 child beliefs → W4 parent behaviors	.10	.08	−.03	−.02	.01	.01	.08	.10
Stability paths								
W3 parent behaviors → W4 parent behaviors	.75***	.90***	.70***	.87***	.87***	.90***	.93***	.79***
W3 child beliefs → W4 child beliefs	.57***	.56***	.49***	.46***	.41***	.36***	.29***	.37***
Within wave covariances								
W3 child beliefs ↔ W3 parent behaviors	.09	.10	.26***	.29***	.51***	.35***	.48***	.31***
W4 child beliefs ↔ W4 parent behaviors	−.01	−.01	.07	.12	.45***	.40***	.73**	.33**
Value								
Cross-lagged paths								
W3 parent behaviors → W4 child beliefs	−.17**	−.19**	.08	.14	.22***	.19***	.47***	.40***
W3 child beliefs → W4 parent behaviors	−.09	−.09	.14	.08	.04	.05	−.02	−.03
Stability paths								
W3 parent behaviors → W4 parent behaviors	.85***	1.01***	.66***	.83***	.87***	.89***	1.02***	.90***
W3 child beliefs → W4 child beliefs	.66***	.58***	.62***	.44***	.52***	.59***	.42***	.48***
Within wave covariances								
W3 child beliefs ↔ W3 parent behaviors	.18***	.35***	.31***	.45***	.43***	.32***	.46***	.35***
W4 child beliefs ↔ W4 parent behaviors	.11	.65	.05	.07	.48***	.49***	.53*	.36*

	Math				Reading			
	Mothers		Fathers		Mothers		Fathers	
Path	Girls	Boys	Girls	Boys	Girls	Boys	Girls	Boys
Self-concept of ability								
Cross-lagged paths								
W3 parent behaviors → W4 child beliefs	−.03	−.03	.18*	.20*	.01	.01	−.04	−.04
W3 child beliefs → W4 parent behaviors	−.06	−.06	.02	.02	−.02	−.02	.05	.05
Stability paths								
W3 parent behaviors → W4 parent behaviors	.91***	.90***	.65***	.83***	.34***	.33***	.29***	.26***
W3 child beliefs → W4 child beliefs	.44***	.43***	.43***	.45***	.50***	.54***	.51***	.57***
Within wave covariances								
W3 child beliefs ↔ W3 parent behaviors	.04	.04	.05	.05	.07	.06	.06	.05
W4 child beliefs ↔ W4 parent behaviors	n/a	n/a	−.07	−.14	**.19**[*a]	**−.29***[a]	−.09	−.07
Value								
Cross-lagged paths								
W3 parent behaviors → W4 child beliefs	.02	.12	.18*	.20*	.08	.07	.20**	.15**
W3 child beliefs → W4 parent behaviors	−.10	−.10	.03	.04	.02	.02	.04	.04
Stability paths								
W3 parent behaviors → W4 parent behaviors	.85***	.83***	.49***	.69***	.34***	.34***	.29***	.26***
W3 child beliefs → W4 child beliefs	.48***	.50***	.51***	.53***	.52***	.54***	.62***	.55***
Within wave covariances								
W3 child beliefs ↔ W3 parent behaviors	.28***	.26***	.12	.11	.05	.05	.07	.07
W4 child beliefs ↔ W4 parent behaviors	−.22	−.16	.01	.01	.04	.04	−.07	−.05

Note. n/a = This covariance was not included because the error variance of one of the Wave 4 latent variables was set to a nonsignificant, positive value. Paths that significantly varied by child gender are bolded. The level of significance of the difference is noted with [a]$p < .05$.
*$p < .05$.
**$p < .01$.
***$p < .001$.

parent education were not consistent predictors. Child IQ positively predicted child self-concepts of music ($\beta = .21–.26$) and reading abilities ($\beta = .13–.16$). In contrast, child IQ negatively predicted child self-concept of sport ability at Wave 3 ($\beta = -.18$ to $-.13$). Teachers' ratings of children's natural abilities consistently predicted children having more confidence in their abilities at Waves 3 and 4 ($\beta = .16–.47$). Teachers' ratings of children's natural abilities also positively predicted children's value of math and sports at Waves 3 and 4 ($\beta = .17–.37$), but only predicted parents' behaviors in sports ($\beta = .30–.41$; and not in the three other domains). Finally, there were several consistent cohort differences. Generally, children in the oldest cohort had lower confidence in their abilities in all four domains compared to children in the youngest and middle cohorts ($\beta = .13–.30$). Consistent cohort differences in children's values were only evident in sports and math ($\beta = .14–.21$), in which older children placed lower value on sports and math than children in the two younger cohorts. Parents' behavior was higher for the two younger cohorts in math compared to the older cohort ($\beta = .19–.40$), but the opposite pattern emerged in instrumental music ($\beta = -.56$ to $-.18$).

Discussion

The majority of hypotheses outlined in the Eccles's model were supported in this set of analyses, although the strength of these findings differed by domain and gender of the parent. As predicted in the Eccles's models, parents' behaviors were associated with changes in children's ability self-concepts and task value beliefs over time across several models in math, sports, and instrumental music. These findings were consistent and strong in instrumental music (effect sizes ranged from moderate to strong). In general, these findings support and extend research specific to each dimension of parenting, including prior research on modeling in sports and music (Davidson et al., 1996; Kahn et al., 2008), studies relating parental encouragement to children's motivational beliefs in math and sports (Bauer et al., 2008; Ferry et al., 2000; Fredricks & Eccles, 2005), and studies linking sports equipment purchases to sport motivational beliefs (Fredricks & Eccles, 2005). Additionally, our findings are consistent with the literature on the impact of parents' involvement on motivational beliefs and participation in sports, instrumental music, and math (Babkes & Weiss, 1999; Davidson et al., 1996; Fredricks & Eccles, 2005; Simpkins et al., 2012).

Interestingly, we found that fathers' behaviors were a more consistent predictor of children's beliefs in math and reading than were mothers. Fathers' behaviors predicted small to moderate increases in their children's math and reading beliefs in three of the four analyses. The parallel analyses for mothers were all nonsignificant. This finding demonstrates the role that fathers play in academic socialization and underscores the importance of including fathers in future research on parenting. This finding may reflect the fact that mothers' involvement in children's school work is more normative than is fathers' involvement (Yeung, Sanberg, Davis-Kean, & Hofferth, 2001). Because fathers tend to be less involved in that aspect of development, those fathers who do support their child in math and reading are likely to have a larger impact on motivation than mothers. It is also possible that fathers support their children in math and reading in qualitatively different ways than do mothers that are particularly helpful during these developmental years. Qualitative research would help test this hypothesis.

We found no evidence of reciprocal influences between parents' behaviors and their children's beliefs during the late elementary and early middle school years in any these domains. It is certainly possible at this developmental point in children's lives that they could be trying to elicit parents' supportive to help them build their competencies and interest in these activity domains, particularly in their leisure activities for which they might request equipment, lessons, parent involvement in transporting them to lessons, and parent attendance at events in which they are playing or performing. We suspect that these nonsignificant paths reflect the very high stability in the parents' behaviors. With cross-time stabilities from .66 to 1.02 in sports and music there was little unexplained variance to predict. The cross-time stability of the parents' behaviors were somewhat low in math, particularly for fathers, and for both parents in reading but even in these models there was no evidence of the children's beliefs predicting changes across time in their parents' behaviors.

Finally, we were particularly interested in the fact that the associations of parents' behaviors with their children's beliefs were the strongest and most consistent in the instrumental music domain. This result could reflect differential timing of parents' most effective engagement in their children's skill development across different domains. There was some emerging evidence of this possibility in Chapter 5 in which the association between parents' beliefs and behaviors increased dramatically between Wave 2 and Wave 3. If this increase reflects an emerging consolidation between parents' beliefs and behaviors in this domain, then it seems very logical that the impact of the parents' behaviors in instrumental music might be particularly strong between Wave 3 and Wave 4 because the children would be benefiting from this consolidation between their parents' beliefs and behaviors.

It also seems quite likely that the period of maximally effective parent socialization processes might come earlier for the other domains, when these competencies are first emerging in their children and the role of parents in the acquisition of these competencies is most supported by larger social forces. For example, interest in reading and books is strongly encouraged during the preschool years by the availability of picture and simple-word

106

books for parent child co-reading, by strong societal norms about the importance of co-reading during the preschool and early school years, and by the wide availability of children's television shows focused on early pre-reading activities. This confluence of opportunities and norms, coupled with this being the time when these skills can develop most rapidly, could lead the preschool and early elementary school years to be a time of maximal impact of parents on children's confidence and interest in reading. The early elementary school years may also be an important period for parent socialization in sports. This is the time period when many parents sign up children for their first sporting experience, coach their child's sport team, and work with their child on learning sport skills. Finally, one might begin to see an analogous situation emerging with early math as efforts are being made to encourage greater parent involvement in early math learning. Focused research across different age periods is needed to test these hypotheses.

SUPPORTING INFORMATION

Additional supporting information may be found in the online version of this article at the publisher's website

VII. YOUTH BELIEF AND PARTICIPATION MODELS

In this chapter, we focus on the question: Do youths' beliefs predict changes in their participation in the activities and courses in each of these domains during their late childhood and adolescent years? According to the Eccles's expectancy-value models, adolescents' choices should be influenced by their prior ability self-concepts and subjective task value. Empirical evidence is growing to support this general hypothesis in mathematics and sports over relatively short periods of time. Much less work has been done in the domains of reading/English and instrumental music and over the longer periods of time encompassing the entire high school period of development. In the CAB dataset, the lag between Wave 4 and Wave 5 was four years and the lag between Wave 5 and the end of high school varies from 2 to 5 years depending on the cohort. Having these longer time lags provides an opportunity to fill these gaps in the literature. We added the link of beliefs at Wave 5 to adolescents' high school history of participation in order to provide the most comprehensive picture possible of links proposed in the Eccles's models. Thus, the time lags in this chapter are larger than the time lags in the previous chapters.

Given the nature of the feedback loop from current participation and performance to subsequent self- and task-related beliefs within the Eccles's model (see Figure 1a), we also expected to find evidence of reciprocal influences between beliefs and behaviors. Engaging in any task provides the actors with new information about how well they are doing at the activity and how much they like doing the activity. Thus, we also test for these reciprocal associations.

We suspect that both directions of possible influence may differ across the four domains we are studying, because the nature of the experiences in each domain changes in different ways across these four domains. For example, the content of instruction in both reading/English and mathematics changes substantially as youth move from elementary into middle and secondary school. These changes may weaken the associations between beliefs and behaviors in these two domains compared to the associations in instrumental music and sport. However, although the content may not change dramatically in leisure domains, the opportunities to participate may change due to increasing competitiveness of team sport participation. We do include participation in school team sports as one of the youth behavioral choices, even though factors other than individual choice will influence this indicator due to the increasing competition for slots on school-based teams. For that reason, we also included indicators of participation in noncompetitive sport activities. One might expect that the evidence for beliefs influencing changes in participation over time will be larger for these more voluntary sport activities than for participation on competitive high school teams. However, it might take higher levels of confidence in one's sport abilities and higher levels of valuing of sports to seek out slots on competitive teams than voluntary sport activities. We also differentiate within instrumental music between participating in high school bands and playing an instrument on one's own. The same predictive dilemma holds for instrumental music as in sports. Thus, in neither case do we make firm predictions about variations in the strength of the predictions across different measures of participation in the leisure domains.

The same is not true for the two academic domains because of different requirements for and availability of various high schools courses. Some form of English, literature, or writing was required each year in the districts we studied. Furthermore, it is impossible to reliably code the difficulty level of the various literature and writing courses offered in the schools we studied; AP courses in English or literature were rare. Thus, the variance in our indicators of high school English/literature/writing courses was constrained and the amount of reading for leisure is not necessarily going to increase over these age periods. In contrast, only 2 years of math was required and AP math courses were much more commonly available in our schools. Thus, we had a strong indicator of variation in math participation during the high school years. Because of the greater variability in math participation we expect to be able to document stronger associations between beliefs and behavior in this domain than reading.

Data Analysis Plan

As in the earlier chapters, we used cross-lagged structural equation models to test our hypotheses within each domain. We ran separate models for ability self-concept and value beliefs. We examined models that included youths' beliefs and participation at Wave 4 and 4 years later at Wave 5 as well as measures of activity participation and courses during the high school years. As shown in Figure 8 (p. 62), these models differ from those presented in the previous chapters as we have the typical cross-lagged model between Waves 4 and 5, but these models also included indicators of youths' activities and courses throughout high school. For example, in sports, the model included youths' motivational beliefs at Waves 4 and 5, time spent in organized sports at Waves 4 and 5, and four indicators of youths' sport activities throughout high school. The high school indicators represent the average of each indicator across the high school years, which spanned Waves 6 to 9 depending on the specific cohort. It is important to note that a slightly different model was tested for math. Because math participation was not collected at Wave 5, these models included youths' math motivational beliefs at Waves 4 and 5, math participation at Wave 4, and the average number of math AP/honors courses per year in high school. As a result, fewer paths were tested in the math models than the other domains.

Eight structural equation models were estimated to test the relations between youths' beliefs and participation over time in each of the four domains and for ability self-concept and value. The high school indicators varied by domain. Sports included four high school outcomes: (a) the average number of school sports per year, (b) the average number of community sports per year, (c) the average time spent in organized sports per year, and (d) the average time spent in other sports per year. Instrumental music included two high school outcomes: (a) the average time spent practicing per year, and (b) whether adolescents ever participated in band. Math included one high school outcome: the average number of AP/honors math courses per year. Reading included three high school outcomes: (a) the average time spent reading per year, (b) whether adolescents ever participated in a literature-related club, and (c) the average number of English/literature courses per year. First, we tested for weak measurement invariance in the models as outlined in the general data analysis plan. Following the tests of measurement invariance, we present the findings for the final models, gender moderation of the relations among youths' beliefs and participation, and the relations including the exogenous control variables.

Results

Measurement Invariance
The model-level statistics testing weak measurement invariance across time and gender are presented in Table S29 in the online material. The unconstrained models fit the data well (i.e., CFI = .980–.998, RMSEA = .009–.034). Five of the eight models evidenced full weak measurement invariance across time and gender when tested simultaneously. These five models were sport ability self-concept, sport value, instrumental music value, math ability self-concept, and reading ability self-concept. The findings suggest that the structure of all the latent variables in each of these five models were similar across Waves 4 and 5 as well as across girls and boys. Thus, we constrained loadings in each of these models to be equal across time and gender.

Three of the eight models evidenced partial weak measurement invariance. These three models were instrumental music ability self-concept, math value, and reading value. In each of the three models, the loadings were similar across girls and boys (i.e., invariant across gender), but one individual loading in each model varied across Waves 4 and 5. The specific item differed across the three models. In the instrumental music ability self-concept model, the item that had a different loading over time was the item asking children to compare their ability in music to other subjects (i.e., item 1c in Table 7). In the reading task value model, the loading for the importance of reading changed over time (i.e., item 2b in Table 7). In the math model, the loading for the interest item varied over time (i.e., item 3a in Table 7). Because only one loading differed over time in these models, we freed that one loading across time in each model (i.e., it was estimated separately at Waves 4 and 5), but constrained these loadings to be equal across girls and boys. All other loadings in these three models were constrained to be equal across Waves 4 and 5 and across girls and boys.

Final Models

As shown in Tables 22 and S30, across all four domains, the final models fit the data well. The standardized paths are shown in Table 23; the standardized and unstandardized estimates are presented in Table S30 in the online material.

The pattern of significant cross-lagged paths varied across domain (Table 23). There was consistent evidence of the predicted associations from Wave 4 beliefs to Wave 5 participation across all domains (except math which was not tested) and for both the youths' ability self-concepts and perceived task value, despite the 4-year lag in time between these two waves. Wave 4 motivational beliefs always predicted small to moderate increases in participation across the 4-year span in sports, instrumental music, and reading ($\beta = .16-.32$, $p < .001$). In addition, Wave 5 motivational beliefs (both ability self-concepts and perceived task value) predicted small to moderate increases in adolescents' overall high school participation in sports, instrumental music, and math ($\beta = .14-.41$, $p < .05$). Because indicators of both Wave 4 participation and an independent indicator of adolescents' ability in each domain were included as covariates, these relations are net of a substantial portion of the variance in actual competencies and prior patterns of participation. In contrast, these cross-lagged paths were much weaker and often insignificant for reading.

Interestingly, the relative predictive associations of both youths' ability self-concepts and their valuing of each domain with increases in participation across time varied somewhat across domains. They were slightly higher for perceived task value than for ability self-concepts in all domains except math. This is particularly true for the analyses spanning Waves 4–5 in sports and

111

TABLE 22

MODEL FIT INDEXES FOR THE MODELS WITH YOUTHS' BELIEFS AND ADOLESCENTS' PARTICIPATION

Model	df	χ^2	CFI	RMSEA
Sports				
Self-concept of ability	297	424.15***	.973	.024
Value	289	323.88	.992	.013
Music				
Self-concept of ability	185	287.02***	.981	.028
Value	176	234.64**	.989	.021
Math				
Self-concept of ability	156	270.07***	.964	.032
Value	139	169.21*	.986	.017
Reading				
Self-concept of ability	246	352.85***	.969	.025
Value	219	265.63*	.980	.017

*$p < .05$.
**$p < .01$.
***$p < .001$.

spanning Wave 5 to overall high school participation in instrumental music. In contrast, for math, Wave 5 ability self-concept was a stronger predictor of high school AP course participation than Wave 5 valuing of math.

There was also weak but significant support for the power of Wave 4 participation in predicting changes in youths' beliefs from Wave 4 to Wave 5 in sports and instrumental music. In these two leisure domains, youths' participation at Wave 4 predicted small changes in youths' sport ability self-concept, music ability self-concept, and music value over the 4-year gap between Waves 4 and 5 ($\beta = .09–.18$, $ps < .05$), supporting the hypothesized reciprocal influences in these two leisure domains. There was no support for the significance of the link between participation and beliefs in either math or reading.

The stability of youths' beliefs and behaviors over time ranged from small to large. Across the 4-year period from Waves 4 to 5, the stability of youths' beliefs in all four domains was typically small to moderate ($\beta = .29–.56$, $ps < .001$), whereas the stability in youths' participation was small over the same 4-year period ($\beta = .07–.21$). The models also included paths for the stability of adolescents' participation from Wave 5 to overall high school indicators. In sports, the stability was small to moderate for time in organized sports and the number of school sports ($\beta = .21–.39$, $ps < .001$) compared to small stability for informal high school sport activities ($\beta = .09–.15$, $ps < .05$). The stability in instrumental music ($\beta = .37–.58$, $ps < .001$) and reading participation ($\beta = .54–.64$, $ps < .001$) were particularly strong across these periods and often stronger than the predictive power of youths' motivational

112

TABLE 23

Standardized Path Estimates for the Models With Youths' Beliefs and Adolescents' Participation

	Models With Youth Ability Self-Concept		Models With Youth Value	
Path	Girls	Boys	Girls	Boys
Sports				
Cross-lagged relations between beliefs and behaviors				
W4 beliefs → W5 time	.20***	.17***	.32***	.24***
W4 time → W5 beliefs	.09*	.10*	.12*	.13*
W5 beliefs → HS time organized sports	.27***	.26***	.24***	.24***
W5 beliefs → HS time other sports	.36***	.30***	.37***	.32***
W5 beliefs → HS # school sports	.31***	.22***	.32***	.24***
W5 beliefs → HS # community sports	.27***	.22***	.31***	.27***
Stability				
W4 beliefs → W5 beliefs	.53***	.50***	.56***	.44***
W4 time → W5 time	.14**	.14**	.07	.07
W5 time → HS time organized sports	.37***	.38***	.37***	.39***
W5 time → HS time other sports	.15**	.14**	.12*	.11*
W5 time → HS # school sports	.30***	.23***	.28***	.21***
W5 time → HS # community sports	.14*	.13*	.10*	.09*
Within wave covariances				
W4 beliefs ↔ W4 time	.38***	.44***	.41***	.52***
W5 beliefs ↔ W5 time	.41***	.37***	.50***	.42***
HS time organized sports ↔ HS time other sports	.25***	.21***	.26***	.22***
HS time organized sports ↔ HS # school sports	.47***	.33***	.48***	.33***
HS time organized sports ↔ HS # community sports	.14**	.12**	.14**	.12**
HS # school sports ↔ HS time other sports	.21***	.12***	.21***	.12***
HS # school sports ↔ HS # community sports	.31***	.18***	.30***	.18***
HS # community sports ↔ HS time other sports	.50***	.35***	.49***	.34***
Music				
Cross-lagged relations between beliefs and behaviors				
W4 beliefs → W5 time	.17***	.20***	.20***	.24***
W4 time → W5 beliefs	.18**	.16**	.11*	.10*
W5 beliefs → HS band participation	.17**	.17**	.17*	.18*
W5 beliefs → HS time	.23***	.21***	.41***	.37***
Stability				
W4 beliefs → W5 beliefs	.32***	.35***	.34***	.40***
W4 time → W5 time	.21***	.19***	.18***	.17***
W5 time → HS band participation	.51***	.49***	.49***	.48***
W5 time → HS time	.58***	.51***	.43***	.37***
Within wave covariances				
W4 beliefs ↔ W4 time	.59***	.57***	.57***	.51***
W5 beliefs ↔ W5 time	.67***	.69***	.76***	.74***
HS time ↔ HS band participation	.50***	.42***	.50***	.41***
Math				

(Continued)

TABLE 23

(Continued)

Path	Models With Youth Ability Self-Concept		Models With Youth Value	
	Girls	Boys	Girls	Boys
Cross-lagged relations between beliefs and behaviors				
W4 time → W5 beliefs	.04	.04	.04	.05
W5 beliefs → HS math AP courses	.26***	.25***	.16***	.14***
Stability				
W4 beliefs → W5 beliefs	.31***	.29***	.37***	.37***
W4 time → HS math AP courses	.08	.08	.07	.07
Within wave covariances				
W4 beliefs ↔ W4 time	.25***	.26***	.35***	.34***
Reading				
Cross-lagged relations between beliefs and behaviors				
W4 beliefs → W5 time	.16***	.16***	.19***	.22***
W4 time → W5 beliefs	.09	.08	.05	.05
W5 beliefs → HS English class	.09	.07	.07	.05
W5 beliefs → HS literature club	.11*	.15*	.02	.02
W5 beliefs → HS time	.02	.02	.05	.05
Stability				
W4 beliefs → W5 beliefs	.32***	.29***	.33***	.36***
W4 time → W5 time	.18***	.18***	.17***	.17***
W5 time → HS English class	.07	.06	.08	.06
W5 time → HS literature club	.08	.10	.09*	.11*
W5 time → HS time	.64***	.54***	.63***	.54***
Within wave covariances				
W4 beliefs ↔ W4 time	.26***	.26***	.25***	.23***
W5 beliefs ↔ W5 time	.16**	.15**	.15**	.15**
HS English class ↔ HS literature club	.07	.08	.09	.10
HS English class ↔ HS time	.05	.04	.05	.03
HS literature club ↔ HS time	−.10*	−.11*	−.09*	−.10*

Note. HS, High school.

*$p < .05$.

**$p < .01$.

***$p < .001$.

beliefs. In math, there was not an indicator of Wave 5 participation. Thus, Wave 4 was used to predict high school courses. There was not a significant relation across waves in math ($\beta = .07–.08$, *ns*).

Gender Moderation

The tests for gender moderation in the relations among youths' beliefs and participation (shown in Figure 8 [p. 62]) are presented in Table S30 online. The overall tests suggested that these relations were similar across gender in every model.

Exogenous Control Variables

As in the previous chapters, we provide a summary of the relations between the exogenous control variables and youths' beliefs and participation from the final models ($ps < .05$). These statistics are not presented in tables, but are available from the authors. Several of the relations between the control variables and youths' beliefs and participation were statistically significant. Teachers' ratings of children's natural ability in a domain often positively predicted adolescents' high school classes ($\beta = .21–.44$) and motivational beliefs ($\beta = .11–.55$); however, the relations were more consistent in predicting ability self-concept compared to value, and in predicting beliefs in math, reading, and sports compared to instrumental music. Youths' IQ was not a consistent predictor. Generally, the oldest cohort had taken more math and reading classes each year in high school ($\beta = -.33$ to $-.10$) as well as spent more time in instrumental music at Waves 4 and 5 ($\beta = -.25$ to $-.22$) than the youngest and middle cohorts. When there were differences in youths' motivational beliefs by cohort, the patterns generally replicated what other studies have found where younger youth have higher self-concepts of abilities ($\beta = .13–.29$) and values ($\beta = .19–.24$) of these domains than older youth (Fredricks & Eccles, 2002; Jacobs et al., 2002). Parents' education positively predicted sports and instrumental music participation at multiple waves for girls ($\beta = .12–.30$), and advanced high school math courses for both boys and girls ($\beta = .11–.16$). Parents' education also predicted higher ability self-concepts in music and math ($\beta = .14–.30$). Parent education did not predict any of the reading indicators. Youths' sport ability and family income rarely predicted the indicators at hand.

Discussion

As we predicted and consistent with prior research, by and large both ability self-concepts and task value predicted participation choices across the four domains and across both time periods, including the number of AP math courses (Simpkins et al., 2006, 2012; Updegraff et al., 1996), participation in sport activities at both Wave 5 and across the high school years (Fredricks & Eccles, 2005; Marsh et al., 2007), and instrumental music participation at both Wave 5 and across high school (Austin, 1990; Klinedinst, 1991; Simpkins et al., 2012). These findings align with theories emphasizing competence beliefs as a predictor of achievement choices, including self-efficacy, self-concept, and self-determination theories (Bandura, 1997; Ryan & Deci, 2000; Marsh & Craven, 2006). Furthermore, these findings support motivational theories that focus on the value construct as the key determinant of choice behavior, including expectancy-value, interest, and intrinsic motivational theories (Deci & Ryan, 1985; Eccles, 1993; Schiefele, 1991).

Interestingly, in some previous work by Eccles and her colleagues using other data sets, subjective task value was a strong predictor of activity choices, whereas ability self-concepts were the strongest predictors of changes in actual performance (see Wigfield et al., 2006, for review). Clearly in this study, both beliefs were significant predictors of participation, though their relative influence varied across different analyses. It is not surprising that youths' math ability self-concepts might be a particularly strong predictor of enrollment in AP math courses because these courses require both very high levels of ability and great confidence in one's ability to master the difficult material. Furthermore, because taking AP math courses is very useful for getting into the best college possible after high school, there may be a great deal of external pressure on those students who have high abilities in math to take these courses, leaving less variance to be explained by the value youth place on these courses. The same pattern emerged for participation in high school literature-related clubs, but the coefficients were much weaker and not even significant for the perceived value of English. These same dynamics would be less true in sports and instrumental music, domains in which perceived valuing is often a stronger predictor than ability self-concepts.

The findings on the direction of influence suggest that there is more support for the reciprocal influence between beliefs and participation in the leisure domains than in the academic domains. In math and reading, participation at Wave 4 did not predict changes in these youths' ability self-concepts or perceived value of these domains 4 years later. These same relations evidenced small effect sizes in sports and instrumental music. Why might participation predict changes in youths' beliefs in leisure and not in academics? It is not because there are consistent differences in the stabilities of either beliefs or participation across the domains. But it could be that the types of activities these youth can participate in each domain change more dramatically in the academic than in the leisure domains. For example, the types of math courses taken during the late elementary and early middle school years were quite different from the types of math courses taken in eighth grade and beyond in these cohorts. Late elementary school and early middle school math consisted primarily of arithmetic; later middle school and high school math courses consisted of algebra and geometry, which are more abstract forms of mathematics. As a result, it seems less likely that the experiences one was having at Wave 4 could influence later math ability self-concepts and the perceived value of the kinds of math they were learning in late middle school and early high school than might be true in sports in which the nature of the experiences are likely to be more similar across these time frames. The same argument could be made for reading/English where the high school course material is much more focused on literature than the reading and writing courses they took in fifth through seventh grades.

116

In addition, the nature of the grading in the academic subjects also changed across this time frame from more mastery based feedback to more relative performance based feedback (i.e., marks that relate to improvement versus marks based on how well one performed relative to other students in one's class). These arguments suggest that assessing beliefs and behaviors more closely in time during the middle school and early high school years might yield a different pattern of results in the academic domains.

In addition, as noted in Chapter 4, youths' free time participation in both math and reading can reflect their enjoyment of the activity or their need to spend time improving their competencies. In the latter case, this could be because they want to excel in this area or because they need to overcome deficits in their current competencies. If participation is for remedial purposes, high rates of participation might not be associated with gains in either one's ability self-concepts or one's interest in the subject area due to frustration and failure experiences associated with remediation efforts. Thus, in order to fully understand the relations between time spent in academic domains and their beliefs, one might also need to understand the goals for their participation (e.g., enjoyment vs. improvement). In leisure, the relation between participation and subsequent beliefs should be more positive than in academic domains (albeit small) because youth who are not skilled in sports and instrumental music can quit. Thus, the heterogeneity in the reasons why one is participating might be larger in academics than in leisure particularly in the late childhood and early adolescent periods of development.

Generally the findings supported the expectancy-value model in all domains except reading. Consistent with prior research (Baker & Wigfield, 1999; Wigfield & Guthrie, 1997), self-concept of reading ability and value predicted reading participation 4 years later from Waves 4 to 5. In addition, self-concept of reading ability at Wave 5 predicted high school participation in literature-related clubs. However, neither English belief predicted high school English coursework or time spent reading. Why might this be so? First some form of English-related coursework was required each year in the high schools sampled in this study. Thus, there was very little variance to explain. Second, the cross-time stability of reading was quite high, the highest of the four domains sampled in this study; leaving little variance to be predicted.

This nonsignificant association between Wave 5 beliefs and high school English-related course work is inconsistent with the work of Durik et al. (2006). Using the same dataset, they found a small, positive relation between value beliefs at tenth grade and language arts course taking throughout high school. In the current study, we examined the relations between Wave 5, which included seventh, eighth, and tenth grade data depending on the cohort, and indicators of high school coursework. In the Durik et al. study (2006), the indicators for values and courses were both measured in high school for everyone. It is possible that a small relation between tenth graders' perceived value of English and their decision to taking extra English- or writing-related coursework during their last 2 years of high school emerged because adolescents' beliefs were measured very close in time to the coursework decisions. Examining the same relation over longer time frames may decrease the likelihood of finding a significant association.

SUPPORTING INFORMATION

Additional supporting information may be found in the online version of this article at the publisher's website.

VIII. DISCUSSION

We had two major goals for this project: (1) To test the predicted socialization pathways from parents to children as summarized in Figure 1b; and (2) to test the pathways from children's motivational beliefs to their behavioral engagement as predicted in Figure 1a in four different achievement domains. Related to these goals, we had three major sub-goals: (1) To rigorously test the direction of effects at each step in the developmental sequence inherent in the Eccles's expectancy-value models of the ontogeny of achievement-related behavioral choices; (2) to explore the variations in the strength of support for the Eccles's models across different activity domains; and (3) to determine whether children's gender predicts mean-level differences and moderates the patterns of associations predicted in Figures 1a and 1b. In this chapter, we summarize and discuss the major findings associated with each of these six goals while avoiding repetition of our discussions in each of the four results chapters.

Major Findings

At the most general level, we found the most consistent support for pathways in the expectancy-value model concerning adolescent's motivational beliefs to their subsequent high school behavioral engagement in sports, instrumental music, and math, even with indicators of elementary school competence and participation in each domain and family social class controlled as noted in Figure 1a. We found a more mixed pattern of support for the predicted socialization pathways from parents' beliefs to their elementary school-aged children's beliefs as noted in Figure 1b. For the most part, we found strong and consistent links from parents' perceptions of children's abilities to the changes in children's beliefs 1 year later. The strength of these associations was highest in the two leisure domains and was not significant for math. We also found little consistent evidence that parents' valuing of these four domains predicts changes in their children's motivational beliefs. Additionally, in only three cases did parents' beliefs

119

predict changes in children's valuing of any domain. However, parents' estimates of their children's ability in instrumental music predicted increases in the value the children attached to instrumental music and mothers' ratings of their children's reading ability predicted increases in the children's valuing of reading. Although parents' beliefs predicted changes in youths' beliefs, we found very limited support for the predicted cross-lagged links between parents' beliefs and their behavior. In contrast, we found stronger and more consistent evidence of a cross-lagged link from parents' behaviors to changes in their beliefs across time.

With regard to our first sub-goal on direction of influence, as predicted, we found consistent evidence that Wave 2 (grades 1, 2, and 4) indicators of children's domain-specific competence levels predicted changes in their parents' perceptions of their children's ability over time in sports and math. This was not true for instrumental music and it was only true for mothers in reading. In contrast, we found little evidence that Wave 2 children's motivational beliefs and participation predict changes in either their parents' estimates of their children's abilities or the value the parents' attached to competence in sports, math, or reading. Thus, although parents beliefs and behaviors were responsive to information about their elementary-school-aged children's competencies, their beliefs and values were not responsive to their elementary school-aged children's beliefs and interests over time except in the domain of instrumental music.

In regard to our third sub-goal, we found fairly consistent evidence that children's gender predicts their parents' concurrent perceptions of their children's ability, the importance of the domain for their child, and parents' supportive behaviors in our two leisure activity domains. The association of children's gender with either the parents' beliefs or supportive behaviors in math and reading was much less consistent, varying by wave and by gender of the parent. When present, however, the differences were in the gender stereotypic direction even when independent indicators of current competence levels were controlled. However, we found no evidence that the patterns of associations among the constructs varied by children's gender. Thus, despite consistent evidence of gender-stereotypic differences in the mean levels of both children's and their parents' beliefs and behaviors, the socialization processes appear to work the same for both girls and boys.

We organize our general discussion of these results around three general themes: (a) direction of influence or the reciprocal relations between parents and children in the ontogeny of achievement-related beliefs and behaviors, (b) the robustness of the findings across different activity domains, and (c) the role of gender in the ontogeny of parents' and children's achievement-related beliefs and behaviors.

120

Direction and Reciprocity of Influence

We looked at two types of possible reciprocal influences. First, and most importantly for the developmental sciences, we examined the direction of predictive influences between parents and children. Second, and most importantly for social cognitive perspectives on motivation, we looked at the reciprocal influences between beliefs and behaviors for both parents and children.

Directions of Influence Between Parents and Children

In many studies of socialization, researchers assume that parents influence children and design their methods and analyses accordingly (e.g., Eccles et al., 1983; Furstenberg et al., 1999; McGillicuddy-DeLisi, 1982; McLoyd, 1990; Simpkins et al., 2012). In contrast, Bell (1979) and others argued that parents adjust their beliefs and behaviors according to their children's beliefs, performance, and participation. Through a stringent test of cross-lagged models with several control variables, we found evidence for both the responsiveness of parents' beliefs about their children based on characteristics of their children and the more unidirectional impact of parents' beliefs on changes in their children's motivational beliefs and behaviors (see Chapter 4). With regard to the first pattern, as predicted, teachers' estimates of a child's natural talents did predict changes in parents' views of their child's domain-specific abilities.

In contrast, during the elementary school years, there was almost no evidence that children's motivational beliefs and participation influence changes in their parents' perceptions of their child's abilities over 1 year (see Chapter 4). There was also no evidence that older elementary school-aged children's motivational beliefs predict changes in their parents' supportive behaviors over 1 year (see Chapter 6). The predominate direction of influence flowed from parents to children during both Waves 2–3 and Waves 3–4, which spanned grades 1 through 6.

We found consistent evidence that parents play an important role in shaping the ontogeny of their children's ability self-concepts during the early elementary school years in sports, instrumental music, and reading (Eccles, 1993; Eccles et al., 2000; Fredricks, 1999; Simpkins et al., 2012; Yoon et al., 1993). The predictive power of parents' beliefs was significant even when the association of the teachers' ratings of each child's natural talent with both the parents' and the children's ability perceptions were controlled. These findings suggest that parents' perceptions of their children's abilities are receptive to information from their children's teachers. In turn, parents' perceptions of their children's abilities influence their children's own developing sense of their abilities particularly in sports and reading.

Why do children's ability self-concepts have so little predictive influence on changes in their parents' beliefs and behaviors? By the early elementary school years, children do have reliable opinions about their abilities in different domains (Wigfield et al., 1997). One might expect that a child would make comments while engaged in different activities that would both reflect his/her developing ability self-concept and inform their parents' developing view of their child's relative abilities across different domains. For example, they might make comments such as "I can't do this" or "It's easy" or "It's too hard for me." If so, we found no evidence that such comments influence parents' estimates of their children's abilities in various domains during the early elementary school years.

This set of findings also could reflect the relative across-time stabilities of parents' versus children's estimates of the child's abilities; parents' ratings were much more stable than children's. As a result, there was little room for change in the parents' ratings by the time their children were in elementary school, particularly in sports and reading. The same argument is true for the link between parents' supportive behaviors and their children's beliefs in all domains except reading because parents' supportive behaviors in math, sports, and instrumental music were very stable across time.

It seems likely that the predominant predictive direction between parents' and children's estimates of children's abilities across different domains will vary across chronological age and in different social or cultural contexts. First, the developmental course associated with the increasing stability of these ability perceptions likely differs for parents and children; parents' greater cognitive maturity and interest in forming these judgments likely leads to greater stability in parents' beliefs during the early elementary school years. However, as children mature, they gain more performance experience in different domains, as well as greater cognitive ability to integrate this information into stable concepts about their relative abilities and interests, and they become more interested in assessing their own competencies in different activity domains. As a result, their ability self-concepts should, and, in fact do, become increasingly stable (e.g., Stipek & MacIver, 1989; Wigfield et al., 2007). At some point, the stabilities of parents' and children's estimates of the children's abilities should become more equivalent.

Second, relative access to performance information should change as children mature. When children are young, parents have more opportunities to observe their children's performance in those activities that are prevalent in the children's life (Furstenberg et al., 1999; Parke et al., 2003). As children get older and begin doing more of these activities away from their parents, children's access to information about their performance will increase and likely surpass that of their parents by the time the children move into and through secondary school. At that point, the predominant direction of influence may change as adolescents interpret their performance histories for their parents rather than the reverse. Unfortunately, our research design does not allow us to test either of these predictions because we did not have the funding to gather parent data during the middle and high school years.

Directions of Influence Between Individual's Beliefs and Behaviors

The second type of reciprocal effects that we investigated was the relation between people's beliefs and their behaviors over time. We tested these relations within both parents and adolescents. Although most social cognitive theorists of motivation, particularly those focused on the self as a causal agent have focused their empirical work on the belief to behavior link (Deci & Ryan, 1985; Dweck, 2006; Eccles et al., 1983; Lerner, 1996; Weiner, 1979), most motivational theorists posit a reciprocal relation over time between self-beliefs and behaviors, performance, or choices (Bandura, 1997; Eccles et al., 1983; Harter, 1999; Marsh, 1990; Marsh & Craven, 2006; Skaalvik, 1997; Weiner, 1979). For example, as outlined in Figure 1a, to the extent that behavior yields performance information that is then interpreted by the actor, behaviors should lead to changes in ability self-concepts and values over time. Similarly, within social psychology, there is a long history of interest in the causal ordering of the relations between attitudes and behavior (e.g., Bem, 1970, Eagly & Chaiken, 1993). Nonetheless, within the area of motivated behavior, few studies have directly tested the possible reciprocal links between self-beliefs and behavioral engagement over time in either parents or children (see Marsh & Craven, 2006, for a recent exception).

We found evidence of both reciprocal patterns and unidirectional patterns of influence at several points. The strongest support for reciprocal influences was in sports for parents' beliefs and behaviors (Chapter 5) and for youths' beliefs and behaviors (Chapter 7), as well as in instrumental music for youths' beliefs and behaviors (Chapter 7). For mothers and fathers, parents' supportive behaviors and perceptions of both their children's sport competence and the value of sports were reciprocally related over time. For youth, their beliefs and their participation in sports and in instrumental music were reciprocally related. With regard to evidence consistent with a unidirectional pattern of influence, the most consistent and strongest findings suggest a predominant flow of influence from beliefs to behaviors among youth in math and from behavior to beliefs among parents in instrumental music.

Variations by Domain

One of our major goals was to investigate domain differences in the applicability of the Eccles's models for explaining achievement-related choices across mandatory academic domains and voluntary achievement-related leisure pursuits. Our findings suggest that the predicted associations are stronger in sports and instrumental music than in math and reading.

There are several possible explanations for this pattern. One is that math and reading are required aspects of the school curriculum, whereas sports and music are more likely to occur outside of the traditional curriculum in voluntary school- and community-based after-school contexts. As a result, motivation and participation in math and reading are more likely to be influenced by school factors, especially in the elementary schools years, whereas sports and instrumental music are more likely to be influenced by experiences provided by families or determined by adolescents' own interests, identities, and self-perceptions as the children get older.

Similarly, these domains differ in the number of ways in which parents can and need to be involved if their children are to acquire strong interests and competencies. For both instrumental music and sports, parents are called upon to play many roles in helping their children acquire skills and interests in these (and other) achievement-related leisure activities, such as driving children to practices and lessons; cheering at games and recitals; paying for lessons, equipment, uniforms, and camps; and watching sports and music together (Fredricks & Eccles, 2004; Simpkins et al., 2015). Thus, if their children are to acquire these skills and interests, parents need to organize and implement the relevant experiences, likely leading to a stronger correspondence between parents' beliefs, parents' behaviors, and children's engagement in these domains than in the domain of academic subjects.

Reading and math, however, differ from sports and instrumental music in the United States as both domains are viewed as key components of academic and, therefore, life-long success. The importance the typical middle class American parents attach to math and reading skills is likely quite high and not particularly diverse. For example, in this sample parents' mean ratings of the importance of reading averaged above 6.4 on a 7-point scale and the standard deviations were much smaller for reading than for either sports or instrumental music. Because of the lower variability, it was not surprising that we found weaker relations between parents' beliefs, parents' behaviors, and their children's ability self-concepts and value in reading and math than in sports and instrumental music.

We also documented interesting differences between math and reading. First, parents' beliefs had a stronger predictive influence on children's beliefs in reading than in math. The stronger relations for reading may reflect the fact that reading is emphasized in the early elementary school grades to a greater extent that is math and the type of reading activities that parents and children do at home may be better aligned with the skills the children are learning in reading in early elementary school. If so, these characteristics could help explain why parents' Wave 2 (grades 1, 2, and 4) beliefs predicted increases in their children's beliefs and leisure activities over the next year in reading, but not in math (Chapter 4). By Wave 3 (grades 2, 3, and 5), the majority of the students in this study were in third or fifth grade. By this time, math is becoming both a more important component of the curriculum and more difficult. At the same time, the kinds of basic reading skills that children need to read with their parents are becoming more routine. To the extent that this is true, then parents may be called upon to provide more substantive academic support in math than in reading, leading to stronger evidence of parent to child influence in math during the Wave 3 to Wave 4 transition (grades 2, 3, and 5 to grades 2, 4, and 6) than during the transition 1 year earlier (Chapter 6).

Interestingly, fathers' Wave 3 (grades 2, 3, and 5) behaviors predicted increases in their children's math ability self-concepts and value, as well as reading value over the next year, but mothers' behaviors did not. The fact that fathers have greater predictive influence than mothers in math could reflect cultural stereotypes about who is better in math as well as likely differences between mothers and fathers in both their confidence and their valuing of math (Eccles [Parsons] et al., 1984).

Additionally, we found that early adolescents' Wave 5 (grades 7, 8, and 10) beliefs were more predictive of high school math course taking than English course taking. We believe this difference reflects culturally grounded differences in the choices students have over course enrolment in math versus English. For this sample, English was required for all four high school years whereas math was only required for 3 of the 4 years. Furthermore, the level of difficulty of the courses selected was easier to code in math than in English. Finally, AP courses were more readily available in math than in English in all of the high schools attended by our participants. Thus, students had more choice in math about how much math to take and the difficulty of the math courses they selected. Consistent with this argument, the students' reading beliefs did predict their participation in high school literature clubs, an area in literature/English domain where students may have more choice.

The final domain difference we want to point out is the uniqueness of the instrumental music. This was the domain in which parents' beliefs and behaviors were most consistently responsive to their children's expressed interests and behavioral engagement. Why? One possibility is that instrumental music is the least universally valued skill of the four we studied in this culture with the least easily available organized opportunities to learn during the first 8–9 years of life. During the early elementary school years, the parents in this sample were much less likely to enroll their children in organized programs, to do the activity with their child, and to model related behaviors in instrumental music compared to sports. Parents of boys also placed less value on instrumental music than on sports. Finally, the rate of provision of opportunities to learn instrumental music went up from Wave 2 to Wave 3 (i.e., grades 1, 2, and 4 to grades 2, 3, and 5) and then declined in later waves. Together, this pattern suggests that most of these parents were not motivated to provide their children with opportunities to learn to play a musical instrument before the middle of their elementary school years. Children may have been key to initiating this opportunity to a greater extent in music than in sport and then perhaps were more key to stopping their instruction if they did not enjoy it and feel competent at it. We know of no other research to evaluate the role of youth in initiating or halting the pursuit of instrumental music. It seems likely that the relative parental valuing of instrumental music versus sport will vary by culture and subculture. Understanding the association of the relative valuing, as well as parents' beliefs about the origins of interest and individual differences in aptitude across different domains for various activities is an important topic for future research.

Gender

We examined both mean differences between boys and girls and differences in the relations among constructs by child gender. Consistent with prior research, we documented stereotypic mean-level gender differences among children, with boys typically having higher scores than girls on sports and math ability self-concepts, value (only for sports), participation, and coursework (Eccles, Wigfield, et al., 1993; Fredricks & Eccles, 2005; Simpkins, Davis-Kean, et al., 2005). In contrast, boys had lower ability self-concepts, value beliefs, participation, and course taking in reading and music than girls (Baker & Wigfield, 1999; Eccles et al., 1993; Jacobs et al., 2005). The mean-level differences were generally stronger in the two leisure domains than in the two academic domains. This may reflect the fact that participation in sports and music tends to be voluntary, whereas math and reading are the two subjects that form the backbone of children's education from kindergarten through the high school years. Mastery of math and reading are important precursors to college achievements and economic success in adulthood.

Although the youth findings were fairly consistent, the evidence of an association of children's gender with parents' beliefs and behaviors was mixed. Just as was true for the youth, both mothers and fathers tended to be gender-stereotyped in their beliefs about their children and their behavioral supports in sports and instrumental music. Consistent with previous studies, parents of sons held more positive beliefs and did more to support their children's engagement in sports than did parents' of daughters (Eccles et al., 2000; Fredricks & Eccles, 2005; Welk et al., 2003). These gender differences likely reflect the internalization of cultural expectations about gender competencies and interest in these domains. In contrast, there were significantly fewer gender differences in parents' beliefs and practices in math and reading.

This study is one of the first to examine gender differences in children's and parents' beliefs and behaviors in instrumental music (see Simpkins et al.,

2012; Wigfield et al., 1997; for exceptions) and our findings run counter to the differential prevalence of males versus females in the professional world of instrumental musicians. By and large, gender-related stereotypes about both ability and interests reflect the gendered differential participation patterns in the adult world (Ruble et al., 2006). By a substantial margin, the majority of professional instrumental musicians are male (Ammer, 2001). Why then do both parents and children see instrumental music as female-typed during the childhood years? We suspect that parents' beliefs and behaviors reflect two cultural phenomena: (a) lay person's assumptions about the patience it takes to study instrumental music coupled with stereotypes regarding gender differences in children's patience and self-control, and (b) the greater emphasis placed on sports for boys. We know of no studies assessing these two predictions.

Despite the fact that girls and boys rated themselves and were rated by parents as being different in several domains, the patterns of associations among the predictors over time were quite similar for girls and boys. Take sports as an example. Girls had less confidence in their sport abilities, spent less time in sports, and experienced fewer supportive sport-related behaviors from parents than boys. However, the predictors of children's sport ability self-concepts or participation were similar for girls and boys. The lack of gender moderation is consistent with the limited number of studies that have investigated gender as a moderator (Marsh et al., 2007; Sabiston & Crocker, 2008; Simpkins et al., 2005, 2006, 2012; Valentine et al., 2004). The relative lack of gender moderation in light of the mean-level differences based on gender is important for interventions aiming to change motivation and participation. On the one hand, these findings indicate that socialization processes operate similarly across gender, suggesting that similar interventions can be used to support both girls' and boys' participation in these domains. On the other hand, these findings suggest that one will need to provide more of these service to girls than to boys if one wants to reduce the mean level gender differences in beliefs and behaviors.

Broader Implications for Research

Researchers make many decisions in designing, implementing, and then analyzing data for large scale, longitudinal datasets like CAB. In this section, we discuss what we learned about the impact of such decisions on the findings from the approach we took in this manuscript.

Developmental Design

Development takes place over time and can be studied using quite different time frames ranging from moment to moment developmental processes to the more distal accumulation of developmental pathways over longer time frames. Developmental scientists make decisions about the time frame they wish to study both when they design their data collection plan and when they design their data analytic strategies. These decisions have several implications for what can be learned from any given data analytic project.

First, Eccles and her colleagues have analyzed the CAB data using various time frames, giving us the opportunity to compare the results of applying different types of statistical analyses on the same data. In 2012, we published a study using the CAB data to test the general Eccles's model of the socialization of achievement-related beliefs and behaviors summarized in Figure 1b. In this study, we used a widely accepted method to analyze longitudinal data to assess a singular set of theoretical predictions. Specifically, using structural equation modeling techniques, we estimated a linear model that captured the central theorized sequences of events that unfold over time. The findings in that paper provided strong evidence that the data fit well with what would be predicted over the long term from the Eccles's models. Although useful, that particular statistical approach does not allow one to rigorously evaluate possible rival hypotheses concerning the direction of influence, examine and predict changes in these phenomena over time, or address the multi-determined origins of parents' beliefs. The detailed, cross-lagged modeling approach used in this monograph is better suited to examine these types of issues and questions.

Additionally, the results of this monograph point to the need to plan carefully for when in the life course these developmentally defined sequences of data should be collected. We found different patterns of relations across the four activity domains we studied. These differences could reflect different developmental time courses for the processes in each domain. We argued that differences in the developmental time course for acquiring skills in instrumental music versus sports might explain the different patterns of relations across these two domains. The same could be true for reading versus math. If this is true, then we would have needed to gather the data when the children were younger in order to capture the power of parental socialization for reading. This issue is directly related to previous research on parents' beliefs about development (Goodnow & Collins, 1990; Sigel, McGillicuddy-De Lisi, & Goodnow, 1992). These scholars argued that parents' beliefs about when various skills should be cultivated should influence the timing of their related socialization behaviors. Our patterns of domain differences could reflect this phenomenon. The timing of various socialization practices should also vary cross-culturally because cultures will vary in their theories about optimal developmental timing (Harkness & Super, 1996; Willemsen & Van de Vijver, 1997).

Effect Size

Our findings also relate to concerns about effect sizes. Many of our effects sizes from the cross-lagged models fall within the range of .10 to .25—a range that would be considered small according to Cohen (1992). Small is often considered to be bad or not significant in the practical sense. We disagree with this assessment. In order to provide as stringent a test as possible of our hypotheses regarding the possible impact of parents on children and the possible impact of motivationally related beliefs on behaviors, we used longitudinal data to test for lagged effects and included several important controls for selection effects. This is a very conservative approach, which coupled with the fact that the "outcomes" we tested at each point are complex and likely to be multi-determined, is very likely to yield small effect sizes. However, as has been shown in the literature on teacher effects (Jussim & Eccles, 1992), such effects can accumulate over time to yield quite marked differences in developmental trajectories (see Rosenthal, Rosnow, & Ruben, 2000, for a similar discussion of the accumulation of small effect sizes).

Second, our study provides just one snapshot of a developmental process that begins at conception. We looked only at the parental socialization processes occurring during the elementary school years and the within-individual selection processes during secondary school. Because our method relies on predicting change over a 1-year gap (Chapters 4 to 6) or 4-year gap (Chapter 7), our effect sizes will be limited in the extent to which we captured the point of maximal change in the predicted variables. The high stability in some of our predicted "outcomes" inevitably leads to lower cross-lagged effect sizes because there is less unexplained variance to predict. Studying both parents and children simultaneously makes this issue particularly problematic because beliefs like those we are studying are likely to stabilize at different developmental points for parents and children due to cognitive and experiential differences between these two groups of people.

Finally, the "outcomes" we are studying at each step in our analyses can be influenced by many forces and experiences. The developmental processes underlying the trajectories of change in these "outcomes" are complex and multifaceted. Consistent with thinking about ecologically embedded developmental systems (e.g., Bronfenbrenner & Morris, 2006; Sameroff, 2000), these processes represent patterns of adaptation of both parents and children to each other over time and across various contexts. Furthermore, these processes include the principles of both multifinality and equifinality (Cicchetti & Rogosch, 1996) with the same precursors leading to multiple developmental outcomes and different precursors leading to similar developmental outcomes. Given these complexities, we should not expect that any one model will yield particularly high effect sizes.

In this monograph, we took a holistic view of parenting in which we tried to capture the more general environment parents create for socializing their children's skill acquisition and interest development. Considering a range of parental behaviors simultaneously supports theoretical perspectives that emphasize the multifaceted and systems nature of parental behaviors in relation to child outcomes (Eccles, 1993; Epstein, 1995; Furstenberg et al., 1999; Grolnick & Ryan, 1989; Sameroff, 2000). However, in general, the extant literature has tended to include a singular aspect of parenting, such as coactivity or encouragement, or to try to isolate the unique effects of specific behaviors or characteristics. Drawing on the work of Sameroff (2000) and our own previous studies (Fredricks & Eccles, 2005), we adopted a different strategy—one that tries to capture family level variations in the broader system of parenting, which includes parents' beliefs, parents' own role modeling behaviors, and parents' direct attempts to manage their children's experiences. More specifically, we included multiple indicators to reflect the multidimensionality of parenting behaviors and the diverse behaviors that parents exhibit to promote children's pursuit of a domain. We utilized two analytic approaches to addresses the multidimensionality of parental behavior: (a) latent variable approach, which was used in the sports, instrumental music, and math models, and (b) the cumulative promotive approach, which was used in the reading models. Both approaches were useful in understanding parents' behavior. We believe such approaches to the study of family influences fits better with natural ecology of family functioning that do statistical models based on unique, additive effects.

To design better family level interventions, it would be helpful for future studies to pinpoint whether there is an optimal fit between particular patterns of parenting behaviors with particular types of children and whether there are particular qualities of parent–child coactivity or encouragement that should be targeted. It is also important for future researchers to complement our type of inclusive analyses with more micro-level and person-centered analyses. Results on parenting behavior at these various levels will be necessary to develop the most effective parenting interventions. The current results provide insight into the breadth of parenting behaviors. Future research on the fit between parents' behaviors and children would provide insight on for whom certain behaviors would be most effective. Findings on the qualities of the interactions would provide the foundation for what skills to teach parents.

Directly related to the issue of the best way to conceptualize and then study parenting and family processes is the issue of conceptualizing and then studying complex systems over time. There is a major effort in current developmental studies to include increasing numbers of control variables presumably to isolate the "causal influence" of particular experiences or characteristics on particular developmental "outcomes." This effort is considered to be key to social policy recommendations because social policies usually target specific interventions and are usually aimed at universal interventions. Although this may true for social policy recommendations, such strategies may not be appropriate for modeling and understanding the complex course of human development. For example, studies on the role of extracurricular programs often try to control for selection into these programs in order to estimate their causal impact on the acquisition of particular skills or interests. It may be the case that those children most likely to benefit from any particular program are those with the highest levels of motivation to enter and then persist in the program or the highest level of aptitude for the skill being taught. Controlling for such "selection" factors as initial motivation or skill level is very likely to substantially reduce the effect size associated with participating in any specific program. Is this a good thing? Rather than simply controlling for selection factors to isolate program effects, researchers could address the complexity of development by understanding the extent to which the impact of the program might vary based on selection factors.

We certainly used this strategy to test the potential impact of parents' beliefs and behaviors on their children's beliefs and behaviors by controlling for teachers' estimates of the children's natural talent in each domain and for the children's scores on the Slosson intelligence test. We included these controls to better isolate the unique effect of parents' beliefs and behaviors. But this strategy did not allow us to investigate the dynamic nature of associations across time of children's abilities and motivation on their self-selection or parent mandated selection into particular learning contexts with their increasing abilities and changing interests and participation. Looking at the cross-lagged associations between teachers' ratings and parents' beliefs about their children's abilities provided an initial look at these complexities. We encourage future studies that focus less on controlling for selection effects and more on the dynamics or these complex developmental processes and reciprocal pathways.

Broader Implications for Applied Work

The findings of this study also have applied implications. With the exception of instrumental music, during elementary school, the results of our cross-lagged models show that parents are more likely to shape children's motivation than vice versa, and that parents' beliefs about their children are quite stable by early elementary school. These findings suggest that targeting parents even prior to elementary school will be a more effective method for increasing children's long-term motivation than targeting parents later in the elementary school years. These interventions can educate parents about how they can shape children's beliefs and activity choices by acting as "interpreters of experiences" and providing their children with inputs about their emerging abilities and the value of different skills for their short and long term developmental goals. Interventions could also highlight the multitude of ways parents can influence children's pursuit of domains through opportunities both inside and outside of the home. Especially at younger ages, parents play a primary role in structuring experiences and exposing children to different domains (Furstenberg et al., 1999; Parke et al., 2003). Such an approach to parenting has been labeled family management.

Directly related to age patterns in the role of parents is the possibility that there are optimal times for parents to try to help their children acquire different skills. As we discussed earlier, parents have ideas about when their children should be learning particular skills and these ideas vary across cultures (Harkness & Super, 1996). It is not clear that these ideas are developmentally accurate and thus parents may not be implementing the best developmental strategies. For example, we now know that learning a second language is easiest during the preschool years (Lightbown & Spada, 2006), but many American parents continue to resist sending their children to multilingual preschools and until quite recently, second language learning was not introduced to American children until secondary school. The same may be true for instrumental music and if so then both parents and schools in the United States are missing the optimal learning period for children's engagement in instrumental music. More research is badly needed on determining if and when optimal periods for learning skills are, so that parents and schools can be better informed about when to introduce experiences to children related to acquiring different types of skills.

Our results also demonstrate the important role that early motivational beliefs play in shaping achievement-related choices in high school. Understanding the ontogeny of activity choices is important because of evidence of the long-term benefits of participation in these domains for educational attainment, choice of college majors, occupational status, and well-being (Eccles, 1994; Fredricks & Eccles, 2006). These results suggest that strengthening competence and value beliefs offer a promising means of intervening to encourage greater participation in these domains for both girls and boys. Such interventions might focus on altering youths' beliefs about their ability and educating both girls and boys about the value of participating for their well-being and for their future educational and occupational pursuits. The importance of such a perspective has recently gained recognition in educational and recreational efforts to increase participation of America's children in STEM.

Our findings also have implications for involvement in leisure domains. Many schools have experienced shrinking budgets. One way schools have addressed these budget concerns is to reduce their instruction in subjects that are not core academic subjects, such as music and sports. The lack of opportunities is particularly problematic in music. Few parents in this study reported spending time by themselves or with their children playing musical instruments. Furthermore, music activities often require purchase or rental of instruments. In contrast, families were more likely to participate in athletic activities together. Moreover, some types of physical activities require minimal equipment and skill (e.g., walking, playing Frisbee). These cuts in instrumental music instruction in the school will likely have more profound implications on youths' pursuit of music than of sports, as our data suggest families were less likely to promote music than they are to promote sports.

Finally, our findings also have implications for child health. We are in the midst of a health crisis related to increases in childhood obesity. Our data suggest that families are critical to youths' motivational beliefs and participation in sports. The Let's Move campaign spear-headed by Michelle Obama is an example of a recent campaign designed to promote healthy lifestyles. The advice directed at families to promote youths' physical activity center on several of the key components of our model, including parental encouragement, coactivity, coaching a child's team, and providing athletic opportunities in home (www.letsmove.gov).

Limitations and Future Directions

The results of this study need to be interpreted in light of several methodological decisions. This study was based on a sample of middle-class European American families, whose children were in the early elementary grades in 1987. This sample was explicitly selected to test the processes by which parents influence children's activity choices and motivational beliefs in families where income and neighborhood resources were not obstacles to supporting activity participation. This decision has implications for the generalizability of our findings. It will be important to test whether these findings replicate across families of different socioeconomic, ethnic, cultural, and national groups. We expect that the associations will hold, though the strength in various domains may vary across these groups. For example, the associations between adolescents' beliefs and participation in sports and instrumental music may be weaker in contexts where there are fewer opportunities for adolescents to engage in these activities.

Another concern is that the data were collected from 1987 to 1999. Although we expect that the basic relations would emerge in data today, cultural changes over time might shift the strength of some of the relations. For example, several prominent book series, including the Harry Potter,

Twilight, and Hunger Games, have increased many children's and adolescents' interest in reading. It will be important in the future for researchers to use multiple datasets collected during different historical periods to understand how such shifts in popular culture impact youth.

Over the last decade, there also have been shifts in the gender patterns in some careers and college majors. From 1996 to 2006, there have been increases in the number of women who have earned graduate degrees in almost all areas of STEM (science, technology, engineering, and mathematics; National Science Foundation, 2009). Some STEM areas that were historically dominated by males are experiencing shifts. For example, the percentage of women who earned a bachelor's degree in chemistry rose from 45% in 1997 to 51% in 2006. As noted in ecological theory (Bronfenbrenner & Morris, 2006), it will be important to understand how such societal and cultural shifts alter micro-processes within youth and families.

Similarly, we made decisions about the testing regimen and the cohorts selected. Because our previous work had focused on the adolescent years and the school context, we decided to move to the elementary school years in order to investigate the family influence on the development of children's self and task related beliefs. We also decided that we could only assess the families once per year due to financial and practical limitations. Finally, we could only get initial funding for 5 years. Although we were able to get funding to collect additional data during the high school years, we were unable to get funding to collect data during the middle school years for most of our sample. As we discussed previously, each of these decisions limited what we could model. Clearly given the importance of the middle school period, more research is needed on the role of families during this period of development.

Another limitation in our study is that all information on parenting behaviors and adolescents' achievement-related behavior was collected with self-report methodologies. Although these parental measures have been validated and used in several in other studies (e.g., Eccles, 1993; Eccles et al., 2000; Fredricks & Eccles, 2005; Simpkins et al., 2012), there are concerns about the accuracy of parents' report of behavior, the level of detail that can be collected with self-report methods, and the types of analyses that can be conducted with this type of data (Holden & Edwards, 1989). The items in this study focused on the frequency of behavior, either more generally or in the past year. No information was collected on the quality of parent-child relations or specific details of their interactions, which likely moderate this relation between parental behaviors and youths' beliefs (Grolnick, 2003). In future research, it will be important to use a range of methodological techniques to collect more nuanced data on other parental behaviors to complement these general measures. Observational data can be used to assess a vast array of behaviors, as well as allowing for sequential analysis between parents' behaviors and children's outcomes (Bakeman & Quera, 2012).

Another methodological decision we made that has implications for the generalizability of our findings was to study mothers and fathers in separate analyses so that we could use the full sample of mothers and fathers. This meant that we could not directly test for mother and father differences and that the samples of mothers and fathers are drawn from overlapping, but not equivalent families. In order to test the implications of these decisions on the comparability of our findings, we replicated 20% of our analyses with mother data on the smaller sample of 541 that matched the father sample. In Chapter 4, we had 24 mother models; we reran 6. In Chapters 5 and 6, we had 8 mother models; we reran 2 in each chapter. We stratified the selection of the models by domain, parent construct, and youth construct (e.g., a model predicting self-concept and a model predicting value). Essentially, there were no substantial differences in the findings, suggesting that limiting the mother sample to only those whose husbands had participated would yield similar results but then these results would only generalize to families in which both mothers and fathers agree to participate. We chose to maximize the sample we had for mothers and for fathers at the outset for several reasons. First, we wanted to include as many cases as possible to examine child gender as a moderator. It is harder to document interactions using longitudinal data because we controlled for prior levels of the outcome variable. In contrast, interactions are easier to finding in the lab because of experimental manipulations. Because it is hard to find significant interactions in non-experimental designs, we needed maximum statistical power. Second, the comparison of mothers versus fathers was not our question. We included fathers because one major weakness of the literature on parenting is the limited information on fathers. Thus, we wanted to present our father data as well as our mother data while maximizing the representativeness within each sample.

We also made the decision to run ability self-concepts and task values in separate models due to issues related to multicollinearity and our desire to present findings relevant to both the ability self-concept/efficacy literature and the interest/value literature. However, taking this strategy prevented us from looking at the interaction of ability self-concepts and values in predicting either parents' behaviors (Chapter 4) or the youths' participation in high school (Chapter 7). For example, Marsh and his coworkers have shown that value increases the predictive power of ability self-concepts on subsequent academic achievement (Marsh, Trautwein, Ludtke, Koller, & Baumert, 2005). Similarly, although this has never been tested, parents' valuing of domain might moderate the association of their socialization behaviors with their perceptions of their children's abilities. For example, if the parents place very high value on skills in particular area, they might be particularly likely to engage in remedial behaviors if their child is having difficulty mastering those skills. In contrast, under similar circumstances, they might be more willing to let their child drop out of a specific skill-based activity domain if they placed low value on that particular skill.

The decision to run the value and ability self-concept models separately also prevented us from testing whether the value parents attach to a particular domain moderates their influence on the ontogeny of their children's beliefs and behaviors. For example, it is possible that children will pay either more or less attention to their parents' socializations attempts if they understand how important a particular skill is to their parents. They might be more compliant and willing to invest their own energies if they both think their parents place high value on a particular skill domain and they have a positive relationship with their parents. Alternative, if their parents become too pushy because they value a particular domain so much, their children's motivation might decline because they are feeling too controlled by their parents (Grolnick, 2003).

One goal of this monograph was to examine whether the relations varied across four domains. These domains varied in academic versus leisure focus and if they were traditionally considered masculine or feminine domains. Inclusion of these four domains provided interesting insights we discussed earlier. However, they do not include all academic and leisure domains. The two academic domains that were included are the two core subjects throughout elementary and secondary school. It is unclear at this point if the relations found with these core academic subjects will generalize to other academic domains that become electives in high school or are not taught throughout early schooling. Science, foreign language, or social studies are examples of these classes. Parent endorsement and support of these classes may differ from math and reading. Furthermore, certain domains, such as science, have been shown to vary by gender (National Science Foundation, 2009). Gender differences may be more pronounced in academic subjects parents view as electives.

Similarly, we only picked two skilled-based leisure activities: sport and instrumental music. We picked sport because it is so pervasive in the US culture. We picked music as a less gender-typed but still skill-based comparison leisure domain. Even within in music, we focused specifically on instrumental music in comparison to other types of music (e.g., choral) to keep the music domain as specific as possible and as similar to sports as possible in terms of the role of organized instruction during the childhood years. Future research is needed on other skill-based leisure activities.

Finally, future research needs to explain parent-child effects across different ages. We found that in elementary school the direction largely went from parent to child. However, it is possible that across development there may be a shift in the relative degree of influence between parent and child. When children are young, parents play a large role in structuring children's experiences by signing them up for activities, co-participating and attending events, and buying them equipment and books to support their involvement.

It is possible that one would find that the lagged effects of children on parents will increase as the children become older and are granted more opportunities to make decisions about how they spend their time (Parke et al., 2003; Savage & Gauvain, 1998). However, it is also possible that as children get older, one would find less child effects on parents because of the waning influence of parents on children and the increasing effects of peers in adolescence. More studies are needed to chart these developmental pathways.

Final Summary

Our goal in this study was to test the central processes theorized in the two Eccles's expectancy-value models (Eccles, 1993; Eccles, Schiefele, & Wigfield, 1998). Although we found that mixed evidence that parents' beliefs predicted changes in their behavior, parents' behaviors predicted changes in youths' beliefs. Finally, youths' beliefs predicted changes in youths' participation. This predictive chain was more prominent in sports and instrumental music than in math and reading. There was also some evidence that youth's beliefs, skills, and participation predicted parents' beliefs and behaviors, as well as that individuals' behaviors predicted their later beliefs. But, these relations also emerged primarily in sports and instrumental music. Our findings on child gender suggest that even though there are some differences between girls and boys, the predictors over time were similar for girls and boys.

REFERENCES

Alexander, K. L., & Entwisle, D. R. (1988). Achievement in the first two years of school: Patterns and processes. *Monograph of the Society for Research in Child Development, 53* (Serial no. 218).

Ammer, C. (2001). *Unsung: A history of women in American music* (2nd ed.) Portland, OR: Amadeus Press.

Andre, T., Whigham, M., Hendrickson, A., & Chambers, S. (1999). Competency beliefs, positive affect, and gender stereotypes of elementary students and their parents about science versus other school subjects. *Journal of Research in Science Teaching, 36*, 719–747. doi: 10.1002/(SICI)1098-2736(199908)36:6<719:AID-TEA8>3.0.CO;2-R

Atkinson, J. W. (1964). *An introduction to motivation.* Princeton, NJ: Van Nostrand.

Atwater, M. M., Wiggins, J., & Gardner, C. M. (1995). A study of urban middle school students with high and low attitudes toward science. *Journal of Research in Science Teaching, 32*, 665–677. doi: 10.1002/tea.3660320610

Austin, J. R. (1990). The relationship of music self-esteem to degree of participation in school and out-of-school music activities among upper elementary students. *Contributions to Music Education, 17*, 20–31.

Babkes, M. L., & Weiss, M. R. (1999). Parental influence on children's cognitive and affective responses to competitive soccer participation. *Pediatric Exercise Science, 11*, 44–62.

Bakeman, R., & Quera, V. (2012). Behavioral observation. In H. Cooper, P. M. Camic, D. L. Long, A. T. Panter, D. Rindskopf, & K. J. Sher (Eds.), *APA handbook of research methods in psychology: Vol. 1: Foundations, planning, measures, and psychometrics* (pp. 207–225). Washington, DC: American Psychological Association.

Baker, L., & Scher, D. (2002). Beginning readers' motivation for reading in relation to parental beliefs and home reading experiences. *Reading Psychology, 23*, 239–269. doi: 10.1080/713775283

Baker, L., Scher, D., & Mackler, K. (1997). Home and families influences on motivation for literacy. *Educational Psychologist, 32*, 69–82. doi: 10.1207/s15326985ep3202_2

Baker, L., & Wigfield, A. (1999). Dimensions of children's motivation for reading and their relations to reading activity and reading achievement. *Reading Research Quarterly, 34*, 452–477. doi: 10.1598/RRQ.34.4.4

Bandura, A. (1977). Self-efficacy: Toward a unifying theory of behavioral change. *Psychological Review, 84*, 191–215. doi: 10.1037/0033-295X.84.2.191

Bandura, A. (1997). *Self-efficacy: The exercise of control.* New York: W.H. Freeman.

Bandura, A., Barbaranelli, C., Caprara, G. V., & Pastorelli, C. (1996). Multi-faceted impact of self-efficacy beliefs on academic functioning. *Child Development, 67*, 1206–1222. doi: 10.2307/1131888

Bates, J. E. (1987). Temperament in infancy. In J. D. Osofsky (Ed.), *Handbook of infant development* (pp. 1101–1149). New York: Wiley.

Bauer, K. W., Nelson, M. C., Boutelle, K. N., & Neumark-Sztainer, D. (2008). Parental influences on adolescents' physical activity and sedentary behavior: Longitudinal findings from project EAT-II. *The International Journal of Behavioral Nutrition and Physical Activity, 5*, 12. doi: 10.1186/1479-5868-5-12

Baumrind, D. (1971). Current patterns of parental authority. *Developmental Psychology, 4*, 1–103. doi: 10.1037/h0030372

Beets, M. W., Vogel, R., Forlaw, L., Pitetti, K. H., & Cardinal, B. J. (2006). Social support and youth physical activity: The role of provider and type. *American Journal of Health Behavior, 30*, 278–289. doi: 10.5993/AJHB.30.3.6

Bell, R. A. (1968). A reinterpretation of the direction of effects in studies of socialization. *Psychological Review, 75*, 81–95. doi: 10.1037/h0025583

Bell, R. A. (1979). Parent, child, and reciprocal influences. *American Psychologist, 34*, 821–826.

Belsky, J. (1984). The determinants of parenting: A process model. *Child Development, 55*, 83–96. doi: 10.2307/1129836

Bem, D. (1970). *Beliefs, attitudes, and human affairs.* Belmont, CA: Wadsworth.

Bentler, P. M. (1990). Comparative fit indexes in structural models. *Psychological Bulletin, 107*, 238–246. doi: 10.1037/0033-2909.107.2.238

Bergman, L. R., Magnusson, D., & El-Khouri, B. M. (2003). *Studying individual development in an interindividual context: A person-oriented approach, Vol. 4. Paths through life.* Mahwah, NJ: Erlbaum.

Bhanot, R., & Jovanovic, J. (2005). Do parents' academic gender stereotypes influence whether they intrude on their children's homework? *Sex Roles, 52*, 597–607. doi: 10.1007/s11199-005-3728-4

Bleeker, M. M., & Jacobs, J. E. (2004). Involvement in math and science: Do mothers' beliefs matter 12 years later? *Journal of Educational Psychology, 96*, 97–109. doi: 10.1037/0022-0663.96.1.97

Bloom, B. S. (1985). *Developing talent in young people.* New York: Ballantine Books.

Bois, J. E., Sarrazin, P. G., Brustad, R. J., Trouilloud, D. O., & Cury, F. (2002). Mothers' expectancies and young adolescents' perceived competence: A year-long study. *Journal of Early Adolescence, 23*, 384–406.

Bradley, R. H. (2004). Chaos, culture, and covariance structures: A dynamic systems view of children's experiences at home. *Parenting: Science and Practice, 4*, 243–257. doi: 10.1080/15295192.2004.9681272

Bradley, R. H., Caldwell, B. M., Rock, S. L., Ramey, C. T., Barnard, K. E., Gray, C., et al. (1989). Home environment and cognitive development in the first 3 years of life: A collaborative study involving six sites and three ethnic groups in North America. *Developmental Psychology, 25*, 217–235. doi: 10.1037/0012-1649.25.2.217

Bradley, R. H., & Corwyn, R. F. (2006). The family environment. In L. Balter & C. S. Tamis-LeMonda (Eds.), *Child Psychology: A handbook of contemporary issues* (2nd ed., pp. 493–520). New York: Psychology Press.

Bronfenbrenner, U., & Morris, P. A. (2006). The ecology of environmental processes. In W. Damon (Series Ed.) & R. M. Lerner (Vol. Ed.), *Handbook of child psychology* (6th ed., Vol. 1, pp. 793–828). Hoboken, NJ: Wiley.

Bruininks, R. H. (1978). *Bruininks–Oseretsky test of motor proficiency.* Circle Pines, MN: American Guidance Service.

Brustad, R. J. (1993). Who will go out and play? Parental and psychological influences on children's attraction to physical activity. *Pediatric Exercise Science, 5,* 210–233.

Bugental, D. B., & Johnston, C. (2000). Parent and child cognitions in the context of the family. *Annual Review of Psychology, 51,* 315–344. doi: 10.1146/annurev.psych.51.1.315

Burton, J., Horowitz, R., & Abeles, H. (2000). Learning in and through the arts: The question of transfer. *Studies in Art Education, 41,* 228–257.

Bus, A. (1994). The role of social context in emergent literacy. In E. M. H. Assink (Ed.), *Literacy acquisition and social context: The developing body and mind* (pp. 9–24). Oxford, England: Harvester Wheatsheaf/Prentice Hall.

Cheung, G. W., & Rensvold, R. B. (2002). Evaluating goodness-of-fit indexes for testing measurement invariance. *Structural Equation Modeling, 9,* 233–255. doi: 10.1207/S15328007SEM0902_5

Cicchetti, D., & Rogosch, F. A. (1996). Equifinality and multifinality in developmental psychopathology. *Development and Psychopathology, 8,* 597–600. doi: 10.1017/S0954579400007318

Cohen, J. (1992). A power primer. *Psychological Bulletin, 112,* 155–159. doi: 10.1037/0033-2909.112.1.155

Coles, M., & Hall, C. (2002). Gendered readings: Learning from children's reading choices. *Journal of Research in Reading, 25,* 96–108. doi: 10.1111/1467-9817.00161

Coltrane, S., & Adams, M. (1997). Children and gender. In T. Arendell (Ed.), *Contemporary parenting: Challenges and issues* (pp. 219–253). Thousand Oaks, CA: SAGE.

Conger, R. D., Wallace, L. E., Sun, Y., Simons, R. L., McLoyd, V. C., & Brody, G. (2002). Economic pressure in African American families: A replication and extension of the family stress model. *Developmental Psychology, 38,* 179–193. doi: 10.1037/0012-1649.38.2.179

Covington, M. V. (1992). *Making the grade: A self-worth perspective on motivation and school reform.* New York: Cambridge University Press.

Cox, K. E., & Guthrie, J. T. (2001). Motivational and cognitive contributions to students' amount of reading. *Contemporary Educational Psychology, 26,* 116–131. doi: 10.1006/ceps.1999.1044

Crandall, V. J., Dewey, R., Katkovsky, W., & Preston, A. (1964). Parents' attitudes and behaviors and grade school children's academic achievements. *Journal of Genetic Psychology, 104,* 53–66. doi: 10.1080/00221325.1964.10532540

Crombie, G., Sinclair, N., Silverthorn, N., Byrne, B. M., Dubois, D. L., & Trinneer, A. (2005). Predictors of young adolescents' math grades and course enrollment intentions: Gender similarities and differences. *Sex Roles, 5/6,* 351–367. doi: 10.1007/s11199-005-2678-1

Csikszentmihalyi, M. (1988). The flow experience and its significance for human psychology. In M. Csikzentmihalyi & I. S. Csikzentmihalyi (Eds.), *Optimal experience* (pp. 15–35) New York: Cambridge University Press.

Dai, D. Y., & Schader, R. M. (2002). Decisions regarding music training: Parents beliefs and values. *Gifted Child Quarterly, 46,* 135–144. doi: 10.1177/001698620204600206

Davidson, J. W., Howe, M., Moore, D. G., & Sloboda, J. A. (1996). The role of parental influences in the development of musical performance. *British Journal of Developmental Psychology, 14,* 399–412. doi: 10.1111/j.2044-835X.1996.tb00714.x

Davis-Kean, P. E., Malanchuk, O., Peck, S. C., Eccles, J. S. (2003, April). *Parental influences on academic outcomes: Do race and SES matter?* Paper presented at the biennial meeting of the Society for Research in Child Development, Tampa, FL.

Davison, K. K., Cutting, T. M., & Birch, L. L. (2003). Parents' activity-related parenting practices predict girls' physical activity. *Medicine and Science in Sport and Exercise*, **35**, 1589–1595.

Deci, E. I., & Ryan, R. M. (1985). *Intrinsic motivation and self-determination in human behavior*. New York: Plenum Press.

Dowda, M., Dishman, R. K., Pfeiffer, K. A., & Pate, R. R. (2007). Family support for physical activity in girls from 8th to 12th grade in South Carolina. *Preventive Medicine*, **44**, 153–159. doi: 10.1016/j.ypmed.2006.10.001

Duncan, S. C., Duncan, T. E., & Strycker, L. A. (2005). Source and type of social support in youth physical activity. *Health Psychology*, **24**, 3–10. doi: 10.1037/0278-6133.24.1.3

Durik, A. M., Vida, M., & Eccles, J. S. (2006). Task values and ability beliefs as predictors of high school literacy choices: A developmental analysis. *Journal of Educational Psychology*, **2**, 382–393. doi: 10.1037/0022-0663.98.2.382

Dweck, C. (2006). *Mindset: The new psychology of success*. New York: Random House.

Eagly, A. H., & Chaiken, S. (1993). *The psychology of attitudes*. Fort Worth, TX: Harcourt Brace Jovanovich College.

Eccles, J. S. (1993). School and family effects of the ontogeny of children's interests, self-perceptions, and activity choice. In J. Jacobs (Ed.), *Nebraska Symposium on Motivation, 1992: Developmental perspectives on motivation* (pp. 145–208). Lincoln: University of Nebraska Press.

Eccles, J. S. (1994). Understanding women's educational and occupational choices: Applying the Eccles et al. model of achievement-related choices. *Psychology of Women Quarterly*, **18**, 585–609.

Eccles, J. S. (2009). Who am I and what am I going to do with my life? Personal and collective identities as motivators of action. *Educational Psychologist*, **44**, 78–89. doi: 10.1080/00461520902832368

Eccles [Parsons] J. S., Adler, T. F., Futterman, R., Goff, S. B., Kaczala, C. M., Meece, J. L., et al. (1983). Expectations, values and academic behaviors. In J. T. Spence (Ed.), *Achievement and achievement motivation* (pp. 75–146). San Francisco: W.H. Freeman.

Eccles [Parsons] J. S., Adler, T. F., & Kaczala, C. M. (1982). Socialization of achievement attitudes and beliefs: Parental influences. *Child Development*, **53**, 322–339. doi: 10.2307/1128974

Eccles [Parsons] J. S., Adler, T., & Meece, J. L. (1984). Sex differences in achievement: A test of alternate theories. *Journal of Personality and Social Psychology*, **46**, 26–43. doi: 10.1037/0022-3514.46.1.26

Eccles, J. S., Freedman-Doan, C., Frome, P., Jacobs, J., & Yoon, S. K. (2000). Gender-role socialization in the family: A longitudinal approach. In T. Eckes & H. M. Trautner (Eds.), *The developmental social psychology of gender* (pp. 333–360). Mahwah, NJ: Erlbaum.

Eccles, J. S., & Gootman, J. A. (2002). *Community programs to promote youth development*. Washington, DC: National Academy Press.

Eccles, J. S., & Harold, R. D. (1991). Gender differences in sports involvement: Applying the Eccles' expectancy-value model. *Journal of Applied Sport Psychology*, **3**, 7–35. doi: 10.1080/10413209108406432

Eccles, J. S., Harold, R., & Wigfield, A. (1993). *Ontogeny of self and task concepts and activity choice* (Grant RO1 HD17553-05). Bethesda, MD: National Institute of Child Health and Human Development.

Eccles, J. S., & Hoffman, R. D. (1984). Socialization and the maintenance of a sex-segregated labor market. In H. W. Stevenson & A. E. Siegel (Eds.), *Research on child development and social policy* (Vol.1, pp. 367–420). Chicago: University of Chicago Press.

Eccles, J. S., Jacobs, J. E., & Harold, R. D. (1990). Gender role stereotypes, expectancy effects, and parents' socialization of gender differences. *Journal of Social Issues, **46***(2), 183–201. doi: 10.1111/j.1540-4560.1990.tb01929.x

Eccles, J. S., Jacobs, J. E., Harold, R. D., Yoon, K. S., Arberton, A., & Freedman-Doan, C. (1993). Parent and gender-role socialization during the middle childhood and adolescent years. In S. Oskamp & M. Constanzo (Eds.), *Gender issues in contemporary society* (pp. 59–83). Newburry Park: SAGE.

Eccles, J. S., & Midgley, C. (1989). Stage/environment fit: Developmentally appropriate classrooms for young adolescents. In R. Ames & C. Ames (Eds.), *Research on motivation and education: Goals and cognitions* (Vol. 3, pp. 139–186). New York: Academic Press.

Eccles, J. S., & Wigfield, A. (1995). In the mind of the actor: The structure of adolescents' academic achievement-related beliefs and self-perceptions. *Personality and Social Psychology Bulletin, **21***, 215–225. doi: 10.1177/0146167295213003

Eccles, J. S., Wigfield, A., Harold, R. D., & Blumenfeld, P. (1993). Age and child differences inchildren's self and task perceptions during elementary school years. *Child Development, **64***, 830–847. doi: 10.2307/1131221

Eccles, J. S., Wigfield, A., & Schiefele, U. (1998). Motivation to succeed. In W. Damon (Series Ed.) & N. Eisenberg (Vol. Ed.), *Handbook of child psychology: Vol. 3, Social, emotional and personality development* (5th ed., pp. 1017–1094). New York: Wiley.

Enders, C. K. (2010). *Applied missing data analysis.* New York: Guilford Press.

Epstein, J. L. (1995). School/family/community partnerships: Caring for the children we share. *Phi Delta Kappan, **76***, 701–712.

Erikson, E. H. (1982). *The life cycle completed: A review.* New York: Norton.

Ethington, C. A. (1991). A test of a model of achievement behaviors. *American Educational Research Journal, **28***, 155–172. doi: 10.3102/00028312028001155

Evans, M. E., Schweingruber, H., & Stevenson, H. W. (2002). Gender differences in interest and knowledge acquisition: The United States, Taiwan, and Japan. *Sex Roles, **47***, 153–167. doi: 10.1023/A:1021055324350

Farmer, H. S., Wardrop, J. L., Anderson, M. Z., & Risinger, R. (1995). Women's career choices: Focus on science, math, and technology careers. *Journal of Counseling Psychology, **42***, 155–170. doi: 10.1037/0022-0167.42.2.155

Farmer, H. S., Wardrop, J. L., & Rotella, S. C. (1999). Antecedent factors differentiating women and men in science/non-science careers. *Psychology of Women Quarterly, **23***, 763–780. doi: 10.1111/j.1471-6402.1999.tb00396.x

Ferry, T. R., Fouad, N. A., & Smith, P. L. (2000). The role of family context in a social cognitive model for career-related choice behavior: A math and science perspective. *Journal of Vocational Behavior, **57***, 348–364. doi: 10.1006/jvbe.1999.1743

Fredricks, J. A. (1999). *"Girl-friendly" family contexts: Socialization into math and sports.* Unpublished doctoral dissertation. University of Michigan, Ann Arbor.

Fredricks, J. A. (2014). *Eight myths of student disengagement: Creating classrooms of deep learning.* Thousand Oakes, CA: Corwin Press.

Fredricks, J. A., & Eccles, J. S. (2002). Children's competence and value beliefs from childhood to adolescence: Growth trajectories in two "male-typed" domains. *Developmental Psychology, **38***, 519–533. doi: 10.1037/0012-1649.38.4.519

Fredricks, J. A., & Eccles, J. S. (2004). Parental influences on youth involvement in sports. In M. Weiss (Ed.), *Developmental sport and exercise psychology: A lifespan perspective* (pp. 145–164). Morgantown, WV: Fitness Information Technology.

Fredricks, J. A., & Eccles, J. S. (2005). Family socialization, gender, motivation, and competitive sports involvement. *Journal of Sport and Exercise Psychology*, **27**, 3–31.

Fredricks, J. A., & Eccles, J. S. (2006). Is extracurricular participation associated with beneficial outcomes: Concurrent and longitudinal relations? *Developmental Psychology*, **42**, 698–713. doi: 10.1037/0012-1649.42.4.698

Fredricks, J. A., Simpkins, S. D., & Eccles, J. S. (2005). Family socialization, gender, and participation in sports and instrumental music. In C. R. Cooper, C. Garcia Coll, W. T. Bartko, H. M. Davis, & C. Chatman (Eds.), *Developmental pathways through middle childhood: Rethinking diversity and contexts as resources* (pp. 41–62). Mahwah, NJ: Erlbaum.

Frome, P., & Eccles, J. S. (1998). Parents' influence on children's achievement-related perceptions. *Journal of Personality and Social Psychology*, **2**, 435–452. doi: 10.1037/0022-3514.74.2.435

Furstenberg, F., Cook, T., Eccles, J., Elder, G., & Sameroff, A. (1999). *Managing to make it: Urban families in adolescent success.* Chicago: University of Chicago Press.

Goodnow, J. J., & Collins, W. A. (1990). *Development according to parents: The nature, sources, and consequences of parents' ideas.* London: Erlbaum.

Greendorfer, S. L., Lewko, J. H., & Rosengren, K. S. (1996). Family and gender-based influences in sport socialization of children and adolescents. In F. L. Smoll & R. E. Smith (Eds.), *Children and youth in sport: A biopsychosocial perspective* (pp. 89–111). Dubuque, IA: Brown & Benchmark.

Grolnick, W. S. (2003). *The psychology of parental control: How well-meant parenting backfires.* Hillside, NJ: Erlbaum.

Grolnick, W. S., Gurland, S. T., DeCourcey, W., & Jacob, K. (2002). Antecedents and consequences of mothers' autonomy support. *Developmental Psychology*, **38**, 143–155. doi: 10.1037/0012-1649.38.1.143

Grolnick, W. S., & Ryan, R. M. (1989). Parent styles associated with children's self-regulation and competence in schools. *Journal of Educational Psychology*, **8**, 143–154. doi: 10.1037/0022-0663.81.2.143

Grolnick, W. S., Ryan, R. M., & Deci, E. L. (1991). Inner resources for school achievement: Motivational mediators of children's perceptions of their parents. *Journal of Educational Psychology*, **83**, 508–517. doi: 10.1037/0022-0663.83.4.508

Grolnick, W. S., & Slowiaczek, M. L. (1994). Parents' involvement in children's schooling: A multidimensional conceptualization and motivational model. *Child Development*, **65**, 237–252. doi: 10.2307/1131378

Guillet, F., Sarrazin, P., Fontayne, P., & Brustad, R. (2006). Understanding female sport attrition in a stereotypical male sport within the framework of Eccles' expectancy-value model. *Psychology of Women Quarterly*, **30**, 358–368. doi: 10.1111/j.1471-6402.2006.00311.x

Guthrie, J. T., & Wigfield, A. (2000). Engagement and motivation in reading. In M. L. Kamil, P. B. Mosenthal, P. D. Pearson, & R. Barr (Eds.), *Handbook of reading research* (3rd ed., pp. 403–422). New York: Longman.

Harkness, S., & Super, C. M. (Eds.), (1996). *Parents' cultural belief systems: Their origins, expressions, and consequences.* New York: Guilford Press.

Harter, S. (1981). A new self-report scale of intrinsic versus extrinsic orientation in the classroom: Motivational and informational components. *Developmental Psychology*, **17**, 300–312. doi: 10.1037/0012-1649.17.3.300

Harter, S. (1999). *The construction of the self: A developmental perspective*. New York: Guilford Press.

Hattie, J., & Edwards, J. (1987). A review of the Bruininks-Oseretsky Test of Motor Proficiency. *British Journal of Educational Psychology*, **57**, 104–113. doi: 10.1111/j.2044-8279.1987.tb03065.x

Herbert, J., & Stipek, D. (2005). The emergence of gender differences in children's perceptions of their academic competence. *Applied Developmental Psychology*, **26**, 276–295. doi: 10.1016/j.appdev.2005.02.007

Holden, G., & Edwards, L. (1989). Parental attitudes towards child rearing: Instruments, issues, and implications. *Psychological Bulletin*, **106**, 29–58. doi: 10.1037/0033-2909.106.1.29

Holloway, S. D. (1988). Concepts of ability and effort in Japan and the United States. *Review of Educational Research*, **58**, 327–345. doi: 10.3102/00346543058003327

Howe, M. J. A., & Sloboda, J. A. (1991). Young musicians' accounts of significant influences in their early lives: The family and the musical background. *British Journal of Music Education*, **8**, 39–52. doi: 10.1017/S0265051700008056

Hu, L., & Bentler, P. M. (1999). Cutoff criteria for fit indexes in covariance structure analysis: Conventional criteria versus new alternatives. *Structural Equation Modeling*, **6**, 1–55. doi: 10.1080/10705519909540118

Hyde, J. S., Fennema, E., Ryan, M., Frost, C. A., & Hopp, C. (1990). Gender comparisons of mathematics attitudes and affect. *Psychology of Women Quarterly*, **14**, 299–324. doi: 10.1111/j.1471-6402.1990.tb00022.x

Jacobs, J. E., & Eccles, J. S. (1992). The impact of mothers' gender stereotypic beliefs on mothers' and children's ability perceptions. *Journal of Personality and Social Psychology*, **63**, 932–944. doi: 10.1037/0022-3514.63.6.932

Jacobs, J. E., Finken, L. L., Griffin, N. L., & Wright, J. D. (1998). The career plans of science-talented rural adolescent girls. *American Educational Research Journal*, **35**, 681–704. doi: 10.3102/00028312035004681

Jacobs, J. E., Lanza, S., Osgood, D. W., Eccles, J. S., & Wigfield, A. (2002). Changes in children's self-competence and values: Gender and domain differences across grades one through twelve. *Child Development*, **73**, 509–527. doi: 10.1111/1467-8624.00421

Jacobs, J. E., Vernon, M. K., & Eccles, J. S. (2005). Activity choices in middle childhood: The roles of gender, self-beliefs, and parents' influence. In J. L. Mahoney, R. W. Larson, & J. S. Eccles (Eds.), *Organized activities as contexts of development: Extracurricular activities, after-school and community programs* (pp. 235–254). Mahwah, NJ: Erlbaum.

Jodl, K. M., Michaels, A., Malanchuk, O., Eccles, J. S., & Sameroff, A. (2001). Parents' roles in shaping early adolescents' occupational aspirations. *Child Development*, **72**, 1247–1265. doi: 10.1111/1467-8624.00345

Johnson, M. M. (1975). Fathers, mothers, and sex typing. *Sociological Inquiry*, **45**, 15–26.

Jöreskog, K. J. (1999). *How large can a standardized coefficient be?* Retrieved November 5, 2006 from Scientific Software International Web site: http://www.ssicentral.com/lisrel/advancedtopics.html

Joyce, B. A., & Farenga, S. J. (1999). Informal science, experience attitudes, future interest in science, and gender of high-ability students: An exploratory study. *School Science and Mathematics*, **99**, 431–437. doi: 10.1111/j.1949-8594.1999.tb17505.x

Jussim, L., & Eccles, J. S. (1992). Teacher expectations II: Construction and reflections of student achievement. *Journal of Personality and Social Psychology*, **63**, 947–961. doi: 10.1037/0022-3514.63.6.947

Kahn, J. A., Huang, B., Gillman, M. W., Field, A. E., Austin, S. B., Colditz, G. A., et al. (2008). Patterns and determinants of physical activity in U.S. adolescents. *Journal of Adolescent Health, 42*, 369–377. doi: 10.1016/j.jadohealth.2007.11.143

Kimiecik, J. C., & Horn, T. S. (1998). Parental beliefs and children's moderate-to-vigorous physical activity. *Research Quarterly for Exercise and Sport, 69*, 163–175.

Klinedinst, R. E. (1991). Predicting performance achievement and retention of fifth-grade instrumental students. *Journal of Research in Music Education, 39*, 225–238. doi: 10.2307/3344722

Klomsten, A. T., Marsh, H. W., & Skaalvik, E. M. (2005). Adolescents' perceptions of masculine and feminine values in sports and physical education: A study of gender differences. *Sex Roles, 52*, 625–634. doi: 10.1007/s11199-005-3730-x

Klomsten, A., Skaalvik, E. M., & Espnes, G. (2004). Physical self-concept and sports: Do gender differences still exist. *Sex Roles, 50*, 119–127. doi: 10.1023/B:SERS.0000011077.10040.9a

Lareau, A. (2003). *Unequal childhood: Class, race, and family life.* Berkeley: University of California Press.

Larson, R., & Verma, S. (1999). How children and adolescents around the world spend time: Work, play, and developmental opportunities. *Psychological Bulletin, 125*, 701–736. doi: 10.1037/0033-2909.125.6.701

LeFevre, J. A., Skwarchuk, S. L., Smith-Chant, B. L., Fast, L., Kamawar, D., & Bisanz, J. (2009). Home numeracy experiences and children's math performance in the early school years. *Canadian Journal of Behavioural Science, 41*, 55–66. doi: 10.1037/a0014532

Lerner, R. M. (1996). Relative plasticity, integration, temporality, and diversity in human development: A developmental contextual perspective about theory, process, and method. *Developmental Psychology, 32*, 781–786. doi: 10.1037/0012-1649.32.4.781

Lightbown, P. M., & Spada, N. (2006). *How languages are learned* (3rd ed.) New York: Oxford University Press.

Little, T. D. (2013). *Longitudinal structural equation modeling: Methodology in social sciences.* New York: Guilford Press.

Little, T. D., Preacher, K. J., Selig, J. P., & Card, N. A. (2007). New developments in latent variable panel analyses of longitudinal data. *International Journal of Behavioral Development, 31*, 357–365. doi: 10.1177/0165025407077757

Loera, G., Rueda, R., & Nakamoto, J. (2011). The association between parent involvement in reading and school and children's reading and engagement in Latino families. *Literacy Research and Instruction, 50*, 133–155. doi: 10.1080/19388071003731554

Lummis, M., & Stevenson, H. W. (1990). Gender differences in beliefs and achievement: A cross-cultural study. *Developmental Psychology, 26*, 254–263. doi: 10.1037/0012-1649.26.2.254

Lytton, J., & Romney, D. M. (1991). Parents' differential socialization of boys and girls: A meta-analysis. *Psychological Bulletin, 2*, 267–296. doi: 10.1037/0033-2909.109.2.267

Maccoby, E. E., & Jacklin, C. N. (1974). *The psychology of sex differences.* Stanford, CA: Stanford University Press.

Mahoney, J. L., & Eccles, J. S. (2007). Organized activity participation for children from low- and middle-income families. In A. Booth & A. C. Crouter (Eds.), *Disparities in school readiness* (pp. 207–222). New York: Erlbaum.

Marinak, B. A., & Gambell, L. B. (2010). Reading motivation: Exploring the elementary gender gap. *Literacy Research and Instruction, 49*, 129–141. doi: 10.1080/19388070902803795

Marjoribanks, K. (2002). *Family and school capital: Towards a context theory of students' school outcomes*. Dordrecht, Netherlands: Kluwer Academic.

Marsh, H. W. (1989). Age and sex effects in multiple dimensions of self-concept: Preadolescence to early adulthood. *Journal of Educational Psychology, 81*, 417–430. doi: 10.1037/0022-0663.81.3.417

Marsh, H. W. (1990). The causal ordering of academic self-concept and academic achievement: A multi wave, longitudinal panel analysis. *Journal of Educational Psychology, 82*, 646–656. doi: 10.1037/0022-0663.82.4.646

Marsh, H. W., Byrne, B. M., & Yeung, A. S. (1999). Causal ordering of academic self-concept and achievement: Reanalysis of a pioneering study and revised recommendations. *Educational Psychologist, 34*, 154–157. doi: 10.1207/s15326985ep3403_2

Marsh, H. W., Chanal, J. P., Sarrin, D. G., & Bois, J. E. (2006). Self-beliefs does make a difference: A reciprocal effects model of the causal ordering of physical self-concept and gymnastics performance. *Journal of Sport Science, 29*, 101–111. doi: 10.1080/02640410500130920

Marsh, H. W., & Craven, R. (1997). Academic self-concept: Beyond the dustbowl. In G. Phye (Ed.), *Handbook of classroom assessment: Learning, achievement, and adjustment* (pp. 131–198). Orlando, FL: Academic Press.

Marsh, H. W., & Craven, R. G. (2006). Reciprocal effects of self-concept and performance from a multidimensional perspective: Beyond seductive pleasure and unidimensional perspectives. *Perspectives on Psychological Science, 1*, 133–163. doi: 10.1111/j.1745-6916.2006.00010.x

Marsh, H. W., Gerlach, E., Trautwein, U., Lüdtke, O., & Brettschneider, W. (2007). Longitudinal study of preadolescent sport self-concept and performance: Reciprocal effects and causal ordering. *Child Development, 78*, 1640–1656. doi: 10.1111/j.1467-8624.2007.01094.x

Marsh, H. W., & Perry, C. (2005). Does a positive self-concept contribute to winning gold medals in elite swimming? The causal ordering of elite athlete self-concept and championship performances. *Journal of Sport and Exercise Psychology, 27*, 71–91.

Marsh, H. W., Trautwein, U., Lüdtke, O., Köller, O., & Baumert, J. (2005). Academic self-concept, interest, grades and standardized test scores: Reciprocal effects models of causal ordering. *Child Development, 76*, 297–416. doi: 10.1111/j.1467-8624.2005.00853.x

Marsh, H. W., & Yeung, A. S. (1998). Longitudinal structural equation models in academic self-concept and achievement: Gender differences in the development of math and English constructs. *American Educational Research Journal, 35*, 705–738. doi: 10.3102/00028312035004705

Masten, A. S., & Coatsworth, J. D. (1998). The development of competence in favorable and unfavorable environments: Lessons from successful children. *American Psychologist, 53*, 205–220. doi: 10.1037/0003-066X.53.2.205

Masten, A. S., Roisman, G. I., Long, J. D., Burt, K. B., Orbadović, J., Riley, J. R., et al. (2005). Developmental cascades: Linking academic achievement, externalizing, and internalizing symptoms over 20 years. *Developmental Psychology, 41*, 733–746. doi: 10.1037/0012-1649.41.5.733

McCullagh, P., Matzkanin, K. T., Shaw, S. D., & Maldonado, M. (1993). Motivation for participation in physical activity: A comparison of parent-child perceived competencies and participation motives. *Pediatric Exercise Science, 5*, 224–233.

McGillicuddy-DeLisi, A. V. (1982). Parental beliefs about development. *Human Development*, **25**, 192–200. doi: 10.1159/000272796

McGrath, E. P., & Repetti, R. L. (2000). Mothers' and fathers' attitudes toward their children's academic performance and children's perceptions of their academic competence. *Journal of Youth and Adolescence*, **29**, 713–723. doi: 10.1023/A:1026460007421

McLoyd, V. C. (1990). The impact of economic hardship on African American families and children: Psychological distress, parenting, and socioemotional development. *Child Development*, **61**, 311–346. doi: 10.2307/1131096

McPherson, G. E. (2009). The role of parents in children's musical development. *Psychology of Music*, **37**, 91–110. doi: 10.1177/0305735607086049

McPherson, G. E., & Davidson, J. W. (2002). Musical practice: Mother and child interactions during the first year of learning and instrument. *Music Education Research*, **4**, 143–158. doi: 10.1080/14613800220119822

McPherson, G. E., & Davidson, J. W. (2006). Playing an instrument. In G. E. McPherson (Ed.), *The child as musician: A handbook of musical development* (pp. 331–351). Oxford: Oxford University Press.

McPherson, G. E., & McCormick, H. (1999). Motivational and self-regulated learning components of musical practice. *Bulletin of the Council for Research in Music Education*, **141**, 98–102.

Meade, A. W., Johnson, E. C., & Braddy, P. W. (2008). Power and sensitivity of alternative fit indices in tests of measurement invariance. *Journal of Applied Psychology*, **93**, 568–592. doi: 10.1037/0021-9010.93.3.568

Millsap, R. E. (2011). *Statistical approaches to measurement invariance.* New York: Routledge.

Millsap, R. E., & Olivera-Aguilar, M. (2012). Investigating measurement invariance using confirmatory factor analysis (pp. 380–392). In R. H. Hoyle (Ed.), *Handbook of structural equation modeling.* New York: Guilford Press.

Mischel, W. (1973). Toward a cognitive social learning reconceptualization of personality. *Psychological Review*, **80**, 252–283. doi: 10.1037/h0035002

Moore, L. L., Lombardi, D. A., White, M. J., Campbell, D. L., Oliveria, S. A., & Ellison, R. C. (1991). Influence of parents' physical activity levels on activity levels of young children. *Journal of Pediatrics*, **118**, 215–219.

Morrow, H. (1983). Home and school correlates of early interest in literature. *Journal of Educational Research*, **76**, 221–230.

Mosteller, F., & Tukey, J. W. (1977). *Data analysis and regression: A second course in statistics.* Reading, MA: Addison-Wesley.

National Science Foundation, Division of Science Resources Statistics. (2009). *Women, minorities, and persons with disabilities in science and engineering: 2009*, NSF09-305. Retrieved from http://www.nsf.gov/statistics/wmpd/

Neuman, S. B. (1986). The home environment and fifth-grade students' leisure reading. *The Elementary School Journal*, **86**, 335–343. doi: 10.1086/461454

Nippold, M. A., Duthie, J., & Larsen, J. (2005). Literacy as a leisure activity: Free time preferences of older children and young adolescents. *Language, Speech, & Hearing Services in Schools*, **36**, 93–102. doi: 10.1044/0161-1461(2005/009)

North, A. C., Hargreaves, D. J., & O'Neill, S. A. (2000). The importance of music to adolescents. *British Journal of Educational Psychology*, **70**, 255–272. doi: 10.1348/000709900158083

O'Neill, S. A. (1997). Gender and music. In D. J. Hargreaves & A. C. North (Eds.), *The social psychology of music* (pp. 46–60). Oxford, England: Oxford University Press.

O'Neill, S. A. (1999). The role of motivation in the practice and achievement of young musicians. In S. W. Yi (Ed.), *Music, mind, and science* (pp. 420–433). Seoul: Seoul National University Press.

Pardini, D. (2008). Novel insights into longitudinal theories of bi-directional issues: Introduction to the special section. *Journal of Abnormal Child Psychology, 36*, 627–631. doi: 10.1007/s10802-008-9231-y

Parke, R. D., Killian, C., Dennis, J., Flyr, M., McDowell, D. J., Simpkins, S. D., et al. (2003). Managing the external environment: The parent as active agent in the system. In L. Kuczynski (Ed.), *Handbook of dynamics in parent–child relations* (pp. 247–270). Thousand Oaks, CA: SAGE.

Pedersen, S., & Seidman, E. (2005). Contexts and correlates of out-of-school activity participation among low-income urban adolescents. In J. L. Mahoney, R. W. Larson, & J. S. Eccles (Eds.), *Organized activities as contexts of development* (pp. 85–109). Mahwah, NJ: Erlbaum.

Pfeiffer, K. A., Dowda, M., Dishman, R. K., McIver, K. L., Sirard, J. R., Ward, D. S., & Pate, R. R. (2006). Sport participation and physical activity in adolescent females across a four year period. *Journal of Adolescent Health, 39*, 523–529. doi: 10.1016/j.jadohealth.2006.03.005

Pluck, M. L., Ghafari, E., Glynn, T., & McNaughton, S. (1984). Teacher and parent modeling of recreational reading. *New Zealand Journal of Educational Studies, 19*, 114–123.

Pugliese, J. A., & Tinsley, B. J. (2007). Parental socialization of child and adolescent physical activity: A meta-analysis. *Journal of Family Psychology, 21*, 331–343. doi: 10.1037/0893-3200.21.3.331

Renninger, K. A. (2000). Individual interest and its implications for understanding intrinsic motivation. In C. Sansone & J. M. Harackiewicz (Eds.), *Intrinsic motivation: Controversies and new directions* (pp. 373–404). San Diego, CA: Academic Press.

Rogoff, B. (1990). *Apprenticeship in thinking: Cognitive development in social context.* New York: Oxford University Press.

Rogoff, B. (2003). *The cultural nature of human development.* Oxford, England: Oxford University Press.

Rosenthal, R., Rosnow, R. L., & Rubin, D. B. (2000). *Contrasts and effect sizes in behavioral research: A correlational approach.* New York: Cambridge University Press.

Rowe, K. J. (1991). The influence of reading attitudes at home on students' attitudes toward reading, classroom attentiveness, and reading achievement. An application of structural equation modeling. *British Journal of Educational Psychology, 61*, 19–35. doi: 10.1111/j.2044-8279.1991.tb00958.x

Ruble, D. N., Martin, C., & Berenbaum, S. (2006). Gender development. In W. Damon & R. M. Lerner (Series Eds.), & N. Eisenberg (Vol. Ed.), *Handbook of child psychology: Vol. 3, Social, emotional and personality development* (6th ed., pp. 858–932). New York: Wiley.

Rutter, M. (1988). *Studies of psychosocial risk: The power of longitudinal data.* New York: Cambridge University Press.

Ryan, R. M., & Deci, E. L. (2000). Self-determination theory and the facilitation of intrinsic motivation, social development, and well-being. *American Psychologist, 55*, 68–78. doi: 10.1037//0003-066X.55.1.68

Sabiston, C. M., & Crocker, P. R. E. (2008). Exploring self-perceptions and social influences as correlates of adolescent leisure-time physical activity. *Journal of Sport & Exercise Psychology, 30*, 3–22.

Sallis, J. F., Prochaska, J. J., Taylor, W. C., Hill, J. O., & Geraci, J. C. (1999). Correlates of physical activity in a national sample of girls and boys in Grades 4 through 12. *Health Psychology*, **18**, 410–415. doi: 10.1037//0278-6133.18.4.410

Sameroff, A. J. (2000). Reflections on the past and planning for the future of developmental psychopathology. *Development and Psychopathology*, **3**, 297–312.

Sameroff, A. J., Bartko, T., Baldwin, A., Baldwin, C., & Seifer, R. (1998). Family and social influences on the development of child competence. In M. Lewis & C. Feiring (Eds.), *Families, risk, and competence* (pp. 161–185). Mahwah, NJ: Erlbaum.

Saracho, O. N. (2002). Family literacy: Exploring family practices. *Early Child Development and Care*, **172**, 113–122. doi: 10.1080/03004430210886

Savage, S. L., & Gauvain, M. (1998). Parental beliefs and children's everyday planning in European-American and Latino families. *Journal of Applied Developmental Psychology*, **19**, 319–340. doi: 10.1016/S0193-3973(99)80043-4

Schiefele, J. (1991). Interest, learning, and motivation. *Educational Psychologist*, **26**, 299–323. doi: 10.1207/s15326985ep2603&4_5

Shumow, L., & Lomax, R. (2002). Parenting efficacy: Predictor of parenting behavior and adolescent outcomes. *Parenting: Science and Practice*, **2**, 127–150. doi: 10.1207/S15327922PAR0202_03

Sigel, I. E., McGillicuddy-DeLisi, A. V., Goodnow, J. J., (Eds.), (1992). *Parental belief systems* (2nd ed.). Hillsdale, NJ: Erlbaum.

Simpkins, S. D., Davis-Kean, P. E., & Eccles, J. S. (2005). Parents' socializing behavior and children's participation in math, science, and computer out-of-school activities. *Applied Developmental Science*, **9**, 14–30. doi: 10.1207/s1532480xads0901_3

Simpkins, S. D., Davis-Kean, P. E., & Eccles, J. S. (2006). Math and science motivation: A longitudinal examination of links between choices and beliefs. *Developmental Psychology*, **42**, 70–83. doi: 10.1037/0012-1649.42.1.70

Simpkins, S. D., Fredricks, J. A., Davis-Kean, P. E., & Eccles, J. S. (2006). Healthy minds, healthy habits: The influence of activity involvement in middle childhood. A. Huston & M. Ripke (Eds.), *Developmental contexts in middle childhood: Bridges to adolescence and adulthood* (pp. 283–303). New York: Cambridge University Press.

Simpkins, S. D., Fredricks, J. A., Eccles, J. S. (2015). Families, schools, and developing achievement related motivations and achievement. In J. E. Grusec & P. H. Hasting (Eds.), *Handbook of socialization: Theory and research* (2nd ed.; 614–636). New York: Guilford Press.

Simpkins, S. D., Fredricks, J. A., & Eccles, J. S. (2012). Charting the Eccles' expectancy-value model from mothers' beliefs in childhood to youths' activities in adolescence. *Developmental Psychology*, **48**, 1019–1032. doi: 10.1037/a0027468

Simpkins, S. D., Ripke, M., Huston, A. C., & Eccles, J. S. (2005). Predicting participation and outcomes in out-of-school activities: Similarities and differences across social ecologies. *New Directions in Youth Development*, **105**, 51–69. doi: 10.1002/yd.107

Simpkins, S. D., Vest, A. E., Dawes, N. P., & Neuman, K. I. (2010). Dynamic relations between parents' behaviors and children's motivational beliefs in sports and music. *Parenting: Science and Practice*, **10**, 97–118. doi: 10.1080/15295190903212638

Skaalvik, E. M. (1997). Issues in research on self-concept. In M. L. Maehr & P. R. Pintrich (Eds.), *Advances in motivation and achievement* (Vol. 10, pp. 51–98). Greenwich, CT: JAI Press.

Sloboda, J. A., & Howe, M. J. A. (1991). Biographic precursors of musical excellence: An interview study. *Psychology of Music*, **19**, 3–21. doi: 10.1177/0305735691191001

Slosson, R. L., Nicholson, C. L., & Hibpshman, T. L. (1991). *Slosson intelligence test-revised manual.* East Amora, NY: Slosson Educational Publications.

Sosniak, L. A. (1985). Learning to be a concern pianist. In B. S. Bloom (Ed.), *Developing talent in young people* (pp. 19–67). New York: Ballantine.

Sosniak, L. A. (1990). The tortoise, the hare, and the development of talent. In M. J. A. Howe (Ed.), *Encouraging the development of exceptional skills and talents.* Leichester: British Psychological Society.

Smetana, J. G. (2010). *Adolescents families and social development: How teens construct their worlds.* West Sussex, England: Wiley-Blackwell.

Steiger, J. H. (1990). Structural model evaluation and modification: An interval approach. *Multivariate Behavioral Research, 25,* 173–180. doi: 10.1207/s15327906mbr2502_4

Steinberg, L., Lamborn, S. D., Dornbusch, S. M., & Darling, N. (1992). Impact of parenting practices on adolescent achievement: Authoritative parenting, school involvement andencouragement to succeed. *Child Development, 63,* 1266–1281. doi: 10.2307/1131532

Stipek, D., & MacIver, D. (1989). Developmental changes in children's assessment of competence. *Child Development, 60,* 521–538. doi: 10.2307/1130719

Thompson, M. S., & Green, S. B. (2013). Evaluating between-group differences in latent variable means. In G. R. Hancock & R. O. Mueller (Eds.), *Structural equation modeling: A second course* (2nd ed., pp 163–218) Charlotte, NC: Information Age Publishing.

Tiedemann, J. (2000). Parents' gender stereotypes and teachers' beliefs as predictors of children's concept of their mathematical ability in elementary school. *Journal of Educational Psychology, 92,* 308–315. doi: 10.1037/0022-0663.92.1.144

Turner, S. L., Steward, J. C., & Lapan, R. T. (2004). Family factors associated with sixth-grade adolescents' math and science career interests. *The Career Development Quarterly, 53,* 41–52. doi: 10.1002/j.2161-0045.2004.tb00654.x

Updegraff, K. A., Eccles, J. S., Barber, B. L., & O'Brien, K. M. (1996). Course enrollment as self-regulatory behavior: Who takes optional high school math courses? *Learning and Individual Differences, 8,* 239–259. doi: 10.1016/S1041-6080(96)90016-3

Valentine, J. C., DuBois, D. L., & Cooper, H. (2004). The relation between self-beliefs and academic achievement: A meta-analytic review. *Educational Psychologist, 39,* 111–133. doi: 10.1207/s15326985ep3902_3

VanSchooter, E., Oostdam, R., & de Glopper, K. (2001). Dimensions and predictors of literacy response. *Journal of Literacy Research, 33,* 1–32. doi: 10.1080/10862960109548101

Vilhjalmsson, R., & Thorlindsson, T. (1998). Factors related to physical activity: A study of adolescents. *Social Science of Medicine, 47,* 665–675. doi: 10.1207/s15326985ep3902_3

Vygotsky, L. S. (1978). *The development of higher psychological processes.* Cambridge, MA: Harvard University Press.

Watt, H. M. G. (2005). Exploring adolescent motivations for pursuing math-related careers. *Australian Journal of Educational and Developmental Psychology, 4,* 107–116.

Weiner, B. (1979). A theory of motivation for some classroom experiences. *Journal of Educational Psychology, 71,* 3–25. doi: 10.1037/0022-0663.71.1.3

Welk, G. J., Wood, K., & Morss, G. (2003). Parental influences on physical activity in children: An exploration of potential mechanisms. *Pediatric Exercise Science, 15,* 19–33.

Whitehurst, G. J., & Lonigan, C. J. (2001). Emergent literacy: Development from pre readers to readers. In S. B. Neuman & D. K. Dickinson (Eds.), *Handbook of early literacy research* (pp. 11–29). New York: Guilford Press.

Wigfield, A., & Eccles, J. S. (1992). The development of achievement task values: A theoretical analysis. *Developmental Review*, **12**, 265–310. doi: 10.1016/0273-2297(92)90011-P

Wigfield, A., Eccles, J. S., Schiefele, U., Roeser, R. W., & Davis-Kean, P. (2006). Development of achievement motivation. In N. Eisenberg, W. Damon, & R. M. Lerner (Eds.), N. Eisenberg (Vol. Ed.), *Handbook of child psychology: Vol. 3, social, emotional, and personality development* (6th ed., pp. 933–1002). Hoboken, NJ: Wiley.

Wigfield, A., Eccles, J., Yoon, K. S., Harold, R. D., Arbreton, A. J., & Blumenfeld, P. C. (1997). Change in children's competence beliefs and subjective task values across the elementary school years: A three-year study. *Journal of Education Psychology*, **89**, 451–469. doi: 10.1037/0022-0663.89.3.451

Wigfield, A., & Guthrie, J. T. (1997). Relations of children's motivation for reading to the amount and breadth or their reading. *Journal of Educational Psychology*, **89**, 420–432. doi: 10.1037//0022-0663.89.3.420

Willemsen, M. E., & van de Vijver, F. J. R. (1997). Developmental expectations of Dutch, Turkish-Dutch, and Zambian mothers—Towards an explanation of cross-cultural differences. *International Journal of Behavioral Development*, **21**, 837–854.

Winterbottom, M. R. (1958). The relation of need for achievement to learning experiences in independence and mastery. In J. W. Atkison (Ed.), *Motives in fantasy, action, and society* (pp. 453–478). Princeton, NJ: Van Nostrand.

Yeung, W., Sandberg, J., Davis-Kean, P. E., & Hofferth, S. L. (2001). Children's time with fathers in intact families. *Journal of Marriage and Family*, **63**, 136–154.

Yoon, K. S., Wigfield, A., & Eccles, J. S. (1993, April). *Causal relations between mothers' and children's beliefs about math ability: A structural equation model.* Paper presented at the annual meeting of the American Educational Research Association Atlanta, GA.

Zdzinski, S. F. (1994). Parental involvement, gender, and learning outcomes among instrumentalists. *Contributions to Music Education*, **21**, 73–89.

Zdzinski, S. F. (1996). Parental involvement, selected student attributes, and learning outcomes in instrumental music. *Journal of Research in Music Education*, **44**, 34–48. doi: 10.2307/3345412

COMMENTARY

ON "THE ROLE OF PARENTS IN THE ONTOGENY OF ACHIEVEMENT-RELATED MOTIVATION AND BEHAVIORAL CHOICES"

Aletha C. Huston

ABSTRACT This monograph offers a comprehensive test of an important theory of motivation. Because the theory is sufficiently precise to permit disconfirmation, the results that support and those that fail to support it are both informative. The finding that parents' influence appears primarily for peripheral subjects (sports and music), but not for reading and math raises many issues for further research. The study also informs our understanding of gender differences in motivation.

In this monograph, the authors offer a summative test of Eccles's theory of achievement motivation, which is a direct descendent of work by McClelland, Atkinson, and Crandall. McClelland originally proposed a general theory of motivation, which was most extensively applied to achievement (McClelland, Atkinson, & Clark, 1953). Atkinson's expectancy-value model systematized the theory, formulating mathematical propositions that could be tested in the laboratory or at least in controlled settings (Atkinson & Feather, 1966). Both theories received extensive empirical support, but their very simplicity was also a limitation. In particular, they were developed and tested on college men. Women were excluded from the populations sampled because the measure of achievement motivation was found not to be valid for college women.

Crandall and his associates were pioneers investigating the development and socialization of achievement motivation in children (Crandall, Katkovsky, & Preston, 1960). Among the many conclusions from their work, perhaps the

Corresponding author: Aletha C. Huston, Department of Human Development and Family Sciences, University of Texas at Austin, 108 E. Dean Keaton Street, Austin TX 78712-0141; email: achuston@utexas.edu most important was the recognition that achievement motivation is content-specific. That is, children's motivation for one content domain is relatively independent of their motivation for another.

Eccles's theory builds upon the basic expectancy-value model, extending and elaborating its components, and it also incorporates both content specificity and the possibility of variation by gender. Developmental and socialization processes are melded with the basic expectancy and value constructs providing a clear articulation of the roles of both parents and teachers. The result is more complexity, as evidenced by the models shown in Figures 1a and 1b, but happily, the theory retains the precision that allows strong empirical tests.

In recent years, much of developmental science has taken one of two paths. Along one path are tightly-constructed theories that limit the range of content and processes investigated in order to gain precision and control. The laboratory experiments favored in this approach generate useful knowledge, but their value for understanding social development came under attack in the 1980s and 1990s from people like Bronfenbrenner who once said that our science was the study of children's reactions to strange people in strange (contrived) situations. Along the second path are broadly "ecological" studies without clear predictions or hypotheses. Bronfenbrenner's ecological model, illustrated in his concentric circle model of development (Bronfenbrenner & Morris, 1998), has become a guide for an expanding empirical literature investigating processes of development in complex, real-world environments, but many of these studies lack a clear theoretical foundation. The concentric circles provide a framework, but a model is not a theory. It does not typically lead to hypotheses that can be disconfirmed—a basic requirement of science.

Eccles's theory and research integrate these two paths by retaining a broad ecological approach along with a precisely articulated theory. The work described in this monograph is a good example, demonstrating the value of a guiding theory as well as the limitations of testing it, even with a large-scale longitudinal investigation. As the authors note, their major contributions are testing the theory over a wide age span, including both mothers and fathers, covering four domains of activity, including both concepts of ability and values, testing reciprocal patterns, and assessing gender differences in means as well as moderation by gender. The fact that the results support some predictions, but fail to support others, is a strength allowing refinement of the theory and contributing new knowledge that generates new research questions.

PARENTAL INFLUENCES

The big question in this monograph concerns whether and how parents' beliefs and behaviors affect their children's beliefs and behaviors. According to the theoretical model, although children may influence parents, the principal direction of effects will be from parent to child. The results for younger children (Waves 2 and 3) support that prediction—children are more apt to increase their own beliefs and participation when their parents think the children have ability and when parents value the activity. The link from parents' beliefs to child beliefs leaves open the question of how parents transmit those beliefs. It seems likely that they convey their beliefs through encouragement and other supportive behavior, which in turn predict children's beliefs (Wave 4). The authors make a plausible case for a reciprocal process running from parent beliefs to parent behavior to child beliefs to child participation. Strangely, however, there is no direct test of parent behavior as a predictor of children's or adolescents' participation, leaving open questions about how the complex processes involved actually operate.

Given the many theoretical and intuitive reasons to assume that parents influence children's achievement, it is striking and surprising that parents have so little influence on academic subjects, especially math. Why? Is it really the case that parents are unimportant influences on their children's beliefs and efforts in core academic subjects? In the case of reading, parents may have conveyed their expectancies and values during the preschool years, so that the child's beliefs in Wave 2 already reflect much of the variation in parents' beliefs. This argument seems less plausible for math. Moreover, some parents begin encouraging their children in sports at an early age, yet the associations of parent beliefs with children's beliefs and participation in sports are strong.

The authors suggest that children get more feedback in school about their skills in reading and math than they do in sports and music. Hence, they may base their expectancies and values on their performance and on feedback from teachers. Whatever the reasons for the discrepancy across content domains, it has important implications for understanding the socialization of achievement motivation and behavior in the academic realm. If not parents, then what are the important influences on children's motivation for reading and math?

The likely importance of parents' behavior (e.g., encouragement, participating in an activity with the child, providing equipment and materials, and coaching) may help to understand the differences in parental influence across content domains. Parents' major contributions to their children's motivation and participation occurred in the nonacademic domains of sports and music. Because these activities are voluntary, they require more active parental involvement than do math and reading. For children to participate in many sports and instrumental music activities, parents often have to find teams and coaches, transport their children to lessons and games, pay for equipment and instruction, and encourage practice at home. By contrast, almost all children go to school, which provides materials, instruction, and opportunities for practice in reading and math well beyond those that may be supplied by parents.

GENDER DIFFERENCES

Eccles's early work was inspired by questions about the origins of gender differences in achievement, particularly in math (e.g., Eccles, Barber, & Jozefowicz, 1999). Funding for her research was part of a federal initiative to understand why females performed less well in math than males on average, and why they were less likely to take advanced math courses. Although gender differences in performance have diminished or disappeared in recent years (Hyde, 2014), the gender disparity in STEM-related occupations remains, suggesting that motivation rather than ability may be an important determinant of participation.

In the investigation described in this monograph, children manifested sex-stereotyped patterns of expectancy and value in all of the domains assessed. Boys had higher assessments of their abilities and they valued sports and math more than girls did. Conversely, girls' ability beliefs and values in reading and music were greater than those of boys. Parents' beliefs about sports and music differed in a similar pattern for their sons and daughters, but parents did not have differential beliefs about reading and math for their elementary-school-aged children. Because parents were not assessed once children reached adolescence, we do not know whether their beliefs became more differentiated by gender as children got older.

The important question in this investigation is whether parents' beliefs and behavior contributed to gender differences in children's beliefs and behavior. At the most basic level, the mean gender differences for both parents and children are consistent with the possibility of parental influence in sports and music; however, mean differences are a necessary but not sufficient condition for inferring parental influence. There are many other possible explanations, including the idea that both adults and children are influenced by broad sociocultural forces. In fact, children held stereotyped beliefs about math and reading even though their parents did not, suggesting that other socialization influences contributed to children's beliefs.

Going beyond mean differences, the findings show that parents' beliefs and behavior were related to children's beliefs and behavior, at least in sports and music for both boys and girls. That is, within each gender, when parents thought their children had high ability, valued an activity, and offered behavioral supports, children were more apt to believe in their own ability, value an activity, and participate in it. This pattern supports the idea that parental socialization processes operate similarly for boys and girls.

One might lose sight of the gender differences in the study because the primary question in the analyses was whether *processes*, not means, differed for males and females. For example, were parents' expectancies and values more important for one gender than for the other? Did parents' behavior matter more for one than for the other? The answer was a resounding "no." Although these questions are of interest, the fact that gender did not moderate the relations found does not mean that gender was unimportant. In fact, as the authors note, it suggests that changes in gender-stereotyped patterns can come about through similar socialization experiences for males and females.

One major strength of this work is inclusion of both fathers and mothers, particularly because some earlier research demonstrated that fathers may play a particularly important role in socializing achievement motivation. In fact, fathers' beliefs and behavior predicted those of their children more consistently and with higher coefficients than did mothers' beliefs and behavior. There was no evidence, however, that fathers mattered more for their sons than for their daughters, or the reverse.

EXPECTANCY AND VALUE

Eccles's theory, along with its forerunners, distinguishes perception of ability from task values for both parents and children. In previous research, there was some evidence that both constructs predicted children's achievement-related behavior, but some investigations indicated that subjective task value influenced participation choices more than ability perceptions did (Eccles et al., 1999). On the whole, in this study, parents' beliefs about children's ability were better predictors of children's beliefs than were parents' values. Why? The authors suggest that external pressures for advanced placement math and possibly literature clubs might operate because these activities are important for getting into college. The same point might be made about sports, but it seems unlikely that these pressures would be operating for elementary-school-age children. Moreover, students can value an activity as a means of achieving another goal. It seems equally likely that values are less well defined and more difficult to measure accurately, especially at early ages, than are perceptions of ability and estimates of likely success.

TO WHOM DO THESE RESULTS APPLY?

The population represented in this study was deliberately limited; it was predominantly White, middle- to upper-middle class, and lived in one area of the country. The data were collected in the 1980s and 1990s. These limitations

156

do not diminish the value of the research, but they do raise questions about the extent to which the results would apply to children born a generation later, to a wide range of ethnic and racial groups, and to families living in or near poverty. Given the core assumption that parent and child values and beliefs are culturally conditioned, it is likely that average levels might vary across groups. There might be cultural differences in children's involvement and in parents' expectancies or values for different content domains.

The more interesting question is whether the relations among parent and child beliefs and behavior would be different. For example, might parent expectancies and values matter more or less for children living in poverty or for immigrant families than for those in more affluent or native-born families? Do different kinds of parent behavior convey expectancies and values in different groups? Do parents' expectancies and values have different impacts in different social and cultural contexts (e.g., when children attend schools of different quality or with different populations)? Do parents' beliefs and behaviors matter more when they are in conflict with the surrounding social culture? What is the role of peers for children in different social-cultural contexts? These and many more questions need to be addressed. In short, like all good science, this investigation not only contributes new knowledge, but generates grist for the future research mill.

REFERENCES

Atkinson, J. W., & Feather, N. T. (Eds.). (1966). *A theory of achievement motivation.* New York: Wiley.

Bronfenbrenner, U., & Morris, P. A. (1998). The ecology of developmental processes. In W. Damon (Series Ed.), W. Damon & R. M. Lerner (Volume Eds.), *Handbook of child psychology: Vol. 1. Theoretical models of human development* (5th ed., pp. 993–1028). New York: Wiley.

Crandall, V. J., Katkovsky, W., & Preston, A. (1960). A conceptual formulation for some research on children's achievement development. *Child Development, 31,* 787–797.

Eccles, J. S., Barber, B., & Jozefowicz, D. (1999). Linking gender to education, occupation, and recreational choices: Applying the Eccles et al. model of achievement-related choices. In W. B. Swann, J. H. Langlois, & L. A. Gilbert (Eds.), *Sexism and stereotypes in modern society: The gender science of Janet Taylor Spence* (pp. 153–192). Washington, DC: APA Press.

Hyde, J. S. (2014). Gender similarities and differences. *Annual Review of Psychology, 65,* 373–398.

McClelland, D. C., Atkinson, J. R., Clark, R. A., & Lowell, E. L. (1953). *The achievement motive.* New York: Appleton-Century-Crofts.

Sandra D. Simpkins is an associate professor at Arizona State University. Her research highlights how settings in which an individual is embedded, such as the peer group and family, are critical determinants of youths' achievement-related choices, namely, STEM engagement/coursework and participation in organized activities. In her recent work with Latino families, she has strived to disentangle the role of SES, immigration, ethnicity, and culture in family functioning and youths' outcomes.

Jennifer A. Fredricks is a professor in the Human Development Department at Connecticut College and director of the Holleran Center for Community Action and Public Policy. Jennifer Fredricks's research focuses on extracurricular participation, positive youth development, school engagement, youth sports, and motivation. She is interested in how to create school and out-of-school contexts that optimize positive academic and psychological outcomes for children and adolescents living in diverse environments.

Jacquelynne S. Eccles is a distinguished professor in the School of Education at University of California, Irvine, and a distinguished professor emeritus of Psychology and Education at the University of Michigan. Over the past 40 years, Eccles has conducted extended longitudinal studies focused on a wide variety of topics including the development and consequences of both gender and racial/ethnic identities; the Eccles Expectancy-Value Theory of achievement related choices, engagements, and persistence (including educational and career choices related to STEM and other fields); family, peer, and classroom influences on student motivation, achievement, and well-being; and the Eccles and Midgley Stage-Environment Fit Theory of the impact of social contexts on human development.

Aletha C. Huston is the Priscilla Pond Flawn Regents Professor Emerita of Child Development at the University of Texas at Austin. She is Past President of the Society for Research in Child Development, the Developmental Psychology Division of the American Psychological Association, and the Consortium of Social Science Associations, and the recipient of the Urie Bronfenbrenner Award for Lifetime Contributions to Developmental Psychology in the Service of Science and Society.

STATEMENT OF EDITORIAL POLICY

The SRCD *Monographs* series aims to publish major reports of developmental research that generates authoritative new findings and that foster a fresh perspective and/or integration of data/research on conceptually significant issues. Submissions may consist of individually or group-authored reports of findings from some single large-scale investigation or from a series of experiments centering on a particular question. Multiauthored sets of independent studies concerning the same underlying question also may be appropriate. A critical requirement in such instances is that the individual authors address common issues and that the contribution arising from the set as a whole be unique, substantial, and well integrated. Manuscripts reporting interdisciplinary or multidisciplinary research on significant developmental questions and those including evidence from diverse cultural, racial, and ethnic groups are of particular interest. Also of special interest are manuscripts that bridge basic and applied developmental science, and that reflect the international perspective of the Society. Because the aim of the *Monographs* series is to enhance cross-fertilization among disciplines or subfields as well as advance knowledge on specialized topics, the links between the specific issues under study and larger questions relating to developmental processes should emerge clearly and be apparent for both general readers and specialists on the topic. In short, irrespective of how it may be framed, work that contributes significant data and/or extends a developmental perspective will be considered.

Potential authors who may be unsure whether the manuscript they are planning wouldmake an appropriate submission to the SRCD *Monographs* are invited to draft an outline or prospectus of what they propose and send it to the incoming editor for review and comment.

Potential authors are not required to be members of the Society for Research in Child Development nor affiliated with the academic discipline of psychology to submit a manuscript for consideration by the *Monographs*. The significance of the work in extending developmental theory and in contributing new empirical information is the crucial consideration.

Submissions should contain a minimum of 80 manuscript pages (including tables and references). The upper boundary of 150–175 pages is more flexible, but authors should try to keep within this limit. Manuscripts must be double-spaced, 12pt Times New Roman font, with 1-inch margins. If color artwork is submitted, and the authors believe color art is necessary to the presentation of their work, the submissions letter should indicate that one or more authors or their institutions are prepared to pay the substantial costs associated with color art reproduction. Please submit manuscripts electronically to the SRCD *Monographs* Online Submissions and Review Site (Scholar One) at http://mc.manuscriptcentral.com/mono. Please contact the *Monographs* office with any questions at monographs@srcd.org.

The corresponding author for any manuscript must, in the submission letter, warrant that all coauthors are in agreement with the content of the manuscript. The corresponding author also is responsible for informing all coauthors, in a timely manner, of manuscript submission, editorial decisions, reviews received, and any revisions recommended. Before publication, the corresponding author must warrant in the submissions letter that the study has been conducted according to the ethical guidelines of the Society for Research in Child Development.

A more detailed description of all editorial policies, evaluation processes, and format requirements can be found under the "Submission Guidelines" link at http://srcd.org/publications/monographs.

Monographs Editorial Office
e-mail: monographs@srcd.org

Editor, Patricia J. Bauer
Department of Psychology, Emory University
36 Eagle Row
Atlanta, GA 30322
e-mail: pjbauer@emory.edu

Note to NIH Grantees

Page numbers in *italics* refer to figures and tables.

parents' behaviors and children's beliefs models, 98–107
participation, 50, 51, 52, *62*, 66, 67, 68–69, 79, *112, 113–114*
-reported indicators, 34
school course choices, 5
self-concept of ability, *3*, 34, *35–36*, 51, 52, 65, 66, 67–68, 69, 79, 80, 98, 99, 101, 102, 105, 110–112, 115–116, 121–122
sociocultural changes, 4–5
task value, 35, 79
temperament, 7
values, *3*, 55, 66, 69, 79, 98, 101, 105, 120
youths' beliefs and participation models, vii, 108–118, 133, 137
youth missing data, 45–46
coaching. *See* parents/parenting
coactivity. *See* parents/parenting
competency. *See* children, ability
computer activities, competence beliefs, 18

Eccle's expectancy–value model, vii, *2*, 6–9, 11, 17, 52, 65, 66, 81, 119, 123, 128, 153, 154, 157
ecological theory, 5, 154
educational achievement. *See* achievement-related choices
encouragement. *See* parents/parenting
English/literature, 7, 10, 18, 45
European Americans, 2, 23, 24
expectancy–value, theories of, 2, 5. *See also* Eccle's expectancy–value model

family income, 23, 24, 42, 45, 46, 49, 50, 51, 60, 81, 83–84, 94, 102, 115
family management, 130, 132
fathers' beliefs/behaviors
    child factors and parents' beliefs, 66
    coaching, 57
    direction of influence, 3
    influence on children, 54, 83
    math domain, 90, 101, 105–106, 125
    missing data, 44–45
    music domain, 16, 50, 51, 69, 79, 89, 101, 102
    reading domain, 67, 68–69, 90, 93, 105–106, 125
    role of, 17, 54, 89, 100–101, 105–106, 157
    sport domain, 16, 57, 67–68, 83, 88, 89, 90, 94, 100–101
    study models, 52–53, 89, 135
    value of activity, 79, 88, 89, 101
feedback systems, 6–7

CURRENT